Bauwelt Fundamente 168

T0311211

Edited by

Elisabeth Blum
Jesko Fezer
Günther Fischer
Angelika Schnell

Douglas Spencer

Critique of Architecture:
Essays on Theory, Autonomy, and Political Economy

Bauverlag
Gütersloh · Berlin

Birkhäuser
Basel

The Bauwelt Fundamente series was founded in 1963 by Ulrich Conrads; it was edited from the early 1980s to 2015 jointly with Peter Neitzke.

Supervising editor of this volume: Angelika Schnell

Layout since 2017: Matthias Görlich

Front cover: Fulton Center Metro, Manhattan, New York. Grimshaw Architects, 2014. Photo: Douglas Spencer, 2016
Back cover: Hyatt Regency Atlanta, Portman Architects, 1967. Photo: Douglas Spencer, 2017

Library of Congress Control Number: 2020950291

Bibliographic information published by the German National Library
The German National Library lists this publication in the Deutsche Nationalbibliografie; detailed bibliographic data are available on the Internet at http://dnb.dnb.de.

This publication is also available as an e-book (ISBN PDF 978-3-0356-2164-8)

© 2021 Birkhäuser Verlag GmbH, Basel
P.O. Box 44, 4009 Basel, Switzerland
Part of Walter de Gruyter GmbH, Berlin/Boston
and Bauverlag BV GmbH, Gütersloh, Berlin

bau‖ ‖verlag

Printed in Germany

ISBN 978-3-0356-2163-1

9 8 7 6 5 4 3 2 1
www.birkhauser.com

Contents

For Cem Dursun

Acknowledgements

I write from stolen land, from Des Moines, Iowa, the traditional, ancestral, unceded land of the Báxoǰe or Ioway, Sauk and Meskwaki (Fox) peoples. I recognize that my presence here is the result of the ongoing exclusions and erasure of Indigenous peoples, the original stewards of this land.

The essays in this book were written over the course of the past decade, during which time I have been supported by too many friends, colleagues and comrades to mention here. Their invitations for me to speak, to write, to share, to travel, to teach and to learn with them have been invaluable. You know who you are.

I want to make special mention here, however, of Deborah Hauptmann, for her support of me as an academic and a friend. I thank David Cunningham, not only for writing the foreword for this book, but for being the most intellectually inspiring figure I have ever had the good fortune to study under. I thank Miloš Kosec, not only for the probing discussion of my work prompted by his questions, but for being a long-term, insightful and stimulating interlocutor. I want also to thank Angelika Schnell for her editorial support and guidance in bringing this book to fruition. Without Neil Brenner, who first suggested, and then so generously provided his help and guidance in realizing this project, it would not have happened. Neil, you are a comrade of the highest order.

Finally, I would like to acknowledge the love, support and patience of Becky Beckett, my fellow traveller and constant companion on a journey that has taken some strange and unexpected turns.

Foreword

David Cunningham

It is widely accepted that, in the current marketplace of ideas, the stock of 'critique' could hardly be lower. Critique and its intellectual lineage is, today, regularly dismissed from all sides as hopelessly outmoded, a cynical and pointless activity of debunking and demystification best consigned to the dustbin of history. Critique has, as one of its most influential opponents has put it, 'run out of steam', exposed and destroyed by its own subjective hubris and will to mastery, its own superior claims to know that which its objects do not know. Irredeemably negative, critique functions not as a facilitator of praxis or social change, creativity or construction, but as a blockage and obstacle, an endless and self-indulgent theoretical loop of melancholic refusal that can only bathe in its own repeated articulations of failure. To the 'No' of critique must be opposed the 'Yes' of building, composition and construction. To the elitist and know-it-all scepticism of critical reflection and interpretation must be opposed the humility and pragmatism of description and care.

Such a 'post-critical' position has rapidly assumed the status of *doxa,* even as it continues to present itself as a plucky David to critique's Goliath, and is one shared by a range of theoretical trends over the last two decades, from 'affect theory' and 'object-oriented ontology', to 'actor-network theory' and 'surface reading', to a variety of post-Deleuzian 'new materialisms'. But perhaps its most ubiquitous poster boy has been the French anthropologist and philosopher Bruno Latour; principal subject of one of the final essays included here. As Latour argues, in a 2010 essay first published in the journal *New Literary History,* summing up the contemporary renunciation of critique: 'With a hammer (or a sledge hammer) in hand you can do a lot of things: break down walls, destroy idols, ridicule prejudices, but you cannot repair, take care, assemble, reassemble, stitch together'.[1] Leaving aside the point that one can indeed 'repair' and 'assemble' with a hammer and a bag of nails (if not perhaps a sledge hammer), the argument is clear enough: critique can destroy or negate, shatter or destabilise, but it cannot build or construct, nor can it improve, repair or add to what is already there.

The appeal of this to architects is obvious, and has been widely met with a mix of relief and glee. Having delivered ourselves from the miserable paralysis of critique and negativity, from the dreaded clutches of Marx or Adorno or Derrida, we can now get on with some real, positive *work* of building (even if it turned out, in the meantime, that there wasn't actually that much work any longer for architects to do …). If criticality is a 'disease', in the words of Jeffrey Kipnis, stopping architecture from fulfilling its proper vocation, the cure lies in an unabashed embrace of an architectural practice 'based on the productive, the positive, the mobile, the new', as Sanford Kwinter described it.[2] Plenty have agreed.

The effort to recover a critical theory for architecture at a time when it is routinely denounced and dismissed as both arrogant and futile, both naively adolescent and insufferably world-weary, could then scarcely be more difficult than it appears today. Yet, cashing out the promissory note of the conclusion to his first book, *The Architecture of Neoliberalism* (2016), titled simply 'The Necessity of Critique', this is precisely what Doug Spencer intends in the collection of essays you have before you. More than this, and here is where one might hope it could have its greatest impact upon the field, he does so, without nostalgia, by seeking to interrogate and challenge the normative idea of critique as sheer negativity and non-productivity held by 'post-critical' thought itself.

As *Critique of Architecture* reminds us, it is bracing to consider for just how long this renunciation of critique has been culturally dominant in architectural discourse now – and how remarkable, in some respects, its blithe survival (like neoliberalism itself) through the ongoing capitalist crises of the late 2000s has been. As Spencer traces in various of the essays comprising this collection, if such a renunciation finds its pre-history in strands of postwar cybernetics and systems thinking, the California ideology of the *Whole Earth Catalog*, Buckminster Fuller and Richard Brautigan, and the paeans to flexibility and openness of the Independent Group, Reyner Banham and

Cedric Price (and the 'anti-plan'), it is in the late 1990s, in particular, that it can be first said to take root as an increasingly unquestioned *doxa*. At the same time, while the original 'post-critical' or 'projective' turn in architectural theory emerged in a somewhat provincial context of debates around the uptake of Jacques Derrida, on the one hand, and Manfredo Tafuri, on the other, in the US academy (associated, particularly, with the *Oppositions* journal and with the work of figures like Peter Eisenman and K. Michael Hays), it also coincided with a broader turn against the 'critical' that unfolded unevenly across different disciplines and which – according to a now familiar and self-serving story – pitted a celebration of affirmation and the 'new' against the torturous analyses and deferrals of deconstruction in general. It is not coincidental, then, that the origins of Spencer's own project, as the opening essay in this collection – originally published in the journal *Radical Philosophy* in 2011 – shows, should lie in a critique of what he was the first to name an 'architectural Deleuzism'. That is, 'a self-styled avant-garde in contemporary architecture claiming and legitimizing the emergence of a mode of spatiality' defined by 'mobility, connectivity and flexibility', 'borderless and reprogrammable', as 'essentially *progressive* through its particular reading of the philosophy of Deleuze and Guattari'.

Of course, in some sense, this recourse to Deleuze (with or without Guattari) in the late 1990s appears as a classic instance of architecture's appropriation of a radical philosophy for the rationalization of existing forms of dominant institutional practice; a pattern of legitimation that is hardly new in itself, and which seems little different as instrumentalized 'theory' from the appropriation of Derrida's work in the previous decade. But precisely in rendering such philosophy *positively* instrumental to a 'neoliberal agenda of subjectification', similarly enthused by the flexible, mobile and emergent, it not only arguably de-fanged or contained but also further recuperated and transformed such philosophy by taking theories originally formed in opposition to capitalism and placing them directly (if sometimes unintentionally) in the service of an emerging neoliberal regime of accumulation and mode of subjection itself. And certainly it is true that many of the initial denunciations of critique in the name of a fundamental affirmationism that developed in the 1960s and 1970s emerged out of a critical impulse of their own. One of the problems, however, with their unthinking repetition today is that the libertarian battles of May 68, framed against a Stalinist Communist Party, technocratic top-down urban planning and a paternalistic, bureaucratic welfare state, are hardly our own. Indeed, too often, supposedly radical calls to networked creativity and a self-organized horizontalism, forged in the revolts of the late sixties, simply mime those ideologies of self-organization and ceaseless connectivity attributed to the neoliberal concept of the market, and, worse, provide further support for its generalization. Deleuze and Guattari's gambit that locating a line of flight entailed a demand, in one oft-quoted passage from *Anti-Oedipus,* to 'go further still, that is, in the movement of the market, of decoding and deterritorialisation', looks very different on the other side of the 'neoliberal' revolution and its own dismantling of state institutions and social-democratic norms.[3]

It is unsurprising, then, that if the turn from supposed critical 'negativity' to 'positive' construction and composition has fitted all-too-neatly, on the one hand, with a wider governmental and academic agenda of impact and knowledge exchange, and with a rhetoric for which the social is simply a series of 'problems' to be solved by the appropriate design solutions, it has also coincided, on the other, with new enthusiasms for models of self-organization, spontaneous order and emergence that, only apparently paradoxically, have been defined by their antipathy to Promethean conceptions of planning and to welfarist or social-democratic projects of social transformation. *Contra* Marx's famous eleventh thesis on Feuerbach, one should try neither to interpret *nor* change the world, only describe and affirm it. This has been subject to a particularly brazen articulation by the likes of Patrik Schumacher, who celebrates, increasingly without reservation, architecture and urbanism's subsumption by the form and logic of the market's deterritorializing force against any attempts at 'political' intervention. But, as the essays in this book show, the basic position is common to 'architectural Deleuzism' and its various post-critical progenies far more generally, as is their more or less willing alignment with neoliberal techniques of governmentality and its modes of subjectification and subjection as result.

Of course, in part, this is simply to observe the always changing historical conditions of any critical project. Somewhat inevitably, Spencer's title, *Critique of Architecture,* recalls for us the great (and greatly misunderstood) writings of the Italian architectural historian and theorist Manfredo Tafuri, whose essay 'L'Architecture dans le boudoir' is one of the subjects of the final essay in this book. In particular, and paying close attention to its careful phrasing – that is to say: 'critique of architecture', rather than, for instance, 'criticism of architecture', 'critical architecture', or 'architecture of critique' – it recalls Tafuri's perhaps most notorious provocation: the 'simple truth', as he describes it, first articulated in the 1969 essay 'Toward a Critique of Architectural Ideology', and repeated in *Architecture and Utopia,* that 'just as there cannot exist a class political economy, [but only a class critique of political economy], so too there cannot be founded a class aesthetic, art, or architecture, but only a class *critique* of the aesthetic, of art, of architecture, of the city itself'.[4] Certainly, if Spencer largely shares, I think, Tafuri's view that to 'search for an alternative within the structures that condition the very character of architectural design is indeed an obvious contradiction in terms',[5] he also shares the emphasis on the *necessity* of critique itself.

Like Tafuri, too, Spencer knows that, as either theoretical or architectural practice, critique is never *in itself* a solution to the contradictions and limitations of architecture's current conditions under neoliberalism, and that the historical function of critique must itself be continually subject to self-criticism if it is to meet the challenges of the present. Yet the necessity of critique remains, as a necessity of bringing into question the apparent 'common sense' of contemporary modes of subjectification and subjection, and of architecture's place within these, without which any politics of de-subjection is impossible. The denigration of a tradition of *ideology critique*, in particular, as a simple exercise in elitism and negativity – whatever broader problems the orthodox concept of ideology bequeathed by Marx may indeed possess – is more than a little convenient for those who would prefer not to interrogate too closely architecture's role in furthering the expansion of neoliberal verities about the 'natural' order of the market into ever more areas of social life. The appeals to 'laws of nature' or to 'natural systems' (or, in another register, to ontology over historical analysis) that have become so characteristic of recent architectural discourse all-too-neatly align with the new naturalism of theories of self-organization and complexity that legitimate the 'natural order' of the socio-economic form of the market itself. The necessity of producing a critical knowledge of these ideological 'truths' is not so as to 'negate' them, in the sense of destroying their social reality altogether, but to suspend their givenness as 'just the ways things are' in order to form them as a potential object of strategic intervention and transformation. If it is neoliberalism that constitutes the central object of these essays – and the publication of this collection should establish Doug Spencer, if he isn't already, as *the* pre-eminent thinker to date of architecture's relations to neoliberalism as a social, cultural and political project – then it is precisely because, as he quotes Philip Mirowski in the earlier *Architecture of Neoliberalism:* 'Neoliberalism as a world view has sunk its roots deep into everyday life, almost to the point of passing as the "ideology of no ideology"'.[6]

To the extent that there are, then, continuities with earlier critical projects like that of Tafuri – unsurprisingly, given, across all different forms and regimes of accumulation and valorization, the continuities of capitalism and of the value form itself – there are equally important differences, and the present collection is far from a straightforward return to Tafuri's own idea of a class critique of architecture, not least because Spencer is concerned to interrogate the former's own model of base-superstructure relations in architecture, and the conception of ideology critique that rests on this. Particularly important in this respect is that, *contra* Latour, the critique of the architectural 'fetish' evidently cannot be reduced in these essays to the elitist and debunking 'exposure' of some simple *illusion* about reality on the part of the unenlightened (as the catholic Latour, for example, sometimes seems to suppose is being argued in his reading of the protestant 'iconoclast' Marx). On the contrary, the phantasmagoria is, as it was for Marx, something that exists out there in the actuality of the object as 'value'; a value which is generated by the social relations of capitalist production and exchange. It is in this way that 'the social character of men's labour appears to them as an *objective* character stamped upon the product of that labour; because the relation of the producers to the sum total of their own labour is presented to them as a social relation, existing not between themselves, but between the products of their labour'. This is no simple projection, then, of human ('false') consciousness onto things, but derives from the commodity *form* itself; that is, from the historically specific and very 'real' ways in which things are related in and by capitalism. For this reason, too, merely seeing through it will not, in itself, suffice to render it any less 'real' as such. Indeed, what Marx terms this 'religious reflex of the real world' could only 'finally vanish', he writes, 'when the practical relations of every-day life offer to man none but perfectly intelligible and reasonable relations with regard to his fellowmen and to Nature'.[7]

One of the reasons why architecture, of course, for better or worse, holds a particular importance here is because its problems of appearance and reality, the 'imaginary' and the 'real', are (without simply being reducible to them) also those therefore of the social appearance and reality of capital itself. Positioned in complex ways between the 'infrastructural' and 'superstructural', and consequently mediating between them, architecture is, it may be argued, a privileged site for an interrogation of the productive operations of capital. To the extent that these essays wish to recover a history of efforts to comprehend the ways in which the real abstractions of capital are manifested in the cultural forms through which they are mediated – from Marx to Adorno – they do so, then, in order to *put these to use* in working through the contradictions and naturalizations of our neoliberal present. Only by revealing the abstract relations of power and exchange, which are not themselves 'visible', which are neither 'objects' nor 'things', and which are, as Marx put it, 'occulted' in the naturalization of capitalist forms as self-evident, is it possible to make the latter available to critical reflection. And in architecture, of course, such 'occultation' is all the more effective where form itself is understood as somehow simply self-generated and emergent, rather than as dependent on relations of labour and capital, and thus of social division, exploitation and inequality, necessary to the reproduction of capitalism.

It's striking in this respect – if I may venture one final point of comparison – that Spencer is one of the very few architectural thinkers, since Tafuri, to place a focus on that dirty and vulgar word 'class' itself as crucial to any understanding of the forms and practices of modern and contemporary architecture. As one of these essays puts it, in the context of a discussion of John Barrell's art-historical writings on Constable's landscapes: 'After a now decades-long period of assault on critical theory, discussions of class, labour and capital sit uneasily with what currently passes for theoretical discourse', and its tendency to 'welcome all agents on the stage as equal partners in the making of worlds'. In seeking to reverse this elision, it becomes crucial to return again to the question of the effacement of *labour*, both as the occluded site of production and exploitation, and as antagonist to capital, in the making of the architectural object. Such reminders are unfashionable, and no doubt considerably less seductive than 'avant-gardist' calls to embrace the mobile and the flexible and to abandon the patient and awkward work of critique. But the discomfort they engender in the face of neoliberal 'common sense' is only, as these essays so richly show, a further indication of their necessity.

London, July 2020

Notes

1   Bruno Latour, 'An Attempt at a "Compositionist Manifesto"', *New Literary History* 41 (2010): 475.

2   See Jeffrey Kipnis, 'On the Wild Side', in Farshid Moussavi, Alejandro Zaera-Polo and Sanford Kwinter, eds, *Phylogenesis: FOA's Ark* (Barcelona: Actar, 2004); Sanford Kwinter, *Architectures of Time: Toward a Theory of the Event in Modernist Culture* (Cambridge, MA: MIT Press, 2001).

3   Gilles Deleuze and Félix Guattari, *Anti-Oedipus*, trans. Robert Hurley, Mark Seem and Helen R. Lane (London: Athlone, 1984), 239–40

4   Manfredo Tafuri, *Architecture and Utopia: Design and Capitalist Development*, trans. Barbara Luigia La Penta (Cambridge, MA: MIT Press, 1976), 179.

5   Tafuri, *Architecture and Utopia*, 181.

6   Philip Mirowski, *Never Let a Serious Crisis Go To Waste: How Neoliberalism Survived the Financial Meltdown* (London: Verso, 2013), 48–9.

7   Karl Marx, *Capital, Volume One*, available at: https://www.marxists.org/archive/marx/works/1867-c1/ch01.htm.

Introduction

We are now nearly two decades into the assault on criticality in architecture.[1] The turn to Deleuze, marking the entrance of this assault onto the stage of architecture theory, has itself been succeeded by subsequent turns; to affect, to actor-networks, to object-oriented ontologies, to the new materialism and the non-referential. Yet each of these turns insists, still, on the need to overcome criticality in order to realize the market value of its own new paradigm, as if critique were some ongoing tyrannical regime, some overbearing presence not only in architecture, but in the world at large. Jeffrey Kipnis wrote in 2004 that he wanted to kill criticality, 'once and for all'.[2] In order for the post-critical and its descendants to live, however, criticality must repeatedly be brought back to life in order to be killed change to over and over again. After dying so many deaths, the spectre of critique haunts the world of the living in ever more strange forms. For Mark Foster Gage it assumes the appearance of Kim Kardashian West. Her performative 'awareness' of political concerns is taken as symptomatic of how '[t]hese critical and awareness-based strategies', like those 'critical tactics in architecture', no longer cut it.[3] Worse still, for Gage, the entire project of criticality operates from a privileged position of intellectuality from which it looks down upon the world. Critical theory, from the mid-twentieth century on, 'blanketed architecture, shifting the landscape of Modernist optimism into a darker shade of problem-infested reality that architecture and its privileged perceivers were tasked with "fixing"'.[4] Critical theory is charged by Gage with lowering the positive tone of the twentieth century, and for the presumption to suggest that anything needs setting right.

Rather than the continued and negative reign of the critical, what has in fact marked the past twenty years in architectural culture, in some of its more prominent expressions at least, is its positive embrace of market forces. Architects have learned to play by, and profit from, the rules of the neoliberal truth game: discredit any and all attempts to address the problems of the world as elitist and despotic; demean human capacities for reasoning, leave everything to the superior calculating powers of the market; resign oneself to enjoying its products rather than interpreting them; don't think, feel; market yourself; market the market as progressive.

Conjuring up the critical as a kind of phantasmagoric figure of oppression, though, also serves to ward off the presence of a counter-tendency: the very real and radical politicization of architecture of recent years. Rather than the privilege of the critical theorist, it is that of the white male architect that has been challenged by this counter-tendency. As I write, in 2020, in the midst of the uprising in the US against the ongoing barbarities of structural racism, the funding of the police, and the prison-industrial complex, architects are exposing their experiences of racism in professional practice, and students are demanding substantial revisions to the overwhelmingly white and West-ern-dominated nature of architectural education. While the patriarchal na-ture of the profession has long been called out from feminist historical and theoretical perspectives, this took on even greater significance and urgency, in 2018, with architecture's #MeToo moment, in which allegations of preda-tory and sexually abusive conduct on the part of certain male architects were made public.[5]

The kind of critical awareness disparaged by Gage has been brought to bear, in recent years, both on the employment practices of architectural firms, and on the conditions under which their projects are constructed. The Architec-ture Lobby, formed in 2013 so as to challenge the precarity of architectural employment, has since gone on to address a number of political, economic, environmental and ethical issues in which architecture is implicated.[6] In 2019 the revelation of the use of unpaid interns by Junya Ishigami + Associates, in their Serpentine Pavilion project for London, escalated and made further vis-ible these discussions about the terms and conditions under which architec-tural labour is undertaken.[7] The group Who Builds Your Architecture? have been engaged in bringing about greater awareness of the circumstances un-der which architecture is constructed, and the Settler Colonial City Project 'seeks to rectify the lack of discussion about indigeneity and settler colonial-ism in architecture and urban studies'.[8] All of these initiatives have the goal not merely of raising awareness as some kind of self-satisfying end in itself, but as part of a larger endeavour to bring about radical change within architecture, and the larger world in which it exists.

These are the circumstances to which a critique of architecture must be equal. As Moishe Postone reminds us, 'critical thought and practice' is not itself 'historically indeterminate',[9] and as Ellen Meiksins Wood wrote, the 'critique of capitalism' requires 'a constantly renewed critique of the analytic instruments designed to understand it'.[10] The analytic instruments employed in the critique of architecture are likewise in need of renewal. The essays in this book, accordingly, are not concerned with defending or ratifying critique as it might once have been, or as its opponents imagine it to be, but with the development of critique as a contribution to the larger struggles that refuse to accept what is 'given' in neoliberal capitalism.

Critique is conceived here as a work of praxis, its relation to its object immanent rather than issued from fixed coordinates. It is itself subject to critical analysis in the process of its operation. Expressed in the idiom of critical theory, critique is simultaneously focused on the 'labour of the concept' and the 'concrete specificity' of its objects. Looking both ways at once, its optic acts in relay between theory and practice, each mobilized to unsettle and rethink the other.

Methodologically, the practice of critique presented here is a materialist one, of the old-fashioned Marxian and not the 'new' variety, meaning that architecture is accounted for in terms of how it is financed, designed and built in the fulfilment of social, economic and political projects. The materialist analysis of architecture, as a site of mediation of and for capitalism, is also addressed with reference to the production of subjectivity. As Marx notes in the *Grundrisse*, production in capitalism 'not only creates an object for the subject, but also a subject for the object'.[11] Concern with the means and conditions of subjection, and with how these are made productive of and for capitalism and power, extends of course beyond Marx to twentieth-century critical theory and to Foucauldian modes of analysis. It has also been further elaborated in perspectives offered by Moishe Postone, in his rethinking of the basis of critical theory,[12] and by Sylvia Wynter in respect of the 'overrepresentation' of

Man in the Western and colonizing figure of *homo economicus*.[13] Addressed and drawn upon in *Critique of Architecture*, these approaches are, at the same time, employed with a consciousness of the need to address the part played by architecture, specifically, in the production of subjectivity within capitalism.

In pursuit of this, *Critique of Architecture* addresses how architecture is employed to individuate subjects, or else to aggregate them within formations affirming the imaginary of capitalism. It addresses how circulation patterns accommodate subjects to certain modes of behaviour, how architecture produces proximities instrumental to new forms of living and working. Architecture is conceived and analyzed as a medium through which habits can be formed and broken, through which attention can be focused or dispersed, through which the subject can be directly addressed or treated with indifference. Opposed to the conventions of treating architecture merely as representative of capitalism, *Critique of Architecture* is premised on the analysis of architecture as a medium for its operations.

Critique of Architecture also follows Marx's imperative that the practice of critique be unremittingly ruthless. This entails reckoning with apparent allies as much as obvious enemies. While the essays of the book's first section address the depoliticization of architecture, those of its second section contest the terms of its re-politicization, taking issue with current theories of architectural resistance, and political and individual autonomy. The enemies of our enemies are, after all, not always our friends. Likewise, the third section of *Critique of Architecture*, focused on the practice of theory, takes on the mystifications of its present objects of fascination – cutting through the jargon of 'new' materialisms and object-oriented ontologies – while also confronting its canonically leftist approaches, specifically those endowed to theory through the work of Fredric Jameson, the Situationist's legacy of 'spectacle' and the 'base and superstructure model'.

In the first section Architecture, Deleuze and Neoliberalism, I address the turn to, and the consequences of, architecture's embrace of neoliberalism. Chapter 1, Architectural Deleuzism: Neoliberal Space, Control and the 'Univer-City' was first published, in 2011, in the journal *Radical Philosophy*.

It charts the discursive manoeuvres through which a prominent tendency in architecture dispensed with Derrida – the last vestige of its long engagement with critical, linguistic and semiotic models – so as take up the (apparently) affirmative and (seemingly) more architecturally translatable philosophy of Deleuze and Guattari. Here I explore how the conceptual vocabulary of Deleuze and Guattari, at least as this was appropriated within 'post-critical' and 'projective' architectural currents, enabled these to present themselves as progressive while serving the ends of neoliberalism. Newly written, Chapter 2, Habitats for *homo economicus:* Architecture, Design and the Environment of 'Man', traces the confluence of design and neoliberalism back to an earlier moment than that of 'architectural Deleuzism'. Here I reflect on how certain of the founding thinkers of environment in design – Buckminster Fuller, John McHale, Ian McHarg, Reyner Banham – constructed conceptions of 'Man', 'environment', and a normative notion of what should constitute the proper relationship between the two. These conceptions, I argue, were passed off as natural in a fashion that served, and continues to serve, racial capitalism, and the unquestioned universalization of *homo economicus* as the ideal of human subjectivity. Chapter 3, Personifying Capital: Architecture and the Image of Participation, is also newly written for this collection. I expand here on the critique of participation, and the circulatory forms of architecture facilitating this, first presented in my *Architecture of Neoliberalism.* I also explore the role of such architectures as platforms for the production of an imagery affirming capitalism's ideals of social conduct, in terms of labour and leisure. Reaching back historically to include in my analysis the early nineteenth-century landscapes of John Constable, and forward to today's platform architectures, I point both to the continuities and to the changes in this imagery, and to the circumstances and conditions of capital accumulation to which they are related.

The essays assembled in the second section, Autonomy: Architecture and the Politics of Depoliticization, represent the opening of a second front in the critique of architecture. Where the first section offers a critique of the more or less openly neoliberal ends to which architecture is attuned in its post-critical, projective, environmental and Deleuzian turns, the second section engages with the forms in which this architecture, and its ideology, are opposed. The critique of this oppositional tendency is focused on how it takes the autonomous individual subject as given, rather than as itself historically and ideologically situated, every bit as much the neoliberal subject. These essays also challenge the equation of the formal with the political on which the resistance to neoliberalism in architecture has tended to rest, as well as the related faith in the essentially insulating and protective capacities it is able to afford the subject from the tyrannies of commerce and exchange.

Chapter 4, Less Than Enough: A Critique of the Project of Autonomy, was originally published under the title 'Less than Enough: A Critique of Aureli' in *This Thing Called Theory*, edited by Teresa Stoppani, Giorgio Ponzo and George Themistokleous. In *Less is Enough* Pier Vittorio Aureli argues that the Franciscan monasteries exemplify the kind of protective secession from the economic that architecture ought now to provide for the contemporary subject. This essay challenges both Aureli's account of monastic practices and the broader implications of his arguments. These, it is shown, lack an effectively critical position. Rather than confronting the complexities of contemporary urban reality, they offer only a retreat to a mystified notion of architectural and subjective autonomy. In doing so, this essay concludes, Aureli inadvertently aligns himself with elements of the neoliberal project he supposes himself to be opposing.

In Chapter 5, The Limits of Limits: Schmitt, Aureli and the Geopolitical Ontology of the Island, which first appeared in *New Geographies 8: Island*, 2016, I critique Aureli's argument that prevailing models of the fluid, connective and self-organizing in design, as well as the broader neoliberal conditions in which they operate, are best contested through an agonistic politics translated into architectural form. To this end, I present an analysis of the roots of Aureli's archipelago model in the thought of Carl Schmitt. Addressing the latter's characteristic polarization of terms such as land-sea, political-economic, friend-enemy and limited-unlimited, and exploring the mythic and fascistic roots of these agonistic binaries, I then turn to a critique of Aureli's project centred on the implications of his own adoption of an agonistic politics of architecture.

Chapter 6, 'Out of the Loop: Architecture, Automation and Cognitive Disinvestment' was originally published (with a slightly different subtitle) in the journal *Volume* 49: Automation, September 2016. In this text I reflect on how arguments against automation and its technologies – such as those authored by Bifo Berardi – typically centre on how these supposedly invade and corrupt the mind and mentality of the individual subject. This essay notes, on the contrary, that individuation is a historically situated practice, itself aided and abetted through technology, and argues that the trajectory of technological usage in capitalism is oriented towards an ever-greater disinvestment in human cognitive capacities, the subject tending more now to be addressed through forms of affective management, and for which the contemporary architectural surface serves as a component of its apparatus.

Originally published in *e-flux architecture* in 2017, Chapter 7, Architecture after California, considers how current affirmations of individual freedom and entrepreneurship in design, and the utilization of technologies and techniques drawn from within capitalist development to achieve these, originate in significant part from the beliefs and mentalities cultivated within its Californian counterculture. The consequent depoliticization of design, it is argued here, results in the translation of a socially radical agenda into a purely formal conception and discourse of what is radical in architecture, an affirmation of autonomy exemplified in the practice of Frank Gehry and his 'liberation of architecture' from the tyranny of the right angle, achieved through his appropriation of the CATIA CAD software system.

The third section of this work, Reckoning with Theory, is addressed both to a critique of architectural theory and practice subsequent to the moment of architectural Deleuzism and the post-critical, and to certain of the problematics of critical theory itself, in its failing to fully capture and account for the relations between architecture and capitalism. Chapter 8, Going to Ground: Agency, Design and the Problem of Bruno Latour, was first published in the collection *Landscape as Territory*, edited by Clara Olóriz Sanjuán. This essay takes aim at questions of agency in the flat ontology and Actor-Network Theory of Bruno Latour, and as applied to architecture in the research and writing of Albena Yaneva. In the seemingly generous gesture of extending agency to the full spectrum of its nonhuman actors, I argue here, these models effectively obscure the very real inequalities of the distribution and access to agency afforded to human subjects, and at the same time actively overlook, from their post-political perspective, the agency of the biggest actor of them all: the 'automatic subject' that is capital.

Originally published in *Harvard Design Magazine* in 2018, Chapter 9, Returns on the City: Detroit and the Design of Late Fordism, takes as its point of departure the then recently announced return of the Ford Motor Company to Detroit, particularly its purchase and proposed transformation of the long-abandoned and derelict Michigan Central Station. Concerned with how Ford's investment in the city is both posited on the economic returns it hopes to reap, and with the related ways in which its architectures and landscapes are designed to actively construct certain forms of subjectivity, I note that such practices are consistent with those employed by this company, and others, in the early twentieth century. On this basis, I explore how capitalism, and its architecture, is often more marked by repetition and continuity than its 'stagist' theorists, such as Fredric Jameson and David Harvey, are able to acknowledge.

In the newly written Chapter 10, Enjoy the Silence: On the Consolations of the Post-political, I reflect on the disappearance of signification and symbolism from public architectures such as mass transit systems. I also consider how this disappearance corresponds to a contemporaneous affirmation, in José Aragüez's *The Building,* of an architecture theory that has no need of mediating concepts, and, in Valerio Olgiati and Markus Breitschmid's *Non-Referential Architecture,* of an architecture with no need for referentiality or signification. In concluding this essay, I suggest that the architectural practice and the theoretical discourse considered here are alike in affirming a mentality of indifference to, and acceptance of, things as they present themselves to the subject in immediate experience; a kind of conditioning to the post-political and the post-ideological.

Chapter 11, Architecture's Abode of Production: Beyond Base and Superstructure, also newly written for this book, addresses the limitations of architectural history and theory in its understanding of the relations between architecture and capitalism. It takes aim, firstly, at the default modes to which the critique of architecture tends to resort, especially in relation to the notion of 'spectacle' derived from Guy Debord, and, from Fredric Jameson, the structuralist-inspired interpretation of architecture as 'symptomatic' of some deeper, and otherwise inaccessible, new stage of capitalism. I then turn, more sympathetically, to Manfredo Tafuri's insistence that one sees architecture as directly productive for and within capitalism, looking not at the outer manifestation of architecture's appearance, but at the class relations implicated in its construction. Even here, though, I argue, we are still operating within the confines of a base and superstructure model of capitalism, with production assigned to the former and consumption to the latter. In order to overcome this limiting conception of how capitalism operates, and of how architecture serves this operation, I turn to Marx so as to elaborate more effectively the dialectical relations between production and consumption, and how architecture is implicated in these.

Critique of Architecture concludes with a conversation conducted over the course of the spring and summer of 2020 with the architect, writer and editor Miloš Kosec. Titled 'On Allegory, the Architectural Imagination and Radical Disillusionment', this conversation ranges across the themes and concerns addressed in this collection and other of my writings, as well as the current conditions in which architecture operates, and the relationship between neoliberal capitalism and the architectural imagination.

Notes

1   I take the publication in 2002 of Robert Somol and
     Sarah Whiting, 'Notes Around the Doppler Effect
     and Other Moods of Modernism', *Perspecta* 33,
     'Mining Autonomy', 72–7, as indicative of the point
     at which the so-called 'post-critical' turn com-
     mences. Of course, however, its roots extend far
     deeper, going back, I would argue, to the pragma-
     tism of Robert Venturi, Denise Scott Brown and
     Steven Izenour's *Learning from Las Vegas* (Cam-
     bridge, MA: MIT Press, 1972).

2   Jeffrey Kipnis, 'On the Wild Side', in Farshid Mous-
     savi, Alejandro Zaera-Polo and Sanford Kwinter,
     eds, *Phylogenesis: FOA's Ark* (Barcelona: Actar,
     2004), 579.

3   Mark Foster Gage, *Designing Social Equality: Archi-
     tecture, Aesthetics, and the Perception of Democ-
     racy* (Abingdon and New York: Routledge, 2019) 43.

4   Ibid., 44.

5   See, for instance, Robin Pogrebin, '5 Women Ac-
     cuse the Architect Richard Meier of Sexual Harass-
     ment', *New York Times*, 13 March 2018 <https://
     www.nytimes.com/2018/03/13/arts/design/rich-
     ard-meier-sexual-harassment-allegations.html>.

6   The Architecture Lobby <http://architecture-lobby.
     org/wp-content/uploads/2016/11/2014_Tactics_
     Pamphlet_01b.pdf>.

7   Tim Jonze, 'Row over Use of Unpaid Interns by
     Serpentine Pavilion Architect', *The Guardian*,
     22 March, 2019 <https://www.theguardian.com/
     artanddesign/2019/mar/22/row-unpaid-in-
     terns-serpentine-london-gallery-pavilion-archi-
     tect-project>.

8   Settler Colonial City Project, 2019 <https://settler-
     colonialcityproject.org>.

9   Moishe Postone, *Time, Labor, and Social Domina-
     tion: A Reinterpretation of Marx's Critical Theory*
     (Cambridge , UK and New York: Cambridge Univer-
     sity Press, 1993), 38.

10   Ellen Meiksins Wood, *Democracy Against Capital-
     ism: Renewing Historical Materialism* (Cambridge,
     UK: Cambridge University Press, 1995), 4.

11   Karl Marx, *Grundrisse: Foundations of the Critique
     of Political Economy*, trans. Martin Nicolaus
     (Harmondsworth: Penguin Books in association
     with New Left Review, 1973), 92.

12   Postone, *Time, Labor, and Social Domination*.

13   Sylvia Wynter 'Unsettling the Coloniality of Being/
     Power/Truth/Freedom: Towards the Human, After
     Man, Its Overrepresentation – An Argument', *The
     New Centennial Review*, Vol. 3, No. 3, Fall 2003,
     257–337.

Maison Folie, Lille, France, NOX – Lars Spuybroek, 2004

Section 1.
Architecture, Deleuze and Neoliberalism

1 Architectural Deleuzism: Neoliberal Space, Control and the 'Univer-City'

For many thinkers of the spatiality of contemporary capitalism, the production of all social space tends now to converge upon a single organizational paradigm designed to generate and service mobility, connectivity and flexibility. Networked, landscaped, borderless and reprogrammable, this is a space that functions, within the built environments of business, shopping, education or the 'creative industries', to mobilize the subject as a communicative and enterprising social actant. Integrating once discrete programmes within its continuous terrain, and promoting communication as a mechanism of valorization, control and feedback, this spatial model trains the subject for a life of opportunistic networking.

Life, in this environment, is lived as a precarious and ongoing exercise in the acquisition of contacts, the exchange of information and the pursuit of projects. As a form of space, this is consistent with what Foucault described as the mode of neoliberal governmentality, operating through environmental controls and modulations, rather than the disciplinary maintenance of normative individual behaviour. It also, as many have noted, resembles the 'control society' forecast some time ago by Gilles Deleuze, in his 'Postscript on Control Societies', in which the movement of 'dividuals' is tracked and monitored across the transversal 'smooth space' of a post-disciplinary society.[1] Developed, in part at least, in response to the growth of Post-Fordist knowledge economies, so-called immaterial labour and the prevalence of networked communications media, this spatial paradigm has been theorized through models of complexity, self-organization and emergence. It has also been serviced, as I want to show in what follows, by a self-styled avant-garde in contemporary architecture claiming and legitimizing the emergence of this mode of spatiality as essentially progressive through its particular reading of the philosophy of Deleuze and Guattari.

What I will term here 'Deleuzism' in architecture – identifiable in the projects and discourse of practices such as Zaha Hadid Architects (ZHA), Foreign Office Architects (FOA), Reiser + Umemoto and Greg Lynn, for example – has tended to read the philosophy of Deleuze and Guattari with a marked bias towards its Bergsonian and Spinozian (rather than Marxian) registers. Filtering from the philosophers' corpus any trace of criticality, it has not, though, renounced the political in this process, but rather reframed it as a matter of organization and affect. Transcribing Deleuzian (or Deleuzoguattarian) concepts such as the 'fold', 'smooth space' and 'faciality' into a prescriptive repertoire of formal manoeuvres, Deleuzism in architecture has proposed, through its claims to mirror the affirmative materialism of becoming and 'the new' which it has found within Deleuze and Guattari's oeuvre, that it shares with that oeuvre a 'progressive' and 'emancipatory' agenda.

In the main part of the article that follows, I want to explore this supposed agenda through the study of an exemplary recent project: FOA's design for the new campus of Ravensbourne College (2010) located on the Greenwich Peninsula in London. This is an especially interesting project in this context, not only because of the ways in which it connects with current concerns regarding the neoliberal marketization of education (particularly in the UK), but also because of the reputation acquired by FOA, and of Alejandro Zaera-Polo, for being at the leading edge of contemporary architectural Deleuzism. Like many other figures from this milieu, FOA initially extracted from the work of Deleuze and Guattari a number of key concepts appearing to lend themselves readily to translation into a set of formal and spatial tropes, but, significantly, they have more recently returned to the question of the political, once denounced by Zaera-Polo as ephemeral to the concerns of architecture,[2] and positioned the building envelope as the organizational and representational medium through which the discipline can now acquire political agency. It is to this turn within architectural Deleuzism, along with its reconception of the political and claims to have advanced beyond a supposedly outmoded and regressive politics of opposition and critique, that this article will attend. Before coming directly to FOA and to the Ravensbourne project, however, I need first to trace the emergence of

Deleuze's dominant position within recent 'avant-garde' architectural theory more generally.

The new architecture

During the period of its initial development in the 1990s, Deleuzism in architecture was driven, primarily, by readings of the philosopher's *The Fold: Leibniz and the Baroque,* and the section on the smooth and the striated, from Deleuze and Guattari's *A Thousand Plateaus: Capitalism and Schizophrenia.*[3] Promoted as an architectural device in the 1993 special edition of *Architectural Design* entitled *Folding in Architecture,* which featured essays and projects by Peter Eisenman, Greg Lynn and Jeffrey Kipnis, among others, Deleuze's 'fold', with its apparent correlation of Leibniz's philosophy with the formal complexity of the architectural Baroque, seemed, in particular, to offer architecture an escape route from its entanglement in linguistic and semiotic paradigms, and opened the way for a return to form, as a concern more proper and specific to its own discipline.[4] Eisenman, for example, claimed to have employed the fold as a generative device in his Rebstockpark project of 1990, a Deleuzian inflected account of which was further elaborated in John Rajchman's *Constructions.*[5] Conceptually related to the fold, the schema of the smooth and the striated was originally elaborated in *A Thousand Plateaus* to articulate the relations between open and closed systems in technology, music, mathematics, geography, politics, art and physics. Smooth space was figured there as topologically complex, in continuous variation and fluid. This was a space – a sea or a desert – through which one drifted, nomadically. Striated space, by contrast, was defined by its rigid geometry, a space carved up into functional categories channelling the movements of its occupants along the pre-inscribed lines of its Cartesian grid. Striated space was standardized, disciplinary and imperial. Again, these concepts, particularly the implicit (though qualified)[6] privileging of smooth space and continuous variation over static geometry, were found to resonate with architecture's engagement with complex topologies while suggesting that its formal experimentation was also

Fig. 1.1: Korean Presbyterian Church of New York, Queens, New York, USA, 1999, Greg Lynn FORM

imbued with philosophically radical implications. Deleuzean 'smoothing' and the pursuit of continuous variation has been referenced in the architectural writings of, variously, Lynn, Reiser + Umemoto, Patrik Schumacher and FOA, for instance, to suggest the philosophical substance of the complex formal modulations that characterize their work.

The usefulness of Deleuze and Guattari's philosophy was not limited, though, to its provision of the formal tropes of folding and smoothing, but also extended to a conception of the 'new' with which architectural Deleuzism could further differentiate itself from the preceding currents of Postmodernism and Deconstructivism in the 1980s and early 1990s. In Kipnis's contribution to the *Folding in Architecture* volume, 'Towards a New Architecture', Postmodernist architecture was hence cast as politically conservative, even reactionary, due to its ultimate inability to produce the new. In its use of collage and historicism, Postmodernism's ultimate effect, he argued, was to 'valorize a finite catalogue of elements and/or processes'. For Kipnis, Postmodern architecture had enabled a reactionary discourse that re-establishes traditional hierarchies and supports received systems of power, such as the discourse of the nothing new employed by Ronald Reagan and Margaret Thatcher for their political ends and by Prince Charles, Roger Scruton and even Charles Jencks to prop up PoMo. Whatever the truth of this, one further marker of the 'new' architecture's own newness was, in turn, its departure from any semiotic or linguistic paradigm, even the most radically conceived (as in deconstruction), in favour of a supposedly new Deleuzean orientation adopted by its theorists such as Lynn and Sanford Kwinter. These, wrote Kipnis, had turned from 'post-structural semiotics to a consideration of recent developments in geometry, science and the transformation of political space, a shift that is often marked as a move from a Derridean to a Deleuzean discourse'.[7]

The proposition that Deleuze could think the new in terms of 'political space', while Derrida was mired in the detached realm of 'post-structural semiotics', though unsustainable as a reading of their actual philosophies, was thus mobilized by Kipnis and others in order to distinguish the new architecture from that of its immediate predecessors such as Bernard Tschumi (or the earlier Eisenman). Where such architects had been identified with Derridean deconstruction, a new generation would need to distinguish itself both from its architectural predecessors and from the philosophy with which these had been associated. Yet in order to ratify this new architecture with the same pedigree of philosophical sophistication as that accorded to Deconstructivist architecture, a comparable counterpart to Derrida had to be found. Enter Deleuze.

As François Cusset has noted, there was a broader trajectory of transition from 'Lacanian–Derridean' to 'Deleuzean–Lyotardian' positions during this period in American academia.[8] So, this is far from unique to architecture. But the shift towards Deleuze, in US architectural culture at least, has also to be understood in terms of how the place of the 'new', or of 'becoming', in the thought of Deleuze could be made amenable to an architecture seeking to establish for itself an image of novelty as its very *raison d'être*. Indeed, for the 'new architecture', the term 'new' operated as a convenient conflation of two senses of the term: one identifying it as succeeding the old (Deconstructivism or Postmodernism), the other as an orientation towards a philosophy of invention itself, putatively derived from Deleuze. At this point philosophy was conjoined to an exercise in academic marketing; the new as invention conflated with the new as the rebranding of an architectural 'avant-garde'. Exemplary of this mobilization of newness is Reiser + Umemoto's *Atlas of Novel Tectonics,* where Postmodernism is employed as the foil against which the novelty of their approach to architecture is contrasted. Here Deleuze, and Deleuze and Guattari, are read, above all, as philosophers of matter, emergence and becoming. Through their allegiance to this philosophy the architects thus pursue, they claim, an agenda of 'difference' and 'the unforeseen': 'The primary and necessary conceit of this work is that beneficial novelty is the preferred condition to stability and the driving agenda behind architectural practice.'[9]

Where Deleuzism in architecture originally undertook, then, to establish its autonomy from the linguistically oriented concerns of post-structuralism, it subsequently sought to distance itself too, as part of its affirmation of the new – indeed, affirmation of affirmation – from any obligation to engage with critique. Through its alliance with the 'post-critical' position emerging, around the same time, in US architectural discourse – marked by the publication of Robert Somol and Sarah Whiting's now near-canonical 'Notes Around the Doppler Effect and Other Moods of Modernism' in the journal *Perspecta* in 2002 – it articulated its opposition to critique as a matter both extrinsic to the 'proper' concerns of architecture, and as a counterproductive form of 'negativity'.[10] In an essay of 2004, 'On the Wild Side', for example, Kipnis describes criticality as a 'disease' that he wants to 'kill', 'once and for all'.[11] For Zaera-Polo, similarly, criticality is anachronistic, and, in its 'negativity', allegedly inadequate to deal with contemporary levels of social complexity:

> I must say that the paradigm of the 'critical' is in my opinion part of the intellectual models that became operative in the early 20th century and presumed that in order to succeed we should take a kind of 'negative' view towards reality, in order to be creative, in order to produce new possibilities. In my opinion, today the critical individual practice that has characterized intellectual correctness for most of the 20th century is no longer particularly adequate to deal with a culture determined by processes of transformation on a scale and complexity difficult to understand ... you have to be fundamentally engaged in the processes and learn to manipulate them from the inside. You never get that far into the process as a critical individual. If we talk in terms of the construction of subjectivity, the critical belongs to Freud [and] Lacan, what I called 'productive', to Deleuze.[12]

Zaera-Polo's remarks here are significant not only in recruiting Deleuze to the affirmative 'productivity' of the new architecture (and in the process eradicating through a crude binary opposition the real continuities between Lacan, and Deleuze and Guattari, to be found, for example, in the concept of 'territorialization'), but also in the proposition that architecture position itself within the complexities of contemporary culture so as to 'manipulate' them from the inside. Where Deleuzism in architecture is to be autonomous from any engagement with linguistic paradigms or critical perspectives, through its own formal and material practices, it will become 'progressive' by making its cause immanent to that of a social culture of complexity.

'Progressive realities'

This kind of proposition is especially evident in the writings of Zaha Hadid and her partner in practice Patrik Schumacher. Their argument for the progressive and emancipatory character of an architecture informed by Deleuzean folding and smoothing rests upon the apparent correspondence between the complexity of their formal strategies and that of the social reality into which these are projected. As Hadid remarked in her 2004 Pritzker Prize acceptance speech:

> I believe that the complexities and the dynamism of contemporary life cannot be cast into the simple platonic forms provided by the classical canon, nor does the modern style afford enough means of articulation. We have to deal with social diagrams that are more complex and layered when compared with the social programs of the early modern period. My work therefore has been concerned with the expansion of the compositional repertoire available to urbanists and designers to cope with this increase in complexity. This includes the attempt to organize and express dynamic processes within a spatial and tectonic construct.[13]

In fact, Schumacher's description of this new 'spatial construct' bears a striking similarity to that used by Deleuze to outline the new conditions of a control society. Deleuze wrote, in his 'Postscript on Control Societies':

> The different internments of spaces of enclosure through which the individual passes are independent variables: each time one is supposed to start from zero, and although a common language for all these places exists, it is analogical. On the other hand, the different control mechanisms are inseparable variations, forming a system of variable geometry the language of which is numerical (which doesn't necessarily mean binary). Enclosures are molds, distinct castings, but controls are a modulation, like a self-deforming cast that will continuously change from one moment to the other, or like a sieve whose mesh will transmute from point to point.[14]

Schumacher, in his *Digital Hadid: Landscapes in Motion*, writes of:

> [...] a new concept of space (magnetic field space, particle space, continuously distorted space) which suggests a new orientation, navigation and inhabitation of space. The inhabitant of such spaces no longer orients by means of prominent figures, axis, edges and clearly bounded realms. Instead the distribution of densities, directional bias, scalar grains and gradient vectors of transformation constitute the new ontology defining what it means to be somewhere.[15]

Between Deleuze's 'sieve whose mesh will transmute from point to point' and 'gradient vectors of transformation', on the one hand, and Schumacher's 'spaces of enclosure' and 'clearly bounded realms', on the other, the account of a transition from a striated to a smooth space can be followed in parallel across both passages. The movement that can be traced between them, however, when the passages are returned to the frame of their respective contexts, is one from critique to valorization; from Deleuze's warning to Schumacher's affirmation. This movement paradoxically turns Deleuze's analysis of a nascent control mechanism into a prescription for its implementation. Critique is absorbed into the very forms of knowledge and power it had sought to denounce in order to reinvent and valorize their operation.

In this respect, arguably, it has something in common with certain strands of contemporary managerialism and its own preference for networked and 'self-organized' modes of operation. Indeed, in what is perhaps the most thoroughly researched and elaborated analysis of this, *The New Spirit of Capitalism*, Luc Boltanski and Eve Chiapello have argued that the orientation of contemporary managerial theories towards de-hierarchized and networked forms of organization originates, in fact, not in the production process, but precisely in a critique of capitalism which is then appropriated by capitalism. In particular, they note:

> autonomy, spontaneity, rhizomorphous capacity, multitasking ... conviviality, openness to others and novelty, availability and creativity, visionary intuition, sensitivity to differences, listening to lived experience and

receptiveness to a whole range of experiences, being attracted to informality and the search for interpersonal contacts – these are taken from the repertoire of May 1968.[16]

This liberatory 'repertoire', Boltanski and Chiapello continue, originally directed against capitalism, has since been seized upon within managerial literature, and detached from the broader context of its attack on all forms of exploitation (not just those concerning the division of labour and its alienating conditions), such that its themes are then 'represented as objectives that are valid in their own right, and placed in the service of forces whose destruction they were intended to hasten'.[17]

In the case of contemporary architecture this process has been historically achieved, first of all, via a recasting of Deleuze and Guattari's 'conceptual personae' of the fold and smooth space as affirmative figures prescriptive of a particular ethos of practice – a process of valorization that is reinforced with reference to the contemporary conditions of fluidity and mobility, to the language of networks, fields, swarms and self-organization, with which Deleuze and Guattari's terms appear to accord in their commitment to 'openness' and 'complexity'.[18] As Schumacher writes in his 2006 essay 'The Skyscraper Revitalized: Differentiation, Interface, Navigation': 'Dense proximity of differences, and a new intensity of connections distinguishes contemporary life from the modern period of separation and repetition. The task is to order and articulate this complexity in ways that maintain legibility and orientation.'[19]

Hadid's commitment, in line with this, to what she terms 'porosity in organization', to the concept of the 'open', is broadly evident throughout her practice, and particularly exemplified in projects such as the Museum of XXI Century Arts in Rome (2010), the Phaeno Science Centre in Wolfsburg and the Central Building for BMW, Leipzig (2005).[20]

Zaera-Polo similarly identifies architecture as a progressive practice of spatial organization due to its capacity to facilitate open and complex systems. 'The proposition here', he writes in his essay 'The Politics of the Envelope', 'is that progressive politics today is enabled through dynamic disequilibrium, not static evenness. Rather than a politics of indifference, independence and

Fig. 1.2: BMW Central Building, Leipzig, Germany, Zaha Hadid Architects, 2005

evenness, progressive politics promote connected unevenness, inducing difference and interdependence.'[21] Deleuzism in architecture's claim to be progressive is thereby defined in terms of an allegiance to a zeitgeist of openness, complexity and difference with which its own practice is perfectly attuned. As such, however, it also tends towards a claim for its progressive status made precisely on the basis of its strategic alliance with more specific tendencies within contemporary culture, such as those of corporate organization and the kind of managerial theory that Boltanski and Chiapello discuss. This is, again, most obvious and explicit in the writings of Schumacher. Hence, for example, in his essay 'Research Agenda: Spatializing the Complexities of Contemporary Business Organization', Schumacher proposed that the research agenda of a unit taught at the Architectural Association, London, titled 'Corporate Fields', constituted an 'emancipatory project', founded upon the 'coincidence of tropes between new management theory and recent avant-garde architecture'. 'New ways of organizing labour are emerging', he wrote in this essay, 'as witnessed in countless new organizational and management theories ... The business of management consultancy is now thriving while the discipline of architecture – with few exceptions – has yet to recognize that it could play a part in this process.'[22] The organizational models employed within the most advanced sections of business represent, for Schumacher, a movement from the rigidly segmented and hierarchical work patterns of the Fordist era towards those that are 'de-hierarchized' and based upon flexible networks.

Architecture, using such 'Deleuzian' formal tropes as 'smoothness' and 'folding', he argued, might make itself 'relevant' by entering into a dialectic with the 'new social tropes' with which business organization and management theory are already engaged, thus allowing 'architecture to translate organizational concepts into new effective spatial tropes while in turn launching new organizational concepts by manipulating space'. Unsurprisingly, then, Schumacher has claimed that there is, 'today no better site for a progressive and forward-looking project than the most competitive contemporary business domains'.[23]

This position is maintained by an insistence that left-wing activism has all but 'disintegrated' to the extent that traditional models and spaces of radicalism 'stagnate' and 'regress'.[24] More contemporary forms and sites of activism, such as the anti-globalization 'movement of movements', within whose broad spectrum of oppositional perspectives might be identified some cause for optimism, are similarly discredited by Schumacher, in so far as their 'critical' form lacks a suitably 'constructive' or affirmative trajectory: 'The recent anti-globalization movement is a protest movement, i.e. defensive in orientation and without a coherent constructive outlook that could fill the ideological vacuum left behind since the disappearance of the project of international socialism.'[25] Only within the business organization, he argues, can the 'progressive realities' – such as 'de-hierarchization, matrix and network organization, flexible specialization, loose and multiple coupling, etc.' – thus be found to fill this 'ideological vacuum'. These 'progressive realities' are, in any case, not seen as the creations of business itself, but as conditions 'forced upon the capitalist enterprise by the new degree of complexity and flexibility of the total production process'.[26] Hence they can be bracketed from their neoliberal context, and then pursued, in themselves, as a means by which architecture can locate and pursue a supposedly emancipatory project.

The argument proposed by Zaera-Polo in 'The Politics of the Envelope' is remarkably close to that constructed by Schumacher. Zaera-Polo, and his one-time partner in FOA, Farshid Moussavi, had, in the creation of their Yokohama Port Terminal in Japan (2002), with its undulating platforms and pleated surfaces, acquired a reputation at the cutting edge of Deleuzism in architecture. More recently he and Moussavi have turned to emphasize other Deleuzoguattarian concepts, such as 'micro-politics' and the 'assemblage'. Yet, the apparent politicization of architectural practice entailed by this has in fact served, first and foremost, to redefine the 'political' so that it is now subsumed within the same concerns for 'material organizations', complexity and fluidity that have always been the focus of FOA's theory and practice. Although then Zaera-Polo evokes the possibility of a 'political ecology' that would enable architecture 'to regain an active political role', this does not actually politicize ecology, as a concern that must be considered socially or economically, but instead attempts to reframe the political as a purely environmental matter. At the same time, the progressive potential of such concepts as 'micro-politics', Zaera-Polo has claimed, is best sought through architecture's engagement with the

Fig. 1.3: South-East Coastal Park, Barcelona, Spain, Foreign Office Architects, 2004

market, since it is today 'the most important medium of power distribution within the global economy'. Not only is the market the 'most important medium of power', but, Zaera-Polo argues, it inherently tends, within its own logic, to break down hierarchical power into heterarchical forms. 'We are witnessing', he writes, 'the emergence of a heterarchical order which increasingly constructs its power by both producing and using diversity.' Compared with older, rigidly bureaucratic and hierarchical forms of power, he proposes, the market 'is probably a better milieu to articulate the current proliferation of political interests and the rise of micro-politics'.[27]

FOA's strategic engagement with the market, as a putatively 'heterarchical order', is perhaps best exemplified in their design of the new campus for the digital media and design university Ravensbourne College (2010), located on London's Greenwich Peninsula. Here, according to the ambitions of the college's directors, creative education is to be released from its artificial enclosures and made immanent precisely to the 'realities' of the market. Aligning themselves with this goal, FOA produced for Ravensbourne, specifically in the name of Deleuzoguattarian perspectives and a progressive agenda, an architecture in which education and business are thus made spatially and experientially coextensive. It is therefore worth focusing upon in some detail.

Learning 2.0

Ravensbourne's relocation to Greenwich in 2010 was, in the words of an internal document composed four years earlier, designed to facilitate and reinforce its institutional adoption of a 'flexible learning agenda'. According to this agenda, the 'vision' for the new Ravensbourne, of which FOA's architecture was to be a part, was to be one where 'space, technology and time will work together to create a new and flexible learning landscape that will support ongoing expansion and change, as well as narrowing the gap between an education and industry experience'.[28] This adoption of so-called flexible learning was driven by broader developments in UK higher education in which the Department for Education and Skills and the Higher Education Funding Council for England had recommended the development of 'blended learning strategies' to universities.[29] 'Blended learning', according to Bliuc, Goodyear and Ellis, 'describes learning activities that involve a systematic combination of co-present (face-to-face) interactions and technologically mediated interactions between students, teachers and learning resources'.[30] These 'learning activities' are more flexible not only since they enable the student to 'time-shift' education to a time and place of their own choosing – since they enable and incorporate access to electronic learning resources outside the regulated times and spaces of the educational institution – but also because they respond to students' existing priorities and predispositions, as described by 'space-planning' consultancy DEGW in their 'User Brief for the New Learning Landscape':

> The ability and motivation of students to learn has changed and will change further as economic pressures compound the effects of new media and new attitudes to learning. Today's students assimilate knowledge vicariously from broadcast and interactive media and through practical application rather than formally from books and many are easily bored by traditional teaching with little visual content ... Most expect time-shifted delivery of learning to accommodate the part-time work that helps them manage student debt. Rapid acquisition of fashionable, marketable skills or commitments to intense personal interests (e.g. bands) can take priority over formal achievements in an academic discipline. Future students are likely to rank educational institutions by their ability to deliver employment and to accommodate diverse approaches to learning.[31]

Ravensbourne has sought not only to use digital media as a support for traditional learning methods but as a means to interpellate the student and their practice within market-based forms of enterprise and competition. In the internal report on the college's 'Designs for Learning Project' its authors argue that '[w]ithin an academic environment, practice takes place in a vacuum, or, rather, an endlessly self-reflecting hall of mirrors'. Insulated from the 'creative dialectic between creator and client (or public) that exists in the 'real world' students problematically 'overvalue individual artistic or creative input, rather than the negotiated creativity of the marketplace'. Students of

Ravensbourne are therefore required to adopt 'web 2.0 values' and use online social networks and blogging in their projects as a means to mediate 'a renewed connection with the audience, or consumers, of creative products'. This practice, it is proposed, should become 'a normative component of creative education'.[32] Perfectly exemplifying the neoliberal extension of the market form throughout the social field, and the 'inseparable variations' of what Deleuze called a control society, student practice is released from the artificial enclosure of the 'hall of mirrors', where the value of creativity was given within a purely educational context, into an environment where its worth can now be valorized according to the terms and 'realities' of the market, and through which can be established a continuous feedback loop informing its future development. As much as the market is posited as the environment through which education is to be modulated, education, in a complementary movement, is proposed as a source of ideas and creativity valuable to the market and its own development. Located on the Greenwich Peninsula, in close proximity to new commercial and business development projects, Ravensbourne was envisaged not only as a receptacle for the surrounding environment's enterprise-based values but as a contributor to the local 'knowledge economy' and as a catalyst for 'urban regeneration'.[33] While the connections, mediations and feedback loops between education and enterprise proposed in this model utilize digital media as their channels of communication in a so-called 'virtual' space, the modulation of physical space too plays a critical role in their realization. In particular, the conventional college building and the university campus are refigured as a 'Learning Landscape':

> The Learning Landscape is the total context for students' learning experiences and the diverse landscape of learning settings available today – from specialized to multipurpose, from formal to informal, and from physical to virtual. The goal of the Learning Landscape approach is to acknowledge this richness and maximize encounters among people, places, and ideas, just as a vibrant urban environment does. Applying a learner-centred approach, campuses need to be conceived as 'networks' of places for learning, discovery, and discourse between students, faculty, staff, and the wider community.[34]

Following this model, architecture is then employed, more specifically, to produce the spatial complement of a 'learning landscape' designed around patterns of circulation, connectivity and informality. In the specific case of Ravensbourne, FOA's architecture is designed both to articulate the building's interior as an atmosphere that will inculcate in the student the requisite connective, flexible and informal modes of conduct, and to render it permeable to its surrounding environment as a mechanism for the integration of education and business.

The 'learning landscape' and the 'univer-city'

In plan, Ravensbourne is a chevron-shaped block whose form responds to the outer curvature of the O2 (former Millennium Dome) building to which it lies adjacent. As designed by FOA, the main entrance is situated at the junction of the building's two wings and opens out onto one of its large atria. This quasi-public space is intended as a bridge between the urban environment and activities of the Greenwich Peninsula and the college itself. Rather than being met immediately upon entry by the reception and security areas that clearly mark the thresholds of other educational institutions, the visitor encounters an informal space which includes a 'meet and greet' area, a delicatessen and an 'event' space hosting public displays and exhibitions. This internal space, combined with the environment immediately exterior to it, then constitutes what DEGW,[35] in their account of 'univer-cities' such as Ravensbourne, describe as a 'third place', existing between home and work and combining 'shopping, learning, meeting, playing, transport, socializing, playing, walking, living'.[36] A place, then, in which the activities of the market appear indissoluble from those of urban life, entertainment and education.

From the atrium the successive floor levels of the college and the connections spanning between the two wings are exposed as if in a cut-away section of a more conventional building. Rather than enclosed in stairwells or embedded between rooms, wire-mesh sided stairways and passages are cantilevered into the atrium. These elements form a complex series of crossings and inter-sections across mezzanine levels whose dynamics are further animated by the movements of the building's occupants. Hence an image is presented to visitors within its public atrium of the college as a hive of activity and move-ment while, to its students and staff, it affords a motivational image of the pub-lic, or market, with which the creativity and value of their work has always to be negotiated. The building's circulation is designed not only to serve as an image of movement, but to organize that movement according to a principle of connective liquefaction. Ascent through the building's floors, for example, is staggered across its two wings so as to accentuate the condition of move-ment over that of occupation. As Zaera-Polo explains: 'The idea is to produce a smoother change of plane, to liquefy the volume of the building so you don't have this notion of being on the third floor or the fourth floor. You are always in between floors.'[37]

The plans for several of the building's integrated levels also reveal this lique-faction of volume within the large floor and undivided floor spans. Differ-entiated only by mobile partitions, the arrangement of teaching studios and open-access studios zoned within these spaces suggests informal access and the integration of programmes within a continuously mobile and flexible whole. While a small number of programmes are allocated clearly demar-cated and discrete spaces within the building, the overarching principle of organization is designed to preclude the establishment of any fixed patterns of occupation or consistent identification of certain spaces with specific pro-grammes. This principle of 'deterritorialization' is consistent with the spatial concepts proposed by DEGW as appropriate to the 'univer-city': 'Traditional categories of space are becoming less meaningful as space becomes less spe-cialized, [and] boundaries blur ... Space types [should be] designed primarily around patterns of human interaction rather than specific needs of particu-lar departments, disciplines or technologies.'[38] Lecturers, for instance, are not provided with a private or fixed office space, but required to use available space in open-plan offices on an ad hoc basis. The organizational diagram of Ravensbourne, then, precisely reflects that of other spaces designed to accom-modate the mechanisms of managerialism, where, as Mark Fisher has argued,

'"Flexibility", "nomadism" and "spontaneity" are the very hallmarks of management',[39] and indeed the school's head of architecture, Layton Reid, reports that he wants his students to behave as 'intelligent nomads'.[40] The 'Learning Landscape' is one in which circulation, encounter and interaction are privileged so as to maximize communicational exchange as a source of value. This internal 'landscape' is also modelled after the urban environment with its intersecting activities and multiple opportunities for encounter and exchange.

Critically, it is, of course, the idealized model of the urban, as the networked and extensive environment of the market form, rather than as a space, say, of social contestation, that is reproduced within Ravensbourne. At the same time, this urban mimesis is intended to render the building functionally coextensive with its immediate environment. The relationship between the two environments, between interior and exterior, is figured as symbiotic: while the market is introjected within the space of the building – the business ventures of students are to be 'incubated' and 'hatched' within its architecture[41] – market-negotiated creativity is projected outward as a source of ideas and services for business.

Tellingly, in an early essay from 1994, 'Order Out of Chaos: The Material Organization of Advanced Capitalism', while appearing to engage with a Marxian analysis in drawing upon David Harvey's account of flexible accumulation to model the contemporary relations between capital and urban form, Zaera-Polo immediately circumvents the wider political implications of Harvey's model through the emphasis he places upon the Post-Fordist city in terms of its morphological novelty. The 'restructuring of the capitalist space', he writes, 'unfolds a 'liquefaction' of rigid spatial structures'. The 'spatial boundaries' of the city, he continues, lose their importance within the new composition of capital. From this proposition he then infers a consequent progressive tendency within contemporary urbanism since, 'through this growing disorganization of the composition of capital, the contemporary city tends to constitute itself as a non-organic and complex structure without a hierarchical structure nor a linear organization'.[42] In other words the urban now operates as a complex system whose organization, like that of any other complex

Fig. 1.4: Ravensbourne College, Greenwich, London, UK, Foreign Office Architects, 2010

system with which it is isomorphic, is composed exclusively of local interactions rather than in any way directed by any larger power, such as the capitalist axiomatic and its continual restructuring of urban space in pursuit of value. From here it is but a short step for Zaera-Polo to claim as 'subversive' the part played by corporate capital within the contemporary city: 'The complex formed by the AT&T, Trump and IBM headquarters in Manhattan', he argues, 'not only integrates a multiple programmatic structure, but also incorporates systematically the public space within the buildings: a subversion of the established urban boundaries between public and private.'[43] The urban and its architecture are subsumed by Zaera-Polo and FOA within a model of complexity so that their politics – if, that is, the term can be stretched to this extent – are redefined in terms of their morphological adherence or resistance to 'openness' and the dissolution of boundaries.

If this anticipates the character of the urban mimesis to be observed within the Ravensbourne design, the latter's organizational diagram is also, however, modelled after the 'virtual' space of web-surfing, blogging and social networking. Circulation within networks, flexible movement across and between activities, opportunistic exchange, engagement in multiple projects and self-promotion are the normative standards of online conduct that find their correlate within the physical space of the college. In both spaces, and in moving between them, the student is to be, just as Foucault described the ideal subject of neoliberalism, 'an entrepreneur of himself'.[44] Spatially continuous with the business of its urban environment and analogous in operation to the 'virtual' spaces of enterprise, the architecture of Ravensbourne thus positions the subject of education within an environment whose behavioural protocols further extend the reach of the market form throughout the social field. Yet it is also on the surface of the 'spherical envelope', as well as its interior, with its 'gradients of publicness', that Zaera-Polo and Moussavi locate the potential for architecture's *political* performance. The architectural envelope, it is claimed, has placed upon it 'representational demands'[45] which offer architecture the potential to produce a 'politics' built upon the Deleuzoguattarian concepts of affect and faciality.

Facing affect

Recent developments in building technology, argues Zaera-Polo, have removed from the architectural envelope the necessity for its traditional forms of articulation. 'Freed from the technical constraints that previously required cornices, pediments, corners and fenestration', he writes, 'the articulation of the spherical envelope has become increasingly contingent and indeterminate.' Citing, as examples of this new tendency, 'Nouvel's unbuilt, yet influential Tokyo Opera, Gehry's Guggenheim Museum, Future Systems' Selfridges Department Store, OMA's Seattle Public Library and Casa da Música and Herzog & de Meuron's Prada Tokyo', he contends that the envelope has now become an 'infinitely pliable' surface 'charged with architectural, social and political expression'.[46] The features of this 'expressive' surface, such as geometry and tessellation, have now, he continues, 'taken over the representational roles that were previously trusted to architectural language and iconographies'.[47] Hence, architectural expression need no longer be channelled through the historical codes of its traditional modes of articulation – such as pediments, cornices and fenestration – but can operate through the supposedly uncoded formal, geometric and tectonic means specific to each particular building envelope. This newly discovered expressive capacity of the envelope coincides historically, claims Zaera-Polo, with a post-linguistic orientation within global capitalism: 'As language becomes politically ineffective in the wake of globalization, and the traditional articulations of the building envelope become technically redundant, the envelope's own physicality, its fabrication and materiality, attract representational roles.' Drawing upon Deleuze and Guattari's concept of faciality in *A Thousand Plateaus*, he hence models this shift of the envelope as a movement from 'language and signification' towards a 'differential faciality which resists traditional protocols in which representational mechanisms can be precisely oriented and structured'. Further, this faciality is claimed as a political capacity for the surface of the envelope, but one that operates 'without getting caught in the negative project of the critical tradition or in the use of architecture as a mere representation of politics'.[48] Rather, this faciality operates through affect:

Fig. 1.5: Ravensbourne College, Greenwich, London, UK, Foreign Office Architects, 2010

the primary depository of contemporary architectural expression ... is now invested in the production of affects, an uncoded, pre-linguistic form of identity that transcends the propositional logic of political rhetorics. These rely on the material organization of the membrane, where the articulation between the parts and the whole is not only a result of technical constraints but also a resonance with the articulation between the individual and the collective, and therefore a mechanism of political expression.[49]

This 'politics of affect', as Zaera-Polo terms it, and its 'differential faciality', are deemed apposite to contemporary social reality not only since they accommodate its supposed post-linguistic turn, but due to their capacity to articulate the changed social relations between the part and the whole, the individual and the social, by which it is organized. As has been elaborated above, these relations are now considered, by Zaera-Polo, to be principally heterarchical as opposed to hierarchical; to be characterized by 'assemblages' and 'atmospheres', where 'the articulation between individual and society, part and whole, is drawn by influences and attachments across positions, agencies and scales that transcend both the individuality of the part and the integrity of the whole'.[50] Where the use of modular systems in architecture, within Modernism, corresponded to an ideal of democracy in which the part was prioritized, as an independent variable, over the whole, differential faciality claims to represent their now more complex, interdependent and mutable relations.

Indicative, for Zaera-Polo, of the affective capacity of the envelope, as a form of contemporary political expression, are the 'emerging envelope geometries' which 'seem to be exploring modular differentiation as a political effect and developing alternative forms of tessellation capable of addressing emerging political forms'. These forms of tessellation are, in turn, exemplified for him in certain of FOA's projects, such as the Spanish Pavilion for Aichi in Japan (2005), as well as the Ravensbourne building, whose 'modular differentiation' is held to produce an 'atomization of the face', a 'seamlessness' and a 'body without organs' expressive of 'changes in intensity rather than figures of organization'. Such geometries are supposed to have bypassed the linguistically coded representations upon which both hierarchical social orders and their critique are based, and to have arrived at a post-linguistic form of expression appropriate to a newly post-ideological historical condition. Expressive of this putatively heterarchical order, the once strict organizations of part-to-whole relations are now dissolved into modulations of intensity corresponding to the paradigm of the swarm, and represented in the envelopes of buildings which 'produce affects of effacement, liquefaction, de-striation'.[51]

Yet to posit a politics of pure affect is to propose that the contents of its expression cannot be grasped by thought. Any distance between subject and political expression, and hence any space in which this might be reflected upon, conceptually or critically, through a shared language, is eliminated. The social subject is reduced to a mere 'material organization' whose affective capacities are immediately joined to those of an environment with which it is supposed to identify at some pre-cognitive level. Such ambitions in architecture are, then, as Ross Adams has put it, 'little more than the spatial complement of an advanced neoliberal project of creating a subject who, having fully accepted reality, has only to give himself over to his senses, immersing himself in an architecture of affect'.[52] This fantasy of architecture as a kind of unmediated signal processing appears in Zaera-Polo's claim that 'the politics of affect bypass the rational filter of political dialectic to appeal directly to physical sensation'.[53] Treated as a means to an end, affect becomes reified and is turned to a use opposite to that suggested by Deleuze and Guattari: rather than a path towards the deterritorialization of subject positions imposed by a molar order, affect serves to reterritorialize the subject within an environment governed by neoliberal imperatives.

Yet, while FOA may claim to have transcended the representational codes of architectural language in their works, these are not placed, as a consequence, beyond interpretation or critique. In fact, rather than articulating the building's interior organization, the facade of Ravensbourne expresses a principle of organization consistent with the connective imperatives supposed to be facilitated by its architecture. The smaller openings on the facade, for instance, are clustered within a hexagrid arrangement, resembling the structure of a honeycomb or an insect's compound eye, which is connotative of both the swarm model privileged in contemporary organizational discourse, and the notion of the college as a space in while businesses can be 'incubated' and 'hatched'. The tiling of the facade is similarly expressive of organizational concepts, such as the production of a coherent whole through the interaction of smaller parts. Composed from a limited palette of shapes and tones, the tessellation pattern unifies the surface while implying the cell-like or molecular basis of its emergence through 'bottom-up' processes.

The composition of the Ravensbourne facade is, though, no less a matter of top-down control and decision making than is involved in any conventional act of architectural design. While the tessellation of the tiles may include, as Zaera-Polo claims, an element of self-computation, the decision to use a tessellating pattern is one consciously made. These are not, of course, solely the decisions of an autonomously operating architect, but ones mediated through negotiation and consultation with the client; one concerned to produce a new model of design education modelled on network principles, in order to facilitate its thorough permeation with the mechanisms of the market. Its significance resides in passing this mediation off as unmediated, as a merely 'emergent' process akin to, and at one with, those to be found in the self-organizing materials and geometries of a world whose 'complexity' is itself presented as given.

Reality check

To return, in conclusion, to the question of the larger progressive and emancipatory claims of Deleuzism in architecture, the very basis upon which these are proposed is significantly misconceived. If the 'progressive realities' of borderless complexity, networking and self-organization do not originate in the contemporary production process, as circumstances 'forced upon the capitalist enterprise', as Schumacher argues, and if they are not coincidentally but rather instrumentally related to neoliberal modes of managing the production of subjectivity, then making architecture immanent to these powers becomes a very different prospect. As has been noted, that the orientation of contemporary managerial theories towards de-hierarchized and networked forms of organization originates, in fact, not in the production process, but in a critique of capitalism which is then appropriated by capitalism has been powerfully argued by Boltanski and Chiapello, among others. If, then, what the latter call the liberatory 'repertoire of May 1968', including many of the conceptual formulations of Deleuze and Guattari, has already been instrumentally subsumed to a neoliberal managerialism, then the proposition that these same formulations are at the same time the best, and in fact the only, means by which architecture can pursue an emancipatory project is seriously undermined. In fact the projects of Deleuzism in architecture have only succeeded thus far in servicing the production of subjectivities whose flexibility and opportunism equips them for the mechanisms and precarities of the market. FOA's Ravensbourne exemplifies all too well architecture's contribution to this cause. The space of education that it specifically fashions from the principles of the 'learning landscape' is one made experientially coextensive with the behavioural imperatives of the market. Its strategy of 'liquefaction' produces a space in which the subject, compelled towards a nomadic and flexible disposition, is schooled in the protocols of opportunism and the realities of precarity. What is presented as an emancipatory release from the confines of a disciplinary model of spatial programmes operates, in fact, as a means through which former spaces of enclosure are opened out to the market as an uncontested mechanism of valorization. The forced exposure of education to these mechanisms, and the continual displacement of the subject throughout its digital and physical networks, render in advance problematic, if not inconceivable, the spatial logic of, for example, occupation, defence and resistance, on which so much of the recent student protest against the marketization of education has been predicated. More generally, the market is not some neutral or accidentally emerging organizational phenomenon, in which new forms of 'complexity' and 'flexibility' happen to find themselves expressed, but, as Foucault argued so presciently, a mode of governmentality which aims, globally, towards the production of 'open' environments in which all are immersed in its game of enterprise. It is thus difficult to conceive of how any architecture which makes strategic allegiance with the market, and at the same time so vehemently disavows the practice of critique, can be 'advanced' or 'progressive' – other than to the extent that it advances or progresses the cause of the generalization of the market form itself.

Notes

1   Gilles Deleuze, 'Postscript on Control Societies' in *Negotiations, 1972–1990*, trans. Martin Joughlin (New York: Columbia University Press, 1995), 177–82.

2   See Alejandro Zaera-Polo and Farshid Moussavi, 'Phylogenesis: FOA's Ark', in Farshid Moussavi, Alejandro Zaera-Polo and Sanford Kwinter, *Phylogenesis: FOA's Ark* (Barcelona: Actar, 2003), 10.

3   Gilles Deleuze, *The Fold: Leibniz and the Baroque*, trans. Tom Conley (Minneapolis: University of Minnesota Press, 1993); Gilles Deleuze and Félix Guattari, *A Thousand Plateaus: Capitalism and Schizophrenia,* trans. Brian Massumi (Minneapolis: University of Minnesota Press, 1987).

4   Greg Lynn, ed., A. D. *Folding in Architecture*. Chichester: Wiley-Academy, 1993.

5   John Rajchman, *Constructions* (Cambridge, MA: MIT Press, 1998), 19–35.

6   Deleuze and Guattari cautioned against any straight-forward notion of smooth space as in itself radical or salvational in *A Thousand Plateaus*: 'Never believe that a smooth space will suffice to save us.' See Gilles Deleuze and Félix Guattari, *A Thousand Plateaus*, (Minneapolis: University of Minnesota Press,1987), 500.

7   Jeffrey Kipnis, 'Towards a New Architecture', in Greg Lynn, ed., *Folding in Architecture* (Chichester, UK: Wiley-Academy, 1993), 56–65.

8   François Cusset, *French Theory: How Foucault, Derrida, Deleuze, & Co. Transformed the Intellectual Life of the United States*, trans. Jeff Fort with Josephine Berganza and Marlon Jones (Minneapolis: University of Minnesota Press, 2008), 62–3.

9   Jesse Reiser and Nanako Umemoto, *Atlas of Novel Tectonics* (New York: Princeton Architectural Press, 2006), 20.

10   See, for example, Robert Somol and Sarah Whiting, 'Notes Around the Doppler Effect and Other Moods of Modernism', *Perspecta* 33, 'Mining Autonomy' (2002), 72–7 and 'Okay, Here's the Plan', *Log*, Spring/Summer 2005, 4–7; George Baird, '"Criticality" and Its Discontents', *Harvard Design Magazine* 21, Fall 2004/Winter 2005, 16–21; Jeffrey Kipnis, 'Is Resistance Futile?', *Log*, Spring/Summmer 2005, 105–9; Reinhold Martin, 'Critical of What? Toward a Utopian Realism', *Harvard Design Magazine* 22, Spring/Summer 2005, 104–9.

'Post-critical' writings have often taken Koolhaas's well-known reservations about the possibility of a critical architecture as a point of reference. See Rem Koolhaas and Reinier de Graaf, 'Propaganda Architecture: Interview with David Cunningham and Jon Goodbun', *Radical Philosophy* 154, March/April 2009, 37–47.

11   Jeffrey Kipnis, 'On the Wild Side', in Farshid Moussavi, Alejandro Zaera-Polo and Sanford Kwinter, eds, *Phylogenesis: FOA's Ark* (Barcelona: Actar, 2004), 579.

12   'Educating the Architect: Alejandro Zaera-Polo in Conversation with Roemer van Toorn', <www.xs4all.nl/ [archive]~rvtoorn/alejandro.html>. See also Zaera-Polo's comment 'I was never really interested in Derrida's work. I find it very obscure and based on its own principles, which is about the idea that reality is made out of the self-referential system of codes and signs. I was much more excited and influenced by the work of Deleuze, precisely because of his interest in material process as the core of reality.' Interview with Vladimir Belogolovsky for Intercontinental Curatorial Project Inc. (2005), <www.curatorialproject.com/interviews/alexandrozaera-Zaera-Polo.html [archive]>. Yet, if Zaera-Polo identifies here with Deleuze's 'materialism', the issue of 'organizational power', conceived by the latter as vested in the axiomatic of the 'social machine', is, in FOA, located *exclusively* in matter and its intrinsic capacity to 'self-organize'. This intrinsic organizational capacity is then figured as one of emergence and complexity. See Zaera-Polo, 'The Politics of the Envelope', *Log 17,*, Fall 2008, 101.

13   Zaha Hadid, Pritzker acceptance speech, 2004. <www.pritzkerprize.com/laureates/2004/_downloads/2004_Acceptance_Speech.pdf. [archive]>.

14   Gilles Deleuze, 'Postscript on Control Societies', *Negotiations, 1972–1990* (New York: Columbia University Press, 1995), 178–9.

15   Patrik Schumacher, *Digital Hadid: Landscapes in Motion* (Basel: Birkhäuser, 2003), 19.

16   Luc Boltanski and Eve Chiapello, *The New Spirit of Capitalism*, trans. Gregory Elliott (London and New York: Verso, 2007), 97.

17   Ibid.

18   In addition to affirming the market as a site of such 'contemporary conditions of fluidity and mobility',

this language of networks, fields, swarms and self-organization – with its obligatory reference to Deleuzean categories – has also found a home in recent 'cutting-edge' military discourse, as Eyal Weizman has shown. See 'Walking Through Walls: Soldiers as Architects in the Israeli–Palestinian Conflict', *Radical Philosophy* 135, March/April 2006, 8–21.

19 Patrik Schumacher 'The Skyscraper Revitalized: Differentiation, Interface, Navigation', in *Zaha Hadid* (New York: Guggenheim Museum Publications, 2006).

20 See Douglas Spencer, 'Replicant Urbanism: The Architecture of Hadid's Central Building at BMW Leipzig', *Journal of Architecture*, Vol. 15, No. 2, April 2010, 181–207

21 Zaera-Polo, 'The Politics of the Envelope', 104.

22 Patrik Schumacher, 'Research Agenda: Spatializing the Complexities of Contemporary Business Organization', in Brett Steele, ed., *Corporate Fields: New Office Environments by the AA DRL* (London: AA Publications, 2005), 75.

23 Ibid., 76, 79.

24 Ibid., 78.

25 Patrik Schumacher, 'Research Agenda: Spatializing the Complexities of Contemporary Business Organization' (2005), <www.patrikschumacher.com/Texts/Corporate [archive]%20Fields-%20New%20Office%20Environments.html>. Note that this sentence, with its strident dismissal of all forms of protest, appears only within the version of the essay which was available online, and does not appear in its published version in Steele, ed., *Corporate Fields*.

26 Ibid., 77, 78.

27 Zaera-Polo 'The Politics of the Envelope', 86, 103–4.

28 Jeanette Johansson-Young, 'The BIG Picture: A Case for a Flexible Learning Agenda at Ravensbourne', internal publication of Ravensbourne College, 2006, <http://intranet.rave.ac.uk/quality/docs/LTR060203–flexlearn_4.pdf>.

29 Department for Education and Skills, 'The Future of Higher Education' (2003), <www.dfes.gov.uk/hegateway/strategy/hestrategy/pdfs/DfES-Higher-Education.pdf>; 'HEFCE strategy for e-learning' (2005), <www.hefce.ac.uk/pubs/hefce/2005/>.

30 A.M. Bliuc, P. Goodyear and R. A. Ellis, 'Research Focus and Methodological Choices in Studies into Students' Experiences of Blended Learning in Higher Education', *The Internet and Higher Education*, Vol. 10, No. 4, 2007, 231–44.

31 DEGW, 'User Brief for the New Learning Landscape' (2004), cited in Johansson-Young, 'The BIG Picture'.

32 Miles Metcalfe, Ruth Carlow, Remmert de Vroorne and Roger Rees, 'Final Report for the Designs on Learning Project', internal publication of Ravensbourne College, 2008, 3–4.

33 John Worthington/DEGW, 'Univer-Cities in their Cities: Conflict and Collaboration', paper presented at OECD Education Management and Infrastructure Division, Higher Education Spaces & Places: For Learning, Innovation and Knowledge Exchange, University of Latvia, Riga, 6–8 December 2009, <www.oecd.lu.lv/materials/johnworthington.pdf>.

34 Shirley Dugdale, 'Space Strategies for the New Learning Landscape', *EDUCAUSE Review*, Vol. 44, No. 2, March/April 2009, <www.educause.edu/educause [archive]+Review/edu causereviewmagazinevolume44/SpaceStrategiesfor theNew-Learni/163820>.

35 DEGW were an architectural and space planning practice. They have now been incorporated into the infrastructural firm AECOM.

36 Worthington/DEGW, 'Univer-Cities in their Cities', 14.

37 Alejandro Zaera-Polo, quoted in Graham Bizley, 'FOA's Peninsula Patterns for Ravensbourne College', *BD Online*, 29 July 2009, <www.bdonline.co.uk/practice-and-it/foa's-peninsula-patterns-for-ravensbournecollege/3144928.article>.

38 Worthington/DEGW, 'Univer-Cities in their Cities', 16.

39 Mark Fisher, *Capitalist Realism: Is There No Alternative?* (Winchester and Washington DC: Zero Books, 2009), 28.

40 As recorded at Ravensbourne's media briefing by the author, 9 September 2010.

41 Lucy Hodges, 'Ravensbourne College Gets Ready to Move in to Eye-catching New Premises', *Independent*, 15 July 2010 <www.independent.co.uk/news/education/higher/ravensbourne-college-gets-ready-to-move-in-toeyecatching-new-premises-2026802.html.>.

42 Alejandro Zaera-Polo, 'Order Out of Chaos: The Material Organization of Advanced Capitalism', *Architectural Design Profile* 108 (1994), 25–6.

43 Ibid., 28.

44 Michel Foucault, *The Birth of Biopolitics: Lectures at the Collège de France, 1978–1979,* ed. Michel Senellart, trans. Graham Burchell (Basingstoke and New York: Palgrave MacMillan, 2008), 226.

45 Zaera-Polo 'The Politics of the Envelope', 87.

46 Ibid., p. 89.

47 Alejandro Zaera-Polo, 'Patterns, Fabrics, Prototypes, Tessellations', *Architectural Design*, Special Issue: *Patterns of Architecture*, Vol. 79, No. 6, November/December 2009, 22.

48 Zaera-Polo 'The Politics of the Envelope', 88, 89, 90.

49 Ibid., 89.

50 Ibid.

51 Zaera-Polo, 'Patterns, Fabrics, Prototypes, Tessellations', 23, 25.

52 Ross Adams, personal correspondence with the author, 1 August 2010.

53 Zaera-Polo, 'Patterns, Fabrics, Prototypes, Tessellations', 25.

2 Habitats for *Homo Economicus:* Architecture, Design and the Environment of 'Man'

Introduction: Which man? Which environment? What nature?

Neoliberalism and environmental design occupy common ground. Each requires renunciation of human-centred hubris and submission to naturalized and law-like orders; the unquestionable 'givens' of ecology, environment, nature, the market. The planetary scale and the degree of complexity at which economic and ecological systems alike operate appear to escape human powers of comprehension or intervention. As the neoliberal economist Friedrich Hayek argued, we are, in our limited human capacities, 'necessarily ignorant', and should act accordingly, abandoning any political projects for society.[1] Natural systems, and naturalized economic systems, are held to be better able to calculate and regulate the relationship between man and environment.

Not only do neoliberalism and environmental design have these features in common, their relationship is mutually self-sustaining, symbiotic, even. It's easy to imagine that it is only by returning to nature, by balancing the relationship between man and environment upset by industrial and fossil capitalism, that we can ward off ecological catastrophe. But which man? Which environment? What nature? Such questions may seem beside the point given the urgencies of our current conditions of crisis, yet they go to the heart of its origins and causes. Racial capitalism, which is to say all capitalism, has been built on and through the power to establish its own representations of the human and the environment from the beginning. It has, since the nineteenth century, operated through, and not against, ecological principles. As literary and decolonial theorist Walter D. Mignolo writes:

> What does it mean to be human is no doubt a fundamental question for
> the twenty-first century. Why? For several reasons but mainly … because
> the very concept of the *Human* is called into question by scholars and

intellectuals who carry in their own bodies the traces of racialization and sexualization ... Human and humanity are not only concepts; they are concepts created by agents who considered *themselves* humans and who were in a position to project their own image of themselves as humanity.[2]

Mignolo argues as well that 'nature and culture are both cultural Western concepts that were established as ontologies'.[3] Once established, these could be used to legitimate the idea of 'natural resources' that framed the settler colonialist conception of the 'New World', and the practices of extraction and subjugation which followed from this.

In what follows I outline a history of environmental and ecological design, from the paternalist and reformist forms this assumed in the early part of the twentieth century, through the development of architecture's 'environmental consciousness' of the 1960s, 70s, and 80s. This is a history of how environmental discourse and design comes to operate as politics by other means. Arriving, in conclusion, at the current convergence of neoliberalism and environmentalism in design, I argue that each is premised on sustaining the figure of *homo economicus:* an entrepreneurial, opportunist, go-getting, and ultimately unsustainable version of humanity.

Biopolitical regulation: from imperial ecology to the *Stadtlandschaft*

If for Michel Foucault power can be understood in terms of biopolitical regulation, of the productive management of the relations 'between the organic and the biological, between body and population', then the sciences of ecology and biology, and alongside them evolutionary, organicist and metabolic models, surely count among its most vital instruments.[4] The science of ecology originates, after all, in nineteenth-century Western imperialism and colonialism. As Peder Anker argues, in his *Imperial Ecology,* the new science served the British Empire with the 'tools for understanding human relations to nature and society in order to set administrative economic policies for landscapes, population settlement, and social control'.[5] The science of ecology was employed to orchestrate and control the productivity of species and subjects, both equally 'botanized', captured, and mobilized within the operations of colonial dominion. London's Kew Gardens, at the epicentre of empire, served as 'the central institution of a global network of scientists specializing in economic botany', writes Lucile H. Brockway in her *Science and Colonial Expansion*.[6] With royal patronage, and parliamentary support, the royal botanic gardens cultivated the plant species looted through imperial conquests and the new sciences through which these could be instrumentalized in making the colonies productive.

In the early twentieth century, botanical, ecological and organicist thinking informed plans to regulate the relations between the city and the country in order to manage the life and welfare of the industrial worker. Industrial production, pathologized for its moral and physiological degradation of the proletarian subject, and for its consequently negative influence upon productivity, was to be relocated, decamped from the city to more seemingly natural locations. This was to be facilitated through the design of environs affording access to sunlight and fresh air, to the ameliorative benefits of landscaped parks and gardens. Ebenezer Howard's Garden City is the prototype of this endeavour. The Garden City diagrams the relations between settlements and landscape, plots out social functions in its geometrical order, prescribes everything its proper place. In Howard's hands this is an essentially paternalistic project, shepherding its subjects towards the positive poles of city and countryside. As Timothy Ivison, writing on the biopolitics of urbanism and planning, notes, 'in the Garden Cities and Regional Planning movements of latter decades, biological doctrines are reiterated time and again as the rationale for myriad regulatory interventions and positivist planning theories'.[7]

In subsequent iterations the Garden City model is directed towards other ends than those of Howard's paternalism. The Garden City idea informs the anti-urban orientation of socialist planning in Soviet Russia and the machine-age modernization of the city envisaged by Le Corbusier. In 1920s Germany it inspires the *Siedlungen* of Ernst May and Bruno Taut, here regulating the relations between the life of the subject and that of the soil along metabolic principles. With the involvement of Leberecht Migge (himself inspired by the botanist Raoul Heinrich Francé's writings on soil fertility and organic farming methods), the residents of these settlements are provided with vegetable allotments from which to sustain themselves, and instructed on recycling their own bodily waste back into the very same soil.[8]

Where the loss of bodily waste from metabolic systems is abjured in the interwar years, the alienation of the psyche later appears as a further pathology of the urban condition, and one likewise requiring organic remediation. In his 1948 *Organische Stadtbaukunst: Von der Großstadt zur Stadtlandschaft* (Organic Urban Design: From the Metropolis to the City Landscape), the German urban planner Hans Bernhard Reichow argues that the urban subject is mentally and spiritually estranged by the chaotic and overcrowded conditions of the metropolis.[9] As a corrective, he argues, the space of the city should be opened up to form a landscape, a *Stadtlandschaft* in which the subject can properly apprehend its environment as an organic whole of which it is an integral part.

Operators' manuals

The environmental consciousness of architecture and design in the 1960s makes the perspective of such projects appear parochial by comparison. Organic, metabolic and ecological processes are now conceived at a planetary scale. The scope of the environment expands from the urban and the regional to the global, from Patrick Geddes's 'valley section' to Apollo 8's *Earthrise*. The development of this global environmental consciousness is driven, in part, by the space-time compression effects of advances in telecommunication and transportation, but also by an increasing awareness of the interrelatedness of ecological systems and their susceptibility to human intervention. The Earth is newly recognized as both smaller and more fragile than had previously been conceived. At the origins of this global ecological consciousness figures such as Buckminster Fuller, John McHale, Ian McHarg and Reyner Banham venture responses that will come to exert a significant influence on landscape, architectural and urban design, promulgating ecological, organic, environmental and other models supposed to guide the conduct of the designer in addressing the environment as a globally manifest condition of crisis.

This crisis is also seized as an opportunity. The turn to the environment facilitates a turn against Modernism in design. Modern architecture and urban planning are denounced as ill-informed projects of human hubris, unsympathetic exercises in the manipulation of nature towards coldly rational ends. The heroic Prometheus is recast as a villain, and human mastery is to be surrendered to the laws of general systems theory. Concurrently, new allegiances are sought out. The roles earlier established for architecture, landscape and urban design within and for the nation state are made to appear anachronistic, as are the politics in which these were implicated. Designers, now recast as steersmen and cybernetic pilots, are encouraged and advised to ally themselves with a universal humanity, to 'Man' and to the attunement of this universalized figure with a correspondingly universalized nature. This prospect is explored, especially, in the allegiances forged between architecture and the counterculture in the 1960s and 1970s. 'Man', as Douglas Murphy notes in his *Last Futures,* 'becomes a word that universalizes humanity through a sense of cosmic distance, where divisions are indistinguishable and patterns of behaviour common to all ... "man" takes on a conspicuousness for its stressing of a (not unproblematic) universality, a world beyond struggle and conflict.'[10] This 'not unproblematic' universality conjured into existence by the word 'Man' will be returned to below.

For Buckminster Fuller, the best hope for Man lay in forecasting the direction in which a global humanity was evolving and to steering it, accordingly, with the guidance mechanisms of general systems theory. In his *Operating Manual for Spaceship Earth* of 1969, he argues that nature itself has designed this spaceship and programmed its passengers for the mission which evolutionary progress has long ago mapped out for them: 'What nature needed man to be was adaptive in many if not any direction; wherefore she gave man a mind as well as a co-ordinating switchboard brain.'[11] Spaceship Earth, in Fuller's account, was 'invented' and 'superbly designed' by, and through, the evolutionary *telos* of nature.[12] Spaceship Earth, carrying and nurturing us on its predetermined course, is likewise strategically programmed. The historical point at which Man becomes conscious of the crisis to which he is subjecting the Earth just so happens – as if by predestination – to be that at which Spaceship Earth reveals to him its true nature.[13] Thus informed, its passengers may continue safely on their journey: 'It is therefore paradoxical but strategically explicable ... that up to now we have been mis-using, abusing, and polluting this extraordinary chemical energy-interchanging system for successfully regenerating all life aboard our planetary spaceship.'[14] Computation, whose emergence at this time also appears as historically fortuitous, also comes to our rescue: 'A new, physically uncompromised, metaphysical initiative of un-biased integrity could unify the world. It could and probably will be provided by the utterly impersonal problem solutions of the computers.'[15] Guided by superior processing powers humans can let go of the wheel and enjoy the journey, surrendering their agency to the impersonal and unbiased integrity of computation. The old ideologies that divided humanity are rendered redundant in the face of a universal computation that will solve our crises for us, and in accord with the *telos* Spaceship Earth has been designed to realize. Capitalism and socialism are, for Fuller, 'extinct'.[16] The turn to computation, the technological fix, is not against nature because nature itself is conceived by Fuller as a pre-programmed, essentially cybernetic, and universal system. The human brain is a 'co-ordinating switchboard' to be steered towards acceptance of the 'generalized principles governing the universe' by which it too operates.[17] Fuller's pronouncements both appear within, and contribute to, a conjuncture between the post-ideological, the ecological, and what Sylvia Wynter refers to as the '*techno-automated*' that marks out the essential dimensions of our own neoliberal period.[18]

John McHale's *The Ecological Context* of 1971 similarly identifies the point at which the ecological crisis first appears as simultaneously the point at which its solutions are made manifest: 'Now capable of destroying his own species many times over through consciously contrived means of war, it suddenly becomes apparent that his [man's] largely unconscious, and uncontrolled, exploitation of the earth's resources may similarly render the planet unliveable.'[19] Humanity is poised, argues McHale, at an epochal point of transition.

Its emerging consciousness of global-scale ecological interconnectedness offers the key to its successful passage through this critical moment. The 'conceptual and value shift – from the local study of plants, wildlife and their surroundings to one which suggests responsibility for the planet as lifespace – is in accord with the kinds of changes in human consciousness and conceptuality that are already underway'.[20] For McHale these 'changes in human consciousness' point us to an awareness of the universal principles of ecology; a universality – echoing that of ecology's imperialist and colonial origins – that captures in its totalizing grasp the 'social behaviours of man' as much as the biological behaviour of plant and animal species. In light of this realization McHale, like Fuller, declares existing political paradigms outmoded. The turn to ecology, and not the radical political currents of the 60s, constitutes the 'real' revolution. In respect of contemporary 'large-scale systems with many and variable factors', McHale also follows Fuller in his enthusiasms for the 'steering' power of cybernetics.[21] Through the timely arrival of computational technologies, he argues, a world now to be understood according to the proper and correct concepts will be cybernetically directed 'in a more positive, efficient, and naturally advantageous manner'.[22]

The landscape architect Ian McHarg also sought out a universal model through which his discipline might address the apparent crises of this period. His 1966 essay 'Ecological Determinism' opens with an account of the huge increases in population and urbanization then predicted for the United States. Attempts to plan for this development through the social and economic sciences, argues McHarg, can only succeed in placing the city on the path to becoming a 'necropolis' of social and environmental breakdown.[23] This fate, he argues, might only be averted if we recognize 'the implications of natural process upon the location and form of development'.[24] 'We need a general theory which encompasses physical, cultural and biological evolution', he writes in his 1968 essay 'Values, Process and Form', and this need is answered by the science of ecology, which should, in turn, now constitute the sole basis from which the landscape architect engages with the environment.[25] 'The role of man', he writes, 'is to understand nature, which is to say man, and to intervene to enhance its creative process.'[26]

This call to understand nature in order to 'enhance its creative process' should, by now, strike a familiar chord, as should McHarg's universalization of 'Man' as a figure that ought properly to be understood according to its essentially biological essence. Folded back within the very same nature he is supposed to creatively intervene within, 'Man' is supposed somehow to be both the subject and object of nature. McHarg, like McHale and Fuller, in disparaging politics and ideology, cannot claim to speak from a political or ideological position. His position *is* political and ideological – in calling for a purely biological concept of 'Man', placed now in proper relation to his ecological environment – but this cannot be acknowledged as such. McHarg is, therefore, bound to think of the agency of 'Man', of his project and role within the 'creative process' he is predestined to engage within, in essentially natural and ecological terms. While McHarg can happily reel off the pathologies of the modern world, especially in respect of the degradation of the American city, he cannot point explicitly to the basic mechanisms of such culprits as the real estate market in capitalism, or to structural racism, in doing so. Neither can he argue for social or political solutions to these pathologies. 'Give us your poor and oppressed,' he laments, 'and we will give them Harlem and the Lower East Side, Bedford-Stuyvesant, the South Side of Chicago and the North of Philadelphia.'[27] 'Observe', he continues, 'the environments of physical, mental and social pathology.' And he can *only* observe, from this perspective, an 'environmental' problem requiring 'environmental' solutions. All considerations external to 'nature' are, correspondingly, exorcised from McHarg's prescriptions for the practice of landscape design, urban design and regional planning. In the essay 'An Ecological Method for Landscape Architecture' he posits that regardless of scale – 'from a continent, a major region, a river basin, physiographic regions, sub-regional areas, and a metropolitan region town to a single city' – 'the place, the plants, the animals and men upon it are *only* comprehensible in terms of physical and biological evolution'.[28] Since the problems of the city, the region and the landscape are for McHarg exclusively environmental, it follows that they are also problems of 'fitness', of what and who properly belongs to a particular environment. His notion of 'fitness' is, notably, informed by biologically determinist and colonial theories of race. When 'the primates abandoned instinct for reason' he writes in 'Man and Environment', this caused a 'negative and destructive' impact upon the environment.[29] Hoping to return 'Man' to a relationship of 'fitness' to his environment he points to the example of today's 'aboriginal people' whose 'ecological role has changed little from that of the primate'.[30] McHarg would have us learn from the example of the 'simpler people who were our ancestors (like primitive peoples today)' how to be at one with our environment, just as he recommends that there is an appropriate habitat for each 'race', because: 'Africans differ from Asians, Eskimo from Caucasoid, Mongoloid from Australoid.'[31]

Ultimately, however, McHarg, doesn't want us to straightforwardly return to the practices of such 'simpler people'. His argument appears, rather, to be that we ought to reset our environments, along the lines of a naturalized notion of fitness, in order that we may continue along our predestined evolutionary/developmental path:

> Our world is aching for the glorious cities of civilized and urbane men. Land and resources are abundant. We could build a thousand new cities in the most wonderful locations – on mountains and plains, on rocky ocean promontories, on desert and delta, by rivers and lakes, on islands and plateaus. It is within our compass to select the widest range of the most desirable lands and promulgate policies and regulations to ensure the realization of these cities, each in response to the nature of its site. We can manage the land for its health, productivity, and beauty. All of these things are within the capacity of this people now. It is necessary to resolve to fulfill the American Revolution and to create the fair image that can be the land of the free and the home of the brave.[32]

In the field of architecture Reyner Banham proposed that the discipline refocus its concerns on the environment and its management. Evidently influenced by the writing of Fuller, Banham argues, in *The Architecture of the Well-tempered Environment* of 1969, for 'the close dialogue of technology and architecture' towards this end.[33] Banham's affinities with countercultural sensibilities, and with the emancipatory promise of an environmentally attuned architecture, are especially apparent here. Arguing that the profession has been tied, traditionally, to monied interests and state patronage, he claims that these ties have taught it to design 'enclosed spaces framed by massive structures'.[34] 'Civilized' architecture, claims Banham, is unable to conceive of 'free' or 'unlimited' space.[35] Echoing McHarg's endorsement of 'simpler' peoples, he argues that in other, non-Western traditions such as those of nomadic peoples, habitation was managed without resorting to the structural segregation of humans from their immediate environment.[36] Contemporary architecture, deploying the latest technologies, might also now cast off the dead weight of its civilizational orthodoxy and provide for the enjoyment of similar environmental liberties. Banham's enthusiasms for the frontier spirit of the campfire speak of his proximity to the libertarian values of the counterculture, especially as espoused by Stewart Brand and as promoted in the latter's *Whole Earth Catalog.* The technologically facilitated liberty to be at one with the immediate environment promoted by Banham is captured, famously, in the photograph of him riding his Bickerton bicycle across a Californian salt flat, taken by Tim Street-Porter in 1981. The architectural historian wrote of the rapturous nature of this experience in his *Scenes in America Deserta:* 'Swooping and sprinting like a skater over the surface of Silurian Lake, I came as near as ever to a whole-body experience equivalent to the visual intoxication of sheer space that one enjoys in America Deserta.'[37] In his *Los Angeles: The Architecture of Four Ecologies* of 1971, Banham glossed the experience of environmental immersion offered by the Los Angeles freeway system in similarly transcendent terms. The cybernetic traffic system operates at a level of complexity that demands the 'willing acquiescence' of the driver to its systemic commands.[38] The human is too slow to calculate and respond effectively in this environment and must give up its own agency to that of the system's superior processing power. In recompense, however, the Los Angeleno is delivered over to the 'mystical' experience of the freeway, released in relinquishing control to the opportunity to be 'integrally identified' with the urban landscape.[39]

Environmental Disneyland

The writings of Fuller, McHale, McHarg and Banham are representative of a broader current of enthusiasm for all things environmental, ecological and cybernetic in design during this period. This turn was not, however, unopposed. At the International Design Conference, organized by Banham and held at Aspen in 1970, the radical French architectural group Utopie delivered a statement in objection to the emerging doxa of 'environments' and 'environmentalism'. Written by Jean Baudrillard and delivered by a delegation calling itself 'The French Group', their paper was titled 'The Environmental Witch-Hunt'. In it was written:

> The burning question of Design and Environment has neither suddenly fallen from the heavens nor spontaneously risen from the collective consciousness: It has its own history. Professor Banham has clearly shown the moral and technical limits and the illusions of Design and Environment practice. He didn't approach the social and political definition of this practice. It is not by accident that all the Western governments have now launched (in France in particular for the last six months) this new crusade, and try to mobilize people's conscience by shouting apocalypse.[40]

Baudrillard and the Utopie group considered the conference representative of an emerging 'environmental ideology', a smokescreen contrived to conceal a deeper crisis within capitalism. 'Aspen', wrote Baudrillard, 'is the Disneyland of environment and design' – a 'Utopia produced by a capitalist system that assumes the appearance of a second nature in order to survive and perpetuate itself under the pretext of nature'.[41] Baudrillard understands the turn to the environment in relation to the escalation of the class struggle, as represented, most visibly and emblematically, by *les événements* of May 68, but also encompassing a broader wave of protests, uprisings and strikes elsewhere in Western Europe and the US at this time. It should be added that this same period is marked as well by other struggles, on numerous fronts, including those for civil rights, feminism, gay liberation and the anti-imperialist movements of Algeria and Vietnam. This tumultuous period has also come to be understood, retrospectively, as marking a crisis point within the existing Fordist model of capitalism; a crisis of accumulation engendering the shift towards so-called Post-Fordist and neoliberal modes of production and accumulation. Baudrillard and the Utopie group situate the turn to the environment in the context of these political and cultural upheavals, but in suggesting this turn serves as a sideshow, a distraction designed to divert attention from the struggles of the 60s and 70s and 'monopolize' our consciousness, they miss the mark. The environment and the environmental, the thing and the discourse, are not distractions from politics so much as their new medium. They serve as a means for power to operate on its subjects while assuming an unquestionable, law-like and 'given' form.

Michel Foucault's *The Birth of Biopolitics* – assembled from his lectures at the Collège de France in 1978–1979 – offers a prescient analysis of the intersection between environmental forms of control and the development of neoliberalism.[42] Here Foucault employs the term 'environment' to articulate the shift in the mechanisms of power appearing in the aftermath of the Second World War. Here, and especially in light of the experience of its most extreme and totalitarian expressions, disciplinary power gives way to a new modality:

> [T]he image, idea, or theme program of a society in which there is an optimization of systems of difference, in which the field is left open to fluctuating processes, in which minority individuals and practices are tolerated, in which action is brought to bear on the rules of the game rather than on the players, and finally in which there is an environmental type of intervention instead of the internal subjugation of individuals ... .[43]

This image of environmental intervention is formulated from within the economic philosophy of German ordoliberalism and Austro-American neoliberalism, and is premised on the conception of the human subject as a fundamentally entrepreneurial being, a *homo economicus*. Rather than disciplined to behave in accord with the dictates of the authority of the state, this subject must be at liberty to pursue its individual entrepreneurial interests within an unbounded environment of opportunities for exchange, competition and accumulation. Even though the term 'environment' is used in this context in reference to the milieu of the market, rather than that of 'nature', neoliberal thought models the market, and the action of its subjects, according to precisely the same cybernetic models as does design at this time so as to naturalize and essentialize its operations. Though not addressed by Foucault, the writings of the economist Friedrich Hayek – the key intellectual of the 'neoliberal thought collective' – reveal the influence of cybernetics and systems theory in the development of neoliberalism.[44] Cybernetics serves, for Hayek, to underwrite his contention that individuals are at liberty to act in accord with their true entrepreneurial natures only when immersed in larger environments.[45] These individuals, however, cannot hope to exercise control of these environments themselves, since any such desire, according to Hayek, can lead only to totalitarianism. This desire must be renounced in favour of recognizing, and giving oneself over to, the superior organizational and processing power of the system, surrendering to its spontaneous self-ordering. The environmental operates as an immanent mode of governance that appears to transcend the political, that serves to guide us 'by habit rather than reflection'.[46] Governmental powers are now invested in the mutually legitimating powers of the economic and the environmental. Both play out their hands naturally and invisibly. The environment of 'Man' is the environment of neoliberalism.

Decolonial theory also provides for a compelling analysis of how representations of Man, nature and environment have come to be configured as forms of domination within neoliberalism. Where Foucault understands biopolitics in genealogical terms, Sylvia Wynter locates the conditions of possibility for a purely 'biocentric' conception of the human in the historical and material conditions of colonialism.[47] For Wynter the very notion of Man is an 'overrepresentation', enacted on the part of Western colonizers, in which their own humanity is constructed as a universal standard. Forged through theories of race and biological determinism, and furthered through Darwinian accounts of evolution, this overrepresentation legitimates Western colonialism, alongside its dispossessing, enslaving, extractive, exploitative and accumulative practices, in the name of the natural destiny of Man himself. 'Our present ethnoclass (i.e., Western bourgeois) conception of the human, Man' writes Wynter in her 2003 essay 'Unsettling the Coloniality of Being/Power/Truth/

Freedom', 'overrepresents itself as if it were the human itself.'[48] In conversation with Katherine McKittrick, Wynter argues that:

> as studies of contemporary neocolonialism as well as of its predecessors colonialism and postcolonialism reveal, the West, over the last five hundred years, has brought the whole human species into its hegemonic, now purely secular ... model of being human. This is the version in whose terms the human has now been redefined, since the nineteenth century, on the natural scientific model of a natural organism. This is a model that supposedly preexists – rather than coexists with – all the models of other human societies and their religions/cultures.[49]

The secular, biocentric and universalized representation of Man is placed at the pinnacle of a hierarchical 'chain of being' in which 'all forms of sentient life' are classified, from lowest to highest. As Wynters argues:

> It is, therefore as the new rational/irrational line ... comes to be actualized in the institutionalized differences between European settlers and Indians/Negroes, that the figure of the Negro as the projected missing link between the two sides of the rational/irrational divide will inevitably come to be represented in the first 'scientific' taxonomy of human populations ...[50]

Such are the conceptions of Man posited in the kind of ecological and environmental models addressed above. Non-Western Man is positioned, as in McHarg's invocation of a contemporary 'primitive' humanity, as barely discernible in its ecological condition from that of the primate. Placed further down the evolutionary chain of being than their Western counterparts, the non-Western, the primitive, the simpler peoples, are positively invoked only for the lessons they might offer to 'us' in being better attuned to nature, closer to this as they are supposed to be.

The insistence of ecological thought on a purely biological conception of humanity obscures the very historical and material conditions through which it was forged, conceals the practices and narratives through which its representations and overrepresentations served to universalize and legitimate a conception of Man made in the image of the colonizer. Over the course of the past five centuries *homo economicus* has come to stand as the only conceivable version of the human, and it is for the putative nature of this universalized idea of the human that the environment should function. All other notions of humanity, and its potentials, have been circumscribed by a hegemonic and purely biocentric account of the human as a naturally entrepreneurial species. As Wynter argues, there has been a 'systemic repression of all other alternative modes of material provisioning', so that there can be no 'alternative to its attendant planetarily-ecologically extended, increasingly techno-automated, thereby job-destroying, postindustrial, yet no less fossil fuel-driven, thereby climate-destabilizing free-market capitalist economic system, in its now extreme neoliberal transnational technocratic configuration.'[51]

Sustaining the unsustainable

The environmentally and ecologically oriented design discourse that first appeared in the 60s and 70s has made a marked return since the 90s. Cybernetics, joined by theories of complexity, self-organization and emergence, have come to occupy a central place in its discourse. The adoption of these models works to legitimate the claims of design to be now in touch with the systemic, ecological and environmental realities of the world, to be speaking the same language as the nature of things themselves. Not coincidentally, the return to environmental, ecological and biological imperatives is accompanied by the turn in design from critique and towards naturalizing accounts of the world, to flat ontologies from whose perspective it is impossible to gain any purchase on systemic change. Neoliberalism, meanwhile, has found work for designers in fashioning itself as a naturalized environmental condition. Networked spaces of labour, learning landscapes, green-roofed shopping malls and 'landform buildings' appear as habitats fit for *homo economicus*.[52] Neoliberalism promises us sustainability, but is committed only to sustaining the version of Man that has brought us to the brink of environmental catastrophe. Architecture and design are condemned to serve as its accomplices so long as they fail to ask if another humanity is possible.

Notes

1   Hayek states in *The Constitution of Liberty* that the primary requisite for understanding society is that 'we become aware of men's necessary ignorance of much that helps him to achieve his aims'.

2   Walter D. Mignolo, 'The Invention of the *Human* and the Three Pillars of the Colonial Matrix of Power: Racism, Sexism, and Nature' in Walter D. Mignolo and Catherine E. Walsh, *On Decoloniality: Concepts, Analytics, Praxis* (Durham and London: Duke University Press, 2018),168.

3   Ibid., 164.

4   Michel Foucault, *Society Must Be Defended: Lectures at the Collège de France*, trans. David Macey (London: Penguin, 2004), 253.

5   Peder Anker, *Imperial Ecology: Environmental Order in the British Empire, 1895–1945* (Cambridge, MA: Harvard University Press, 2001), 2.

6   Lucile H. Brockway, *Science and Colonial Expansion: The Role of the British Royal Botanic Garden* (New Haven and London: Yale University Press, 2002), 77.

7   Timothy Ivison, *Developmentality: Biopower, Planning, and the Living City*, unpublished PhD Thesis, London Consortium, Birkbeck College, University of London (2016) <https://pdfs.semanticscholar.org/686f/a5023051797a8fbc6282e14a8ed60ace417a.pdf>, 3.

8   For a thorough historical account of Migge's involvement in the design of the German Modernist *Siedlung*, see David Haney, *When Modern Was Green: Life and Work of Landscape Architect Leberecht Migge* (London and New York: Routledge, 2010). See too, for an analysis of the relationship between Modernism and the organic, environmentalism and biocentrism, Oliver A. I. Botar and Isabel Wünsche, eds, *Biocentrism and Modernism* (Farnham, Surrey and Burlington, VT: Ashgate, 2011).

9   Hans Bernhard Reichow, *Organische Stadtbaukunst: Von der Großstadt zur Stadtlandschaft.* (Braunschweig, Georg Westermann Verlag, 1948).

10   Douglas Murphy, *Last Futures: Nature, Technology and the End of Architecture* (London and New York: Verso, 2016). See too Chapter 5, 'Cybernetic Dreams', 105–36, on the relationship between design and the counterculture.

11   R. Buckminster Fuller, *Operating Manual for Spaceship Earth* (Baden, Switzerland: Lars Müller, 2008/2011), 25.

12   Ibid., 59.

13   In gendering Man as male I am reproducing Fuller's practice. This gendering is, of course, significant, and I address this later in the essay with reference to the practice of what Sylvia Wynter refers to as 'over-representation'.

14   Ibid., 59–60.

15   Ibid., 45.

16   Ibid., 48.

17   Ibid., 66.

18   Sylvia Wynter and Katherine McKittrick, 'Unparalleled Catastrophe for Our Species: Or, to Give Humanness a Different Future: Conversations', in Katherine McKittrick, ed., *Sylvia Wynter on Being Human as Praxis* (Durham and London: Duke University Press, 2015), 22.

19   John McHale, *The Ecological Context* (London: Studio Vista, 1971).

20   Ibid., 2.

21   Ibid., 89.

22   Ibid., 89.

23   Ian L. McHarg, 'Values, Process and Form', in Ian L. McHarg and Frederick R. Steiner, eds, *To Heal the Earth: Selected Writings of Ian L. McHarg* (Washington, DC and Covelo, CA: Island Press, 1998), 40.

24   Ibid., 40.

25   Ibid., 63.

26   Ibid., 59.

27   Ibid. 59.

28   Ian L. McHarg, 'An Ecological Method for Landscape Architecture' in Paul Shepard and Daniel McKinley, eds, *The Subversive Science: Essays Towards an Ecology of Man* (Boston, MA: Houghton Mifflin Company, 1969), 328. Emphasis in italics mine.

29   Ian L. McHarg, 'Man and Environment' in McHarg and Steiner, 13.

30   Ibid., 13.

31   McHarg, 'Values, Process and Form', 68.

32   Ibid., 60.

33   Reyner Banham, *The Architecture of the Well-tempered Environment*, 2nd edn (Chicago, IL: University of Chicago Press, 1984), 28.

34   Ibid., 21.

35   Ibid., 20.

36   '... architects, critics, historians and everyone else
      concerned with environmental management in civi-
      lized countries, lack a range of spatial experience
      and cultural responses, that nomad people have
      always enjoyed'. Ibid., 19.

37   Reyner Banham, *Scenes in America Deserta*
      (London: Thames & Hudson, 1982), 99.

38   Reyner Banham, *Los Angeles: The Architecture of
      Four Ecologies* (Berkeley and Los Angeles, CA:
      University of California Press, 2001), 199.

39   Ibid., 197.

40   Jean Baudrillard/The French Group, 'The Environ-
      mental Witch-Hunt', in Reyner Banham, ed., *The
      Aspen Papers: Twenty Years of Design Theory from
      the International Design Conference in Aspen* (New
      York: Praeger, 1974), 208.

41   Ibid., 210.

42   Michel Foucault, *The Birth of Biopolitics: Lectures at
      the Collège de France, 1978–1979,* M. Senellart ,
      ed., trans. Graham Burchell (Basingstoke, UK and
      New York: Palgrave Macmillan, 2008). For an inci-
      sive reading of Foucault's analysis of environmental
      modes of control in relation to architecture and de-
      sign, see Manuel Shvartzberg, 'Foucault's "Environ-
      mental" Power: Architecture and Neoliberal Subjec-
      tivization', in Peggy Deamer, ed.,*The Architect as
      Worker: Immaterial Labor, the Creative Class, and
      the Politics of Design* (London: Bloomsbury, 2015),
      181–206.

43   Ibid., 259–60.

44   Philip Mirowski, *Never Let a Serious Crisis Go to
      Waste: How Neoliberalism Survived the Financial
      Meltdown* (London: Verso, 2013).

45   For a more extensive analysis of the common ground
      shared between neoliberalism and design thinking
      in relation to systems theory and cybernetics, see
      Douglas Spencer, *The Architecture of Neoliberalism:
      How Contemporary Architecture Became an Instru-
      ment of Control and Compliance* (London: Blooms-
      bury, 2016).

46   F. A. Hayek, *The Constitution of Liberty* (Abingdon
      and New York: Routledge, 2006), 66.

47   Sylvia Wynter 'Unsettling the Coloniality of Being/
      Power/Truth/Freedom: Towards the Human, After
      Man, Its Overrepresentation – An Argument', *The
      New Centennial Review*, Vol. 3, No. 3, Fall 2003,
      257–337. See too Sylvia Wynter and Katherine
      McKittrick, 'Unparalleled Catastrophe for Our
      Species? Or, to Give Humanness a Different Future:
      Conversations' in McKittrick, ed., *Sylvia Wynter: On
      Being Human as Praxis* (Durham and London: Duke
      University Press, 2015) 9–89. For an analysis of the
      relationship between the thought of Foucault and
      that of Wynter in relation to 'Man', see, in the same
      volume, Denise Ferreira da Silva, 'Before Man: Syl-
      via Wynter's Rewriting of the Modern Episteme',
      90–105.

48   Wynter, 'Unsettling the Coloniality of Being', 260.

49   Wynter and McKittrick 'Unparalleled Catastrophe',
      21.

50   Wynter, 'Unsettling the Coloniality of Being', 306.

51   Wynter and McKittrick 'Unparalleled Catastrophe',
      22.

52   For a more thorough analysis of architecture,
      post-criticality and neoliberalism see the preceding
      essay in this collection, 'Architectural Deleuzism:
      Neoliberal Space, Control and the "Univer-City"'.

3 Personifying Capital: Architecture and the Image of Participation

'In the course of our investigation we shall find, in general, that the characters who appear on the economic stage are but the personifications of the economic relations that exist between them.'[1]

Karl Marx, *Capital: A Critique of Political Economy*, Volume 1

Introduction

Certain forms of social appearance are welcomed onto the stage of capitalism. Others are less well received. The acceptable face of social existence, that of free participation and unbounded opportunity, is fleshed out in the form of a platform architecture, a landscaped surface peopled with entrepreneurial actors and citizen consumers. Its other face, formed from structural inequalities and precarious conditions of existence, is largely obscured, though no less designed. Conditions of social existence are least visible where most difficult to endure. Struggle against these conditions, enacted in the form of occupations, strikes, protests, iconoclasm and riots is also a struggle over representation and meaning. These struggles, and the schism between acceptable and unacceptable forms of social appearance, are long-standing, reaching back to the conditions and practices through which capitalism first sought to establish its order, and the images of the English landscape through which these were represented.

In his *The Dark Side of the Landscape: The Rural Poor in English Painting 1730–1840,* the art historian John Barrell analyzes the 'social landscapes' painted by John Constable between 1809 and 1821.[2] In these paintings – including *Boat-building near Flatford Mill* and *Stour Valley and Dedham Church* of 1815, and *The Hay Wain* of 1821 – Constable is said to be concerned with the expression of 'a social vision – the image of a productive and well-organised landscape, as it relates to the idea of a well-organised society'.[3] Constable arrives at the expression of this vision, Barrell argues, through the perspective of class, and in relation to the economic and political struggles being played out on the terrain of early nineteenth-century agrarian capitalism in England.

Constable's 'political attitudes', Barrell tells us, were 'unsurprisingly enough in view of his birth and the position of his family', those of an 'old-style rural Tory, convinced that the social and economic stability of England depended on a flourishing agriculture'.[4] Often the land depicted in Constable's paintings of East Anglia, moreover, was that owned by his family. The barge being built in *Boat-building near Flatford Mill*, for instance, is one of a number of commercial vessels constructed and used by the family's business to transport its grain to market. The land-owning class responsible for the industrial transformation of agricultural production in England, to which Constable and his family belonged, was, at the same time, 'threatened', Barrell remarks, 'by a new fear of the power of the labouring class'.[5] Constable's visions of a 'well-organised' rural landscape were haunted by the spectre of organized labour, of the 'combine' and its emerging capacity to contest the terms and conditions under which agricultural production, and the wider social order, was then being transformed. The threat to the established order – a very real one in this era of agrarian unrest – is warded off in such visions of land and labour as were offered up by Constable.

Barrell describes how Constable conjures up these visions of order, stability and productivity. Scenes of collective labour are evacuated from his paintings. Labour that would have necessarily required the work of many – reaping a field of corn, manufacturing a barge – is represented by solitary figures. Isolated, these figures can then appear harmoniously absorbed within a natural order, rather than as agents in a social or political one. Constable, in his effort to recreate 'an older, georgic image of the flat and productive land of East Anglia', writes Barrell, had to 'reduce his figures until they merge insignificantly with the landscape ... to evade the question of their actuality. The labourers do not step between us and the landscape – they keep their place, and it is a very small place, a long way away'.[6] While figures of labour may only make their appearance under such conditions, other figures are prohibited from appearing at all. Beggars, those subjects dispossessed and displaced by the political and economic transformations then under way in the country, both despite and because of their real and frequent presence in the landscape that Constable's paintings idealize, have no place in his vision. Where artists of the eighteenth century had, in their depictions of rural life, pictured vagrants as sympathetic, if romanticized, figures, their presence in Constable's vision of industrious and contented labour is inadmissible. At the opposite pole of the class spectrum, the nobility and the gentry are equally noticeable by their absence; 'there are no rural portraits of landowners asserting their authority over the landscape behind them'.[7] The presence of this class in Constable's painting would likewise break the spell of the natural order of labour, identifying all too clearly its sources of compulsion and exploitation.

The concerns with which Barrell's analysis of Constable's landscape painting is occupied, those of class, labour, land and property, and their representation, also animate the work of other art historians of this period, notably John Berger, T.J. Clark and Linda Nochlin (the latter, especially, also factoring into her analyses issues of gender representation).[8] Of Thomas Gainsborough's mid-eighteenth-century painting *Mr and Mrs Andrews,* Berger, for example, wrote of its subjects: 'They are not a couple in Nature as Rousseau imagined nature. They are landowners and their proprietary attitude towards what surrounds them is visible in their stance and their expressions.'[9]

Such concerns may seem remote, on multiple counts, to the subject of this essay, concerning the origins of the architectural platform, and its role in facilitating contemporary cultures of participation. Aside from the subject matter, and its historical distance, it is the theoretical apparatus employed in this moment of art history that likely seems anachronistic. After a now decades-long period of assault on critical theory, discussions of class, labour and capital sit uneasily within what currently passes for theoretical discourse. The focus on the subject, on figures and their representation, and the attention given to the antagonistic relations of the various social actors implicated in the scenes depicted, must appear outdated. Our theories of actor-networks now welcome all agents on stage as equal partners in the making of worlds.

Our object-oriented ontologies (OOO) displace human beings from the centre of things, unsettling the hubris of the anthropocentric perspective. A 'new materialism', celebratory and affirmative of the 'vibrancy' of things in themselves, has put paid to an older, darker, and altogether more negative variety of 'historical materialism'. Our new, post-political, and post-critical positions seem to have relieved us of the burdens of critique.

But these positions have themselves to be recognized, critically, as power grabs on the practice of theory; discursive manoeuvres valorized in the currency of the current. The temporality of displacement and succession in which claims to the 'new' are always cashed out, alongside the concomitant demand that critique acquiesce to its supposed obsolescence, is itself something to be critically contended with. Indeed, the possibility of critique holds so long as the gap between what capitalism promises and what it delivers remains. As Moishe Postone notes in his *Time, Labor, and Social Domination,* 'the structurally generated gap between what is and what could be' is what 'allows for the possible historical transformation of capitalism and, relatedly, provides the immanent grounds for the possibility of the critique itself'.[10] Critique, as an immanent and reflexive practice, is not then about to be put into early retirement by the same, and essentially capitalist, temporality of progress and improvement that it is reckoning with. This does not mark critique as immune to history, but as dialectically implicated within it, as the 'immanent grounds' for its own possibility. Critique, as Neil Brenner remarks, 'is not simply an oppositional orientation towards extant spaces, institutions and ideologies; it requires a continual interrogation of the changing historical conditions of possibility for such an orientation'.[11]

Positions valorized in the name of the 'new' and the 'post' mark out for critique the theoretical terrain on which it has to operate. The flattened ontologies of Actor-Network Theory and OOO have to be contested as attempts to dislodge critique, to compress the multiple dimensions through which its analyses pass into a horizontal plane of false equivalence.[12] The 'new' materialism, in turn, in thrall to the innate 'vibrancy' of things, and invested in the affirmation of unmediated experience, can be considered a revived romanticism, a re-enchantment of the world – as it simply *is* – serving to dissuade us from engaging in conceptual and reflexive thought on *why* it is, and *how* it could be otherwise.[13]

It might seem, as well, that the time in which Constable's painting was practised is too remote from our own for us to draw from its analysis any useful lessons. Again, we need to attend to questions of history and temporality. While critique has to be alert to the 'changing historical conditions of its own possibility', it has also to be attentive to the patterns of repetition in that history, to the continuities constitutive of capitalism understood in terms of its *longue durée*. Whatever may be gained in the practice of periodization, in the declaration and divination of each new 'turn' taken by capitalism – late, postmodern, post-industrial, Post-Fordist, financialized, digital, algorithmic, affective – such attempts to define what is particular and unique to the moment are themselves typically valorized in an effectively capitalist currency of the 'new': the discovery that 'changes everything', the special insight rendering all past efforts passé. This form of periodization tends to present the history of capitalism as a series of more or less discrete stages, but while the means through which capital produces value may vary, its orientation towards the production of value, as an end in itself, is unwavering. Extraction, circulation and accumulation are its enduring features.

If the history of capital can be understood as always unfolding through this dialectic of change and consistency, then we might take Barrell's concerns, in his analysis of Constable's painting, as being as much contemporary as they are of their own time. How is 'the image of a productive and well-organised landscape' used today to stand for 'the idea of a well-organised society'? Within what play of social and historical forces does this image appear? What contradictions does its appearance attempt to resolve? Under what terms and conditions can it represent labour, and what kind of work is the image itself engaged in? The posing of such questions around the politics of representation also have their own histories, and their own historical motivations. As T.J. Clark notes in the preface to the 1982 edition of his *The Absolute Bourgeois: Artists and Politics in France 1848–1851*, this, and its companion volume, *Image of the People: Gustave Courbet and the 1848 Revolution* (both first published in 1973), were written 'in ignominious but unavoidable retreat'.[14] Clark was, briefly, a member of the Situationist International (SI), whose ideas and perspective had played such a prominent role in the events of May 68 in France. These books were researched by a committed radical, in the midst of student and worker protests that threatened to overturn the existing social order, and then ultimately published in the aftermath of their defeat. This was, Clark conveys, 'a desolate, exultant time',[15] and the sense of this affective antinomy is all too evident in his accounts of the ultimately failed attempts, on the part of artists of the mid-nineteenth century, to produce a revolutionary or realist art adequate to its own historical moment.[16]

While Clark was working through the experience of defeat, retreating to an earlier moment of class struggle, the order that had survived the events of May 68 was working out what lessons could be drawn from these for the future, figuring out how to fashion its own affirmative 'image of the people'. This would be an image of participation; both a representation of and a mechanism for the kind of conduct required of the emergent neoliberal subject. It would not appear on canvas, but be presented as a real-time performance enacted by figures assembled within and mobilized by the architecture of the platform; the stage on which a new configuration of the public could effectively appear as 'personifications of the economic relations that exist between them'. The Centre Pompidou would be its prototype.[17]

Pompidou: an architecture of feedback

Designed by Renzo Piano and Richard Rogers and located on the Plateau Beaubourg, in Paris's fourth arrondissement, the Centre Pompidou opened in 1977. Architecturally, as Reyner Banham noted at the time of its opening, the project owed a significant debt to the megastructural projects of the 60s. Comprising a stack of five vast floor plates, each measuring 48 x 170 metres, and sporting its multi-coloured structures and services on its exterior, the Pompidou appeared to draw on a number of recent precedents. 'Even that colour scheme', wrote Banham in the *Architectural Review,* 'seems to say "Archigram" (if not "Yellow Submarine"!), the concept of a stack of clear floors that can be adapted to a variety of cultural and recreational functions seems to recall the 'Neo-Babylon' of Constant Niewenhuis [sic], or the Fun Palace of Cedric Price and Joan Littlewood'.[18] With its promise to provide for flexible programming, and the ambition of its architects to have the building serve as a '"Live Centre of Information" covering Paris and Beyond', the project was evidently informed by the cybernetic and multimedia inclinations of the period.[19] 'The building was conceived as a tool', as Rogers and Piano said of the project in 1977, 'whose exterior should have been the contact surface ... a surface of screens – TV screens, movie screens, written messages, newsreels.'[20]

While the ambition to have the building's exterior serve as a vast multimedia screen did not come to fruition, the Pompidou would still serve to mobilize information, only now by having its occupants provide the raw data. From the sloping plaza facing the building, the centre would appear animated by the visitors being transported between floors by escalators sheathed in transparent tubing. Through the plate glass windows occupants might be seen moving between exhibits. Conversely, the plaza itself, dotted with small groups casually seated on its incline, and figures strolling across its open space, would appear to those inside the centre as a reciprocating affirmation of openness and accessibility.

The appearance of accessibility, engagement and participation staged at the Centre Pompidou forms a counter image to that of the events of May 1968. It serves to dispel memories of strikes, occupations, running street battles and barricades, repopulating the imaginary with pictures of free assembly, mobility and institutional generosity. The centre, conceived in 1969 by France's President Georges Pompidou, after whose death it was subsequently named (originally the Centre Beaubourg), is a gesture towards the demands of May 68, but in a form made serviceable to an emergent neoliberal order. This order is driven by a vision of society comprised of self-mobilizing subjects, freely roaming the economic stage in pursuit of opportunities to valorize their individual enterprises. The state, particularly in its more overt and coercive actions, should absent itself from this stage in order to allow the free play of market forces to thrive, and the entrepreneurial mentalities of its actors to flourish.

Fig. 3.1: Centre Pompidou, Paris, France, Renzo Piano and Richard Rogers, 1977

The project for the Pompidou answered, in its own fashion, the calls for participation issued by the avant-garde elements of those in revolt. As Claire Bishop notes her *Artificial Hells: Participatory Art and the Politics of Spectatorship,* a number of political and artistic practices converged at this time in their demands for access and participation; the 'eroticized and transgressive Happenings' of the artist Jean-Jacques Lebel, the public participation projects of the Groupe Recherche d'Art Visuel, and, perhaps most significantly, the SI and their critique of the separation between art and everyday life.[21]

Conceived as a project to breach the divide between high culture and everyday life, the Pompidou was designed to encourage popular forms of public participation, and to level out class distinctions implicated in access to art in the process. As the centre's Secretary General, Claude Mollard stated: 'The President of the Republic himself wished for the centre to be established in a working-class neighbourhood and open to a very broad public: the cultural events

Fig. 3.2: Centre Pompidou, Paris, France, Renzo Piano and Richard Rogers, 1977

should not remain in spirit the privilege of a small, elite [group].' As Rebecca J. DeRoo notes of the Pompidou, in her *The Museum Establishment and Contemporary Art: The Politics of Artistic Display in France after 1968:*

> ... many of the center's visitors came for the kind of sites and activities that [Pierre] Bourdieu had approved of as a means to draw in visitors, such as the cafe, store and view of the city from the top floor. While high art was shown, the curators downplayed the scholarly background that was necessary to understand to make it seem accessible to all. The museum's collection prominently featured works of Pop Art that were embedded in the vocabulary of the mass media and advertising, evoking a resonance with contemporary, urban culture with which the curators contended all could identify.[22]

As a palliative against elitism, this curatorial agenda was, however, tempered with a redefinition of 'everyday life' at odds with those of the SI, and of Henri Lefebvre (from whom the SI had derived its theory of this term). The 'everyday life' with which art would now be integrated was not the contested and contradictory terrain of habits, practices and experiences situated, as Lefebvre wrote, at 'the intersection of the sector man controls and the sector he does not control', but a realm now absolutely assimilated to the norms of the market, itself now presented as a progressive force.[23] Art would be intertwined with a notion of the quotidian for which the hypermarket stood as ideal symbol. It would be made popular by being subsumed into a model of consumption.

Jean Baudrillard observed of this commodification of art, in his essay 'The Beaubourg Effect: Implosion and Deterrence', that 'for the first time, Beaubourg is at the level of culture what the hypermarket is at the level of the commodity'.[24] The correlation between the centre as a 'multidisciplinary cultural centre of an entirely new type' and the supermarket had, though, been consciously contrived.[25] As Ewan Branda has argued, stores such as FNAC, selling books, records and electronic goods, had acquired a reputation as progressive institutions that had been influential in the conception of the Pompidou.[26] Baudrillard held that these attempts to model the Pompidou on the popularity and accessibility of the hypermarket had been nothing less than disastrous. He writes in 'The Beaubourg Effect':

> The masses rush toward Beaubourg as they rush toward disaster sites, with the same irresistible élan. Better: they are the disaster of Beaubourg. Their number, their stampede, their fascination, their itch to see everything is objectively a deadly and catastrophic behaviour for the whole undertaking. Not only does their weight put the building in danger, but their adhesion, their curiosity annihilates the very contents of this culture of animation. This rush can no longer be measured against what was proposed as the cultural objective, it is its radical negation.[27]

From our own perspective Baudrillard's faith in the radically negative powers of the masses must appear misplaced. The Centre Pompidou stands, still, as a prototype for the animation of the public as both image and practice of participation. As such, it affords certain insights pertinent to the architecture that follows in its wake, and the part this has had to play in producing an image of the people in neoliberalism.

The Centre Pompidou, and its architecture, is designed to produce the performative affirmation of participation, access and mobility. The project is pivotal in folding the circulation of the subject into patterns of information distribution, economic valorization and new norms of spatial experience. These are, at the same time, advertised to the immediate urban environment. The architecture of Piano and Rogers, animated by its figures of circulation, serves as a pedagogy of participatory conduct. It is in this performative capacity that the Pompidou is effectively cybernetic, rather than in the extroverted display of its mechanical services. In its self-amplifying circuits of conduct and display, and in folding the events of May 68 into an emergent neoliberal agenda, the Pompidou is an architecture of feedback: 'the property', as defined by Norbert Wiener, 'of being able to adjust future conduct by past performance'.[28]

While the Centre Pompidou stands as prototypical for an architecture of neoliberalism, it exists as well within a genealogy of architectures of circulation; a product of capitalism's dialectic of change and consistency rather than a novelty that comes out of nowhere. As Meredith TenHoor notes, the market area of Les Halles, immediately adjacent to the Pompidou, had traditionally been conceived as the 'stomach of Paris', a central organ placed under longstanding obligation to 'showcase the ability of the government to manage the circulation of products from agricultural land to the city'.[29] In her essay 'Architecture and Biopolitics at Les Halles', TenHoor argues that 'shifting beliefs in the ability of architecture and urbanism to manage the relationship between the city, the market, and the bodies of Parisian citizens have generated new biopolitical roles for architecture and urbanism at Les Halles and beyond'.[30]

Constructed in the mid-eighteenth century, and designed by architect Nicolas Le Camus de Mézières, the Halle au blé grain market and storage facilities, for example, are described by TenHoor as an 'architecture to incite circulation ... of grain and money'.[31] The architect Victor Baltard's mid-nineteenth-century renovation of the markets at Les Halles, with its 'tectonic allusion to the then-modern rail station', in turn, 'suggested that Les Halles were a place for new circulatory freedoms'.[32] Les Halles, for TenHoor, has from the eighteenth to the twentieth century, been a site on which architecture has facilitated flows of food, money, bodies and information, while at the same time integrating these with governmental forms of control and surveillance.

The Centre Pompidou sits, then, within this lineage of circulatory architecture. Yet in its particular mobilization and management of the flow of and distribution of bodies – rendering them sources of information and valorization, channelling their flows into productive feedback loops – the project also points towards the trajectory of more recent architectures of circulation, and the ways in which these serve to control and valorize the subject within specifically neoliberal forms of capitalism.

Becoming infrastructural: a platform architecture

Postmodernism, in the conventional historiography of twentieth-century architecture, is placed as the immediate successor to Modernism. In Postmodernism architecture is reacquainted with the uses and pleasures of ornament, signs and symbols. Rejecting the austere and functionalist aesthetics of Modernism, alongside its universalizing tectonics, Postmodernist architecture is playful, sensitive to context and regionally differentiated. While Postmodernism, and its architectural discourse, also include more wide-ranging social criticisms, particularly of bureaucratic planning, its focus has fallen on architectural style, 'language' and meaning. Obscured from this periodization is a deeper and more substantial shift in the agenda of architecture. Beginning in the mid-1960s, and corresponding to the transition from welfare state to neoliberal modes of capitalism, a certain current in architecture becomes particularly concerned with the mobilization and management of circulation.

The sources and manifestations of this architectural current are multiple. They include Claude Parent and Paul Virilio's Architecture Principe group, and their experiments with the 'function of the oblique';[33] the internally ramped, sometimes labyrinthine structures of Rem Koolhaas/OMA – the

Fig. 3.3: Oslo Opera House, Oslo, Norway, Snøhetta, 2008

Kunsthal in Rotterdam, the Deux Bibliothèques Jussieu, in Paris, the Casa da Música in Porto; the philosophy of Gilles Deleuze's *The Fold: Leibniz and the Baroque*,[34] and the folded geometries of Foreign Office Architects' Yokohama Port Terminal; Gilles Deleuze and Félix Guattari's notion of 'smooth space' from their *A Thousand Plateaus: Capitalism and Schizophrenia*,[35] and the smoothed spaces of Zaha Hadid Architects' MAXXI museum in Rome; the 'landform' architecture touted by Stan Allen,[36] and the roofscape of Snøhetta's Oslo Opera House. Thomas Heatherwick's Vessel at Hudson Yards in Manhattan is its hyperbolic form; an architecture of pure circulation.[37]

Taking upon itself the tasks of mobilizing and managing circulation, architecture exhibits its drive towards becoming infrastructural. The 'organizational diagram' of OMA's 1996 Universal Headquarters project – a precursor to their CCTV building in Beijing – is described as resonating with that of 'subway map' rather than a building plan.[38] The telescoping structure of

Diller Scofidio + Renfro's cultural centre, 'The Shed', in Manhattan's Hudson Yards, runs on rails, its credentials – flexibility, adaptability – recalling those claimed for the Centre Pompidou, or, as Shannon Mattern has noted, Cedric Price's unbuilt Fun Palace project of 1961.[39] These tasks are carried out, it should be noted, within the shift from welfare state to neoliberal capitalism with which they historically coincide. Bodies are mobilized within and between buildings according to new entrepreneurial imperatives of contingency, spontaneity, adaptability and opportunism. The folded, fluid-formed, smooth-spaced architectures of Greg Lynn, Zaha Hadid, Reiser + Umemoto, Foreign Office Architects, are informed by the same models of complexity, self-organization and spontaneous ordering as is the neoliberal economic theory of Friedrich Hayek.[40]

This relationship is not merely coincidental. Architecture – at least some architecture – is instrumental to the political economy of neoliberalism. In neoliberalism the capitalist imperative to accumulate comes to be invested in each subject as its own economic project; an entrepreneurial self supposed to valorize its projects in relation to those of a society modelled as a spontaneously self-organizing market of atomized individuals. Those subjects – their bodies, their calculating rationality, their patterns of attention, their opportunistic impulses – have to be trained and mobilized; aggregated into flows, steered towards attractor points. These are the tasks served by architecture's infrastructural orientation.

The mobilization of bodies is also now mediated and governed through data. In her 2018 essay 'Databodies in Codespace', anthropologist Shannon Mattern addresses the operationalized convergence between bioengineering and cities, a condition in which citizens 'assume the role of "participatory sensors", using their own smartphones to collect data and helping build and install ambient sensing devices', and where 'our bodies and environments are already data – both public and proprietary'.[41] The convivial spaces of the 'smart city' operate, within this condition, as zones from which to seed and harvest data. The subject as 'databody' and the platforms – architectural and media-based – through which it participates, are sites upon which capitalism's procedures of extraction, circulation and accumulation are trained.

Fig. 3.4: The Vessel, Hudson Bay, New York, USA, Heatherwick Studio, 2019

It is not only data that is extracted, circulated and accumulated from such sites, however. An image of participation is also culled from contemporary architectures of conviviality; a performative scenography of well-ordered interaction, amplified through feedback loops of enactment and display. Architecture provides a platform both for participatory conduct and its representation, circulated within the immediate environment and beyond, into the spheres of social media.

The affordances of representation: EDP, MAAT and the call centre worker

John Barrell notes that in one of Constable's preparatory sketches for *Boat-building near Flatford Mill* the artist more faithfully records the labour of barge construction than in his painting, depicting the multiple figures involved in this task. This sketch, writes Barrell, 'is thronged with figures – at least ten men at work on the barge or near it. In the painting these are reduced to four, and all but two of them have been moved away from the foreground'.[42] The final painting is depopulated, warding off the threat of organized labour, allowing the isolated worker to be harmonized within a naturalized landscape. The contemporary scenography of the architectural platform, in contrast, conforms to an order of interaction rather than of isolation, its harmonizing principle that of participation. There appears no need now to depopulate the image in order to render it a harmonious representation of a natural order, perhaps because the order of entrepreneurial participation has itself been normalized, the appearance of the crowd at last reconciled with a legitimate and legitimating appearance of social conduct. Yet this image, just as much as that of Constable's painting, works to undermine the possibility of another and more radical image of the people, one contesting the terms of the existing order.

This ongoing schism in the forms of social appearance assumed or disavowed by capital, and its articulation in the built environment, are exemplified in a recent example of a platform architecture. The MAAT – Museum of Art, Architecture and Technology – is located on the riverfront of the Belém district of Lisbon, Portugal. Designed for the EDP (Energias de Portugal) Foundation by Amanda Levete Architects, and opened in 2016, the MAAT is supposed to serve both as an exhibition centre and a publicly accessible space for the city. This project sits in the context of the ongoing regeneration of the city, under way since 2011, when, in the form of the 'Economic Adjustment Programme for Portugal', the country received a €78 billion bail-out from the IMF and the EU in response to the financial crisis. For the EDP Foundation, a 'private non-profit institution' created in 2004 by the energy company EDP, the MAAT is exemplary of its 'commitment to promoting citizenship' and its goals in 'the promotion, development and support of social, cultural, scientific, technological, educational, environmental and legacy-protecting initiatives'.[43] For its architect, Amanda Levete, the MAAT stands as a 'social place of intersections and conversations across thresholds, one that people can pass through or just be in; a place visitors can use and programme in the way they want'.[44]

Fig. 3.5: The Museum of Art, Architecture and Technology, Lisbon, Portugal, Amanda Levete Architects, 2016

The wave-like form of Levete's architecture is reminiscent of Foreign Office Architects' Yokohama Port Terminal, or their S-E Coastal Park in Barcelona. Its accessible roof recalls that of Snøhetta's Oslo Opera House. As with these precedents, the form of the MAAT – its landscaped, gently contoured geometry – is used to underwrite more broadly encompassing claims around its performance as a socially progressive architecture. The formal capacity of the structure to dissolve spatial distinctions, to signal continuity and connection, is held as well to provide for the exercise of new personal liberties affirmed in the familiar discourse of the blurring of boundaries, or the crossing of thresholds. The popularity of the MAAT, for Levete, speaks of 'the need for spaces that help us overcome the thresholds that could otherwise divide us'.[45] Her building, she claims, provides for the 'vibrancy' that stands as the mark of 'great cities', namely 'those that create countless opportunities to connect across thresholds, connecting people of different nationalities and from different walks of life, with different ideas and different experiences'.[46]

The image for which the MAAT provides a platform, that of a cosmopolitan public, enjoying unhindered access to the opportunities of social connection, belies the fact of other and contrary forms of social existence, ones not afforded institutional or architectural representation. The call centre worker, for instance, experiences the purportedly revitalized economies of the neoliberal city through precarious conditions of employment, and within an architecture that serves to contain and organize their labour, rather than providing for its public display. Where the architectural platform offers a positive representation of flexibility – the promise of a space which the visitor can 'use and programme in the way they want' – flexibility, for the precarious worker, takes on an entirely different aspect.

Following Portugal's 2011 bail-out, and its accompanying austerity measures, the country's workers were left particularly vulnerable to exploitative conditions of employment. These were especially marked in Portugal's call centres. As the sociologist Isabel Maria Bonito Roque remarks, the country is 'on the radar and agenda of international decision makers in attracting foreign investments for the installation of call centres', in part because Portugal is 'strategically positioned on the intercontinental routes that present the best technological infrastructures'.[47] The companies positioned to take advantage of this situation, she notes, operate through agencies for temporary work, subcontracting from other companies, and offering only 'short-term contracts which allow workers to be easily dismissed or seasonally replaced by others more profitable to the company'.[48] Portugal's call centre workers, argues Roque, are subjected to a situation that is 'unstable, flexible, and precarious'; one that 'reinforces individualism, decreasing trade union membership and the weakening of professional and social bonds'.[49] Not only is the employment situation 'flexible' – in this negative sense – but the labour of the call centre also demands 'flexibility' in the physical and emotional performance of the worker. 'The operator', observes Roque, has to be 'fast, attentive, friendly, emotionally balanced, and flexible, that is, being able to deal with unexpected situations.' While undertaking this affective labour, the operator is confined for long hours to the small space of their cubicle, and, Roque reports, subjected to frequent verbal abuse and other forms of harassment.[50]

These conditions have been contested through union-organized strikes and protests, much of this undertaken by the South and Islands Electric Industries' Trade Union (SIESI), and focused on the subcontracting practices of EDP, the company whose foundation financed the design and construction of the MAAT. Roque explains of SIESI that '[t]he main goal of this trade union is to avoid temporary agency companies from employing EDP call centre workers, allowing them instead to be part of the company'.[51] In the very same month in which the MAAT was opened – October 2016 – SIESI call centre workers staged a strike, and protested outside EDP's headquarters in Lisbon.[52]

Through the platform architecture of the MAAT, EDP offer up an image advertising flexibility and connectivity; qualities afforded a generic 'public' through its philanthropic investment. This representation stands, though, as the alibi for the economic conditions of flexibility which it is happy to exploit at the expense of those with whom it refuses to connect contractually.

Conclusion: on the anthropomorphism of capital

What remains true of the image of capital – from the early-nineteenth-century landscape paintings of Constable, to the contemporary architecture of the platform – is the contradiction between those forms of appearance constructed to affirm its operation, and those that must be disavowed. What has changed is the content of the affirmative image, from naturalization to humanization, and its medium, from painting to architecture.

Constable painted *Boat-building near Flatford Mill* when the appearance of massed figures – whether of the 'unruly mob' or of organized labour – could only be taken as threat to the order capital was in the process of attempting to establish. This period, in which capital merely appropriates pre-existent forms of labour for its own ends, is gradually succeeded by one in which it creates the world over in its own image and to its own ends, producing the forms and practices that presuppose and sustain it operations.[53] Within certain traditions of Marxism this is known as the 'real domination' of capital, and is effected, in significant part, by what the Italian Left Communist Jacques Camatte describes as its 'anthropomorphism'.[54] What Camatte argued in the 1970s was that capital had succeeded in re-creating and representing itself as a 'community' from which all contradictions between capital and humanity had disappeared.[55] As he argues in the essay 'Marx and *Gemeinwesen*', 'Religion itself loses its function because it no longer serves to connect beings, a matter left to capital as representation.'[56] This 'community of capital' and its representation, allows capital to address and resolve its own contradictions, as its own ersatz form of the political. As Giorgio Cesarano wrote in 'Apocalypse and Revolution':

> The transition to real domination, however, leads capital to produce a politics – the new image through which it smuggles itself ... Yet the problems of the day, in the apparent forms of an openness to the demands and needs of the people, are always capital's problems. The people are increasingly capital in person ...[57]

Under these circumstances the 'image of the people' becomes the 'image of capital'. The figures in its landscapes – literal or architectural – are no longer likely to be harmonized within nature as solitary beings, but to be mobilized as participatory figures in a shared 'humanity'. May 68 is a decisive hinge point in this process, a critical juncture at which the politics of antagonism are replaced by the image of politics as participation, a conciliatory 'openness to the demands and needs of the people' whose representation is architecturally enacted by the prototypical platform architecture of the Centre Pompidou. Current iterations of this architectural form continue to serve as the alibi of the opportunism of capital, and the inhuman conditions on which it thrives.

Notes

1 Karl Marx, *Capital : A Critique of Political Economy*, Volume 1, trans. Ben Fowkes (London: Penguin, 1976), 178.

2 John Barrell, *The Dark Side of the Landscape: The Rural Poor in English Painting 1730–1840* (Cambridge: Cambridge University Press, 1980).

3 Ibid., 133.

4 Ibid., 134.

5 Ibid., 137.

6 Ibid., 137.

7 Ibid., 133.

8 See, John Berger, *Ways of Seeing* (London: BBC/Penguin, 1972); T. J. Clark, *The Absolute Bourgeois: Artists and Politics in France 1848–1851* (Thames and Hudson, 1973); T. J. Clark, *Image of the People: Gustave Courbet and the 1848 Revolution* (Thames and Hudson, 1973); Linda Nochlin, *The Politics of Vision: Essays on Nineteenth-Century Art and Society* (New York and London: Routledge, 1989).

9 Berger, *Ways of Seeing*, 107.

10 Moishe Postone, *Time, Labor, and Social Domination: A Reinterpretation of Marx's Critical Theory* (Cambridge and New York: Cambridge University Press, 1993), 360.

11 Neil Brenner, *Critique of Urbanization: Selected Essays* (Basel: Bauwelt Fundamente/Birkhäuser, 2017), back cover.

12 For a sustained critique of Actor-Network Theory see Douglas Spencer, 'Going to Ground: The Problem of Bruno Latour', in Clara Olóriz Sanjuán, ed., *Landscape as Territory: A Cartographic Design Project* (Barcelona: Actar, 2019), 150–7. Also included in this collection.

13 See Jane Bennett, *Vibrant Matter: A Political Ecology of Things* (Durham, NC: Duke University Press, 2010). For a recent critique of flat ontologies and the 'new materialism' with which these are associated, see the collection by Russell Sbriglia and Slavoj Žižek, eds, *Subject Lessons: Hegel, Lacan, and the Future of Materialism* (Evanston, IL: Northwestern University Press, 2020).

14 Clark, *Absolute Bourgeois*, 5.

15 Ibid., 5.

16 As Alastair Wright writes, 'Clark's pessimism – "after Courbet, is there any more 'revolutionary art'?" may reflect the bitter aftermath of May 1968 as much as that of February 1848. But I would wager that was his sense of the contradictions of his own time that allowed Clark to think as deeply as he did both in Courbet's own life and in the society around him.' 'T.J. Clark's "Image of the People: Gustave Courbet and the 1848 Revolution", 1973', *The Burlington Magazine*, Vol. 153, No. 1298, Art in France (May 2011), 334.

17 For an extended treatment of the Centre Pompidou as prototypical for neoliberal architecture, see Douglas Spencer, *The Architecture of Neoliberalism: How Contemporary Architecture Became an Instrument of Control and Compliance* (London and New York: Bloomsbury Academic,, 2016), 111–21.

18 Reyner Banham, 'Enigma of the Rue du Renard', *Architectural Review* 963, Vol. CLXI (May 1977), 277.

19 Richard Rogers, competition submission text, cited in Nathan Silver, *The Making of Beaubourg: A Building Biography of the Centre Pompidou, Paris* (Cambridge, MA and London: MIT Press, 1994), 33.

20 Richard Rogers and Renzo Piano, cited in Rebecca J. DeRoo, *The Museum Establishment and Contemporary Art: The Politics of Artistic Display in France after 1968* (New York: Cambridge University Press, 2006), 177.

21 Claire Bishop, *Artificial Hells: Participatory Art and the Politics of Spectatorship* (London and New York: Verso, 2012), 77–104.

22 DeRoos, *The Museum Establishment,* 175.

23 Henri Lefebvre, *Critique of Everyday Life: The One Volume Edition* (London and New York: Verso, 2014), 41.

24 Jean Baudrillard, *Simulacra and Simulation*, trans. Sheila Faria Glaser (Ann Arbor, Michigan: University of Michigan Press, 1994), 69. Richard Rogers, later reflecting on this criticism of the centre, observed that '[c]ertain critics, disoriented by the multiplicity of its activities and the resulting perception of disorder, have complained about its resemblance to a "supermarket"; this comparison has never bothered me: a supermarket is always more lively than a museum'. Richard Rogers, interviewed by Antoine Picon in 1987, cited in Ewan Branda, *The Architecture of Information at Plateau Beaubourg*, University of

California, Los Angeles, PhD thesis (2012).
<https://escholarship.org/uc/item/0w-w309s3#page-1>, 82.

25   'History of the Centre Pompidou', official website of the Centre Pompidou. <https:// www.centrepompidou.fr/en/The-Centre-Pompidou#586>.

26   'FNAC's aim was to improve the lives of workers by access to free cultural events and to the latest technology and cultural products – a revolution if not of higher salaries then of lower prices and open information.' Branda, *Architecture of Information*, 25.

27   Baudrillard, *Simulacra*, 66.

28   Norbert Wiener, *The Human Use of Human Beings: Cybernetics and Society* (London: Free Association Books, 1989), 33.

29   Meredith TenHoor, 'Architecture and Biopolitics at Les Halles', *French Politics, Culture & Society*, Vol. 25, No. 2, Summer 2007, 73.

30   Ibid., 73.

31   Ibid., 76.

32   Ibid., 79.

33   Pamela Johnston, ed., *The Function of the Oblique: The Architecture of Claude Parent and Paul Virilio 1963–1969* (London: AA Publications, 1996).

34   Gilles Deleuze, *The Fold: Leibniz and the Baroque*, trans. Tom Conley (London: The Athlone Press, 1993).

35   Gilles Deleuze and Félix Guattari, *A Thousand Plateaus: Capitalism and Schizophrenia*, trans. Brian Massumi (London and New York: Continuum, 2004).

36   Stan Allen and Marc McQuade, eds, *Landform Building: Architecture's New Terrain* (Zurich: Lars Müller Publishers, 2011).

37   For an extensive treatment of this architectural current, and its relationship to the political economy of neoliberalism, see Douglas Spencer, *The Architecture of Neoliberalism: How Contemporary Architecture Became an Instrument of Control and Compliance* (London and New York: Bloomsbury Academic, 2016).

38   Project description at OMA website, <http://www.oma.eu/projects/1996/universalheadquarters>.

39   Shannon Mattern, 'Instrumental City: The View from Hudson Yards, circa 2019,' *Places Journal*, April 2016 <https://doi.org/10.22269/160426>.

40   See, for example, Hayek, 'Degrees of Explanation', in *Studies in Philosophy, Politics and Economics* (Chicago: University of Chicago Press, 1967), 3–21.

41   Shannon Mattern, 'Databodies in Codespace', *Places Journal*, April 2018, <https://doi.org/10.22269/180417>

42   Barrell, 'Dark Side', 133.

43   EDP Foundation Mission Statement, <https://www.fundacaoedp.pt/en/content/about-us>

44   Amanda Levete, 'There has never been a more important time to celebrate what unites us', CNN Style, 14 September, 2017 <https://www.cnn.com/style/article/amanda-levete-architecture-social-division/index.html>.

45   Ibid.

46   Ibid.

47   Isabel Maria Bonito Roque, 'Trade Unionism and Social Protest Movements in Portuguese Call Centres', *Journal of Labor and Society,* Vol. 21 (2017), 58.

48   Ibid., 58.

49   Ibid., 58.

50   Ibid., 59.

51   Ibid., 61.

52   As SIESI delegate Anna Catarino Romão told reporters at the protest, EDP practices 'false outsourcing'. TPN/Lusa, *The Portugal News*, 'Call Centre Employees on EDP Contract Demand End to Casual Work' (20 October 2016), <https://www.theportugal-news.com/news/call-centre-employees-on-edp-contract-demand-end-to-casual-work/39909>

53   Marx writes in the *Grundrisse* that: 'The separation of *public works* from the state and their migration into the domain of the works undertaken by capital itself, indicates the degree to which the real community has constituted itself in the form of capital', Karl Marx, *Grundrisse: Foundations of the Critique of Political Economy*, trans. Martin Nicolaus (Harmondsworth: Penguin Books in association with New Left Review, 1973), 531.

54   Jacques Camatte, *Capital and Community: The Results of the Immediate Process of Production and the Economic Work of Marx*, trans. David Brown (London: Unpopular Books, 1988).

55   Jacques Camatte 'Marx and Gemeinwesen', *Revue Invariance* (1977), translated and republished in *Endnotes, No. 5: The Passions and the Interests*, Autumn 2019, 275–89.

56   Ibid., 82.

57   Giorgio Cesarano, *Apocalypse and Revolution* (1973), translated and republished in *Endnotes, No. 5: The Passions and the Interests*, Autumn 2019, 298.

EUR District, Rome, Italy, Marcello Piacentini et al, 1937, interrupted by Second World War

Section 2.
Autonomy: Architecture and the Politics of Depoliticization

4 Less Than Enough: A Critique of the Project of Autonomy

Differentiating 'the project' from mere design has been crucial to the architectural theory of Pier Vittorio Aureli, not least since his own oeuvre consists of something like a project for the affirmation of the project.[1] In *The Possibility of an Absolute Architecture* he states, 'Design reflects the mere managerial praxis of building something, whereas the project indicates the strategy on whose basis something must be produced, must be brought into presence'.[2] Aureli's discourse is nothing if not decisive. Decision – from the Latin *decaedere,* 'to cut off', as he reminds his readers – in fact constitutes the form and the content of his project.[3] The separation of the project from design is just one in a series of cuts from which the project itself is fashioned. The political is separated from the economic, the architectural from the urban, the limited from the totality, the object from the field, the fixed from the circulating. The positive terms of each opposition – the political, architecture, limit, object, fixity – are stacked up to one side, forming the basis of the project. The procedure seeks out fundamentals and establishes identities, the fixed points of origin for words, meanings and practices; the essential loci around which architecture and its political potential should be understood and refounded as a formal project. Its case is argued through exemplars – Boullée, Hilberseimer, Red Vienna, Ungers. Architecture is understood as the possibility of establishing the limits that protectively frame the life of the subject and its small-scale communal relations, securing its integrity from the economic currents circulating in the realm of the urban. Its object is autonomy – individual, political, architectural.

In some sense, Aureli's project stands in direct confrontation with the projective, post-critical and Deleuzian turns undertaken by architecture since the mid-1990s. It contests their fetishisation of circulation and their affirmation of continuous connectivity. Patrik Schumacher, for instance – certainly the most vocal contributor to this tendency – has come to openly endorse the market order of neoliberalism as the condition to be unquestioningly served by an architectural culture renouncing any political agency of its own.[4] Diametrically opposed to Aureli's political project for architecture, Schumacher has recently written that '[t]he concept of a "critical" or "political" architecture is either due to the delusion that the revolution has arrived or an atavism that dreams about small "brotherhood" style societies'.[5] Those motivated to contest Schumacher's embrace of the market, and the broader depoliticization of architecture his position represents, might be inclined to endorse Aureli's position in response. Nevertheless, Schumacher touches a nerve. His charge of atavism is not so easily dismissed, exposing as it does something of an issue in the way that the argument against architecture's embrace of neoliberal urbanization has typically been articulated. At issue here is a strategy that simply reverses the polarity of its enemy's affirmations; negating what it valorizes, and vice versa. The strategy of decisive contradiction consigns what aspires to be a critique of capitalist urbanization to a project of redemption. It adopts a position whose roots, going back to the earliest appearance of monetization in fifth century BC Athens, are originally aristocratic. Characterized by the historian Richard Seaford as the 'ideology of self-sufficiency', this seeks to contest forms of unfettered circulation through an appeal to the restorative order of socio-spatial limits.[6]

As Alain Badiou notes in his *Logics of Worlds,* '[e]ndorsing an aristocratic idealism has tempted many a good mind'. The aim of this endorsement – as is to be found, for instance, in Heidegger – is 'practically to safeguard … the possibility of a Return'. The nostalgia of this position, he notes, is however 'always already lost … it cannot partake in the creation of a concept for the coming times'.[7] In the case of the project of autonomy, this is because the formal absolutes and identities from which it is forged are transhistorical. History, for Aureli, appears as a repository from which moments confirming the possibility of an absolute architecture can be recovered; an archipelago of exemplars in which architecture, somehow, realized its proper essence in isolating the subject from the economic imperatives of urban circulation. Where architecture has maintained its formal limits, refusing the dissolution of these within the field of urbanization, it has secured the separation of the subject from the deformities to which it would otherwise be vulnerable within capitalism. The self is protectively framed so as to ensure its enjoyment of the already extant fullness of its being.

There is no real treatment of the production of subjectivity, as such, in this project. Unlike Foucault, for whom subjectivity is a process of production in which discursive and non-discursive practices are always implicated – from ancient Greece and Rome to twentieth-century neoliberalism – Aureli posits an essential form of life whose conditions of possibility are not themselves critically examined, but taken as read, given, transcendent to history.

For Badiou, subjectivisation is an achievement, a temporal event that enables escape from the normative bounds of convention by which the mere individual is constrained.[8] For Aureli, however, an architecture of limits is conceived as the means to ward off subjectivisation as threatening the already identified idea of being to which the self must be adequate. The formal essence and the essentializing formalism of the project are, then, pre-critical.

If this project appears unable to produce concepts critically adequate to contemporary conditions, however, this is above all because of its insistence on the separation of the political from the economic. This renders the project especially compromised in relation to the current conditions of neoliberalism in which the political and the economic are strategically rendered indistinguishable from one another. Aureli's resort to an appeal to escape from these conditions that focuses on the self apart from the economic, articulated in his extended essay *Less is Enough*, is especially revealing of the problematics inherent to his project.[9] Here, the compromised nature of the project of autonomy, and the limitations of its transhistorical and pre-critical approaches, becomes particularly apparent. Its affirmations – its identification of architecture with form, and forms of life, the idea of the self as project, and the privilege of isolation from the urban – begin to converge with those promoted by neoliberalism and its architecture.

'Asceticism,' writes Aureli in *Less is Enough*, 'allows subjects to focus on their life as the core of their own practice, by structuring it according to a self-chosen form made of specific habits and rules.'[10] Asceticism also enables the self to achieve 'autonomy from systems of power'[11] in a process that 'often involves architecture and design as a device for self-enactment'.[12] Monasticism and its architecture, particularly that of the early Franciscans, exemplify this possibility. 'From the outset monasticism manifested itself as an inevitable and radical critique of power, not by fighting it, but by leaving it.'[13] The monastic single cell is the 'quintessential representation of interiority: it is here that the single body finds its proper space, the space in which it can take care of itself'.[14] The Franciscans best exemplify a critique of power since they eschew the concern of other orders with entrepreneurialism and production. Above all, their rule of voluntary poverty enables them to escape corruption from the economic order emerging in the towns and cities of thirteenth-century Europe. The Franciscan 'refusal to own things' is a refusal of their 'economic value and thus the possibility of the exploiting of others'.[15] The architecture of the monastery, its individual cells and cloistered common spaces, holds the monks in protective isolation from the economic powers circulating beyond its walls. Aureli, following the arguments of Agamben's *The Highest Poverty*, maintains that the form of the monastery sustained a 'form of life' in which one's life and the habits through which it was lived were in perfect agreement, the one becoming indistinguishable from the other through the sharing of a common rule.[16] The architecture of the monastery is in perfect consonance with this form of life, it is 'simply an extrusion of the ritual activities that take place within'.[17]

The argument of *Less is Enough* builds upon that of *The Possibility of an Absolute Architecture*. Architecture is only 'resolutely itself' when separated from the managerial paradigm of urbanization associated with the rise of capitalism.[18] An absolute architecture achieving formal autonomy from the economic forces that surround it is, in its very essence, a political architecture: '[t]he very condition of architectural form is to separate and be separated'.[19] An architecture of formal autonomy is political because politics is, in its very essence, 'agonism through separation and confrontation'.[20] The architectural and the political are defined through formal categories in which the one serves to realize the essence of the other. In combination they constitute a project that escapes urbanization with its 'economic logic of social management'.[21] In *Less is Enough* Aureli introduces an essential form of life as a third term within this schema. 'Human nature' is identified with 'its most generic substratum', that of 'life itself–bios' – and human subjects are argued to be properly themselves only when allowed to 'focus on their self as the core of their activity'.[22] What are claimed as the essential properties of the architectural, the political and the human, are held to be perfectly aligned in Franciscan monasticism.[23] This is proposed as a paradigm of resistance-through-escape from the economic and the managerial. And this, in turn, is how Aureli arrives at his concluding argument concerning what is proper to the conduct of the contemporary architect. Whereas architects and designers today often concern themselves with a social agenda, 'they rarely,' Aureli laments, 'look at their own existence, which is what really constitutes the main source of their production'.[24] They would do better, and be more effectively political, were they to focus on their own lives, as formal projects, rather than concerning themselves with an architecture of good intentions. This is Aureli's Franciscanism. Through asceticism the self might realize its properly autonomous essence, a project, in Aureli's words, of 'fundamental liberation from [the] social structure'.[25]

Aureli's Franciscanism, however, constitutes an effectively pre-critical turn in its insistence on fundamental essence and normative identity. No less so than the now near-hegemonic and post-critical architectural discourse of emergence, self-organization and complexity, it identifies life and architecture with form, and the redemption of their essence in restoring the absolute consonance of the one with the other. What Aureli sets out to oppose is only inverted. The extroverted and the open, the flexible, the intensively networked and the hyper-connective, are challenged by an opposing set of morphological principles – the introverted and the closed, the separate and the fixed, the cloistered and the bounded. Each party – the post-critical and the pre-critical – stakes a claim to what is proper to life and to architecture, and each articulates this claim in formal terms. But neither party concerns itself with the conditions under which the proper, in terms of life, architecture and the political, is itself produced, historically, politically, economically. Their respective positions, that is, are not critical but dogmatic. Neither party, though for quite different reasons, seems willing to acknowledge the ways in which architecture and life, and what is supposed to be proper to them, are mediated by the economic. Indeed, for Aureli the redemption and realization of the essential forms of architecture and life are held to be the very means by which both, together, escape the economic. Here the terms of the concept of a 'political economy' are decisively prised apart so that the political is seen as the means through which autonomy from the economic can be achieved. As David Cunningham has recently remarked of this project, 'there is something profoundly formalist about this definition of "the sphere of the political" itself, which in rendering "separation and confrontation" solely internal to politics, merely brackets off the central "context" of actual, historical capitalist social relations themselves'.[26] It might be added that this bracketing off of the economic also serves to obscure the ways in which the seemingly redemptive project of the autonomous self is also mediated by the economic and managerial imperatives of neoliberalism.

Franciscanism does not elude the economic and its managerial operations, it elides them. In fact it even obscures the relationship between capitalism, architecture and religion at work in the case of the early Franciscans. Looked at from a historical perspective, as opposed to a transhistorical one, the relationship between the Franciscans and their architecture reveals precisely the ways in which this was mediated by, and indeed contributed to, the emergence of an urban managerialism driven by the rise of capitalism.

Giacomo Todeschini writes, in his *Franciscan Wealth: From Voluntary Poverty to Market Society,* that 'the Franciscans' approach to the market reveals that it was the most rigorous Christian religiosity that formed a large part of the vocabulary in western economics … the Christian world was never extraneous from the market … nor was there a clear separation between morality and business'.[27] Todeschini is not alone in arguing that the Franciscans were implicated in the development of the market society emerging in thirteenth-century Europe. In *Money and the Middle Ages,* Jacques Le Goff remarks that the early Franciscans 'were better integrated into the new money economy than into the old rural economy'.[28] Caroline Bruzelius reports, in her recent *Preaching, Building, and Burying: Friars in the Medieval City,* that '[e]conomic historians have noted that in time the orders that adopted the idea of evangelical poverty came to have an intimate acquaintance with wealth'.[29] 'Indeed', she continues, 'Franciscans were among the first economic theorists of the Middle Ages.'[30]

The implication of the Franciscan order in the economy of the emerging market society derives in significant part from the fact that it tended, in contrast to the rural locations of earlier monastic orders, to situate its monasteries within the existing urban territory, often at its core. In the early decades of the thirteenth century the order began to insinuate itself into the gaps it found within this environment. It occupied abandoned buildings within towns and cities experiencing rising population growth and the rapid development of mercantile trade. From these footholds it grew its monasteries piecemeal, taking further ground building by building. As Bruzelius suggests, '[w]e can think of mendicant architecture, like cities, as in a constant state of "becoming"'.[31] The architecture of the Franciscan friary was not derived from a logic of isolation internal to the order, or the expression of a plan generated, 'simply', from the rituals it was supposed to accommodate. It resulted from the order's ongoing tactical manoeuvres in the urban environment in which it was embedding itself. The Franciscans fought for urban space from which to save the souls of citizens. Their activities were oriented outward, not inward, towards engaging with the public, the emergent bourgeoisie in particular. Rather than preaching to the choir they evangelized among the urban laity. As C.H. Lawrence notes in his *Medieval Monasticism*, '[t]he Mendicant Orders broke free from one of the most basic principles of traditional monasticism by abandoning the seclusion and enclosure of the cloister in order to engage in an active pastoral mission to the society of their time'.[32] Bruzelius writes that '[o]ne of the radical aspects of the mendicant movement was the externalisation of religion into the open spaces of cities as well as into the private spaces of homes'.[33] Not only did the Franciscans build large conventual structures in the towns and cities, but they projected their message out into the surrounding urban environment. Pulpits were placed on the exterior walls of their buildings so that they could preach to those in the street below.[34] They built piazzas from which to proselytize. They ventured out from their monasteries to visit the laity in their homes – 'usurping the traditional role of the secular clergy', as

Bruzelius notes – in a practice derided by their contemporary, Saint-Amour, as a *penetrans domus*.[35]

The extroverted and expansionary practices of the Franciscans were driven by their rule of poverty, meaning that they had to evangelize in order to receive donations to sustain themselves, as well as to expand their built presence in the city. In return for donations the laity were offered salvation, the assurance that their passage through purgatory in the afterlife would be hastened. What they left in their wills bought intercessionary prayer on their behalf, and space for their burial within the order's convents.[36] Bruzelius observes that the architecture of the Franciscans 'came to resemble ... "warehouses" or "hangars" for tombs and other kinds of interventions of the faithful: paintings, banners, coats of arms, and other paraphernalia'.[37] Death, as Le Goff argues, was 'monetarized'.[38] In burying the bourgeoisie within its convents, death was also, as Bruzelius argues, newly 'democratized'. The monastic architecture of the Franciscans, then, is not 'simply an extrusion of the ritual activities that take place within', but one shaped through financial exchange. The area it occupies registers the extent of their economy, it forms a direct index of the success of their entrepreneurial habits. Trading between donations and services, between life and the afterlife, the Franciscans become, Todeschini argues, socially esteemed for their abilities in calculating value and the management of exchange and wealth.[39] In turn, the Franciscans themselves positively evaluate the emergence of the market society, seeing trade as a kind of evangelical social glue:

> [The] dynamics of evangelical poverty, experienced again in the climate of economic ferment of the thirteenth century, led Franciscans to discover the logic of the market as a keystone of Christian relationships. From the center to the suburbs of the system of cities and territories concretely forming this market society, trading professionals appeared to friars as possible mediators of a life in common that was recognizable both as a common good and as belonging to the Christian world.[40]

Rather than offering a critique of power by leaving it, the Franciscans, and their architecture, are implicated in exactly the kind of economic and managerial operations that Aureli seeks autonomy from, and precisely at the historical locus of the emergence of these. This case, in particular, points to a broader issue for any theory premised on the belief that salvation lies in secession from the economic in order to realize a notion of the political transcendent to history. Positing life and architecture as essential, and essentially formal, categories, it then seeks to locate what will stand as exemplary of these across the history of architecture. The archipelago of exemplars is sustained by identifying those instances, ranging across the centuries, where architecture momentarily realizes its potential to provide protective enclaves in which the economic is held at bay, and where the sacralized individual is thus able to focus on its being, on a life lived in common among small and isolated communities – Schumacher's atavistic brotherhoods. The possibility of an absolute architecture appears as a transhistorical canon of ideal instances, a constellation in which each point illuminates precisely the same promise to be redeemed. There appears no need to be concerned with the ways in which these instances, and thus the forms of life and the forms of architecture with which they are concerned, might be mediated by a history of the economic, the managerial or the governmental. These historical, if not absolute, determinants, are unconsidered because it is supposed that they can be eluded through the redemption of an absolute architectural essence. These determinants are, ultimately, not matters of concern other than in their role in constituting the eternal antagonist of a project of autonomy. But this project of autonomy is itself inescapably mediated by economics, by managerialism, by governmentality. This is what is most troubling about Aureli's insistence that architects might be more genuinely political in focusing their attention on themselves as the source of their own production. It resonates all too well with the doxa of neoliberalism, with the imperative to make of one's own life an ongoing project, with the apparent dissolution of the political in the absolute economization of the self. As Nick Dyer-Witheford has written, 'the insistence that the world be understood only as a set of individual projects, is one of the most powerful and destructive weapons for the current economic system in a "class war" waged from above by capital'.[41]

And what is most prized within this class war is to earn, through working on oneself as an entrepreneurial project, the means to isolate oneself from the dangers and precarities circulating in an urban condition figured as hostile, as a threatening externality. The successfully managed self achieves the privilege of securing its integrity within the private courtyards and securitized common spaces of the gated community. Understood within a historical context it is unable to countenance – the neoliberal mobilization of the economic as the political – the formal project of autonomy comes to share the values of what it supposes itself to oppose.

Notes

1   In his insistence on this differentiation between 'the project' and design, Aureli invokes a long-standing concern within Italian architectural culture, especially as this developed in the 1950s and 1960s within the IUAV (Institute of Architecture of the University of Venice). In this context, the term 'project' (in Italian, *progetto*) is possessed of multiple and variously nuanced meanings. As Marco Biraghi notes, *progetto* 'can mean project, plan, and even architecture. It can also imply a projection or an intention', see Marco Biraghi, *Project of Crisis: Manfredo Tafuri and Contemporary Architecture* (Cambridge, MA, and London: MIT Press, 2013), xi.

2   Pier Vittorio Aureli, *The Possibility of an Absolute Architecture* (Cambridge, MA, and London: MIT Press, 2011), xiii.

3   Ibid., 165.

4   Patrik Schumacher, 'The Historical Pertinence of Parametricism and the Prospect of a Free Market Urban Order', in *The Politics of Parametricism: Digital Technologies in Architecture*, eds, Matthew Poole and Manuel Shvartzberg (London, New Delhi, New York, Sydney: Bloomsbury Academic,, 2015), 19–44.

5   Ibid., 21.

6   Richard Seaford, *Money and the Early Greek Mind: Homer, Philosophy, Tragedy* (Cambridge: Cambridge University Press, 2004), 247–8.

7   Alain Badiou, *Logics of Worlds: Being and Event, 2*, trans. Alberto Toscano (London and New York: Continuum, 2009), 2, 3.

8   As Peter Hallward writes of Badiou's account of subjectivity, '[o]rdinary individuals are constrained and justified by relations of hierarchy, obligation, and deference; their existence is literally bound to their social places. True subjects, by contrast, are first and foremost free of relation as such, and are justified by nothing other than the integrity of their own affirmations'. Peter Hallward, *Badiou: A Subject to Truth* (Minneapolis and London: University of Minnesota Press, 2003), xxxi.

9   Pier Vittorio Aureli, *Less is Enough: On Architecture and Asceticism* (Moscow: Strelka Press, 2013), 4.

10   Ibid., 4.

11   Ibid., 12.

12   Ibid., 4.

13   Ibid., 5.

14   Ibid., 7.

15   Ibid., 9–10.

16   Giorgio Agamben, *The Highest Poverty: Monastic Rules and Form-of-Life*, trans. Adam Kotsko (Stanford: Stanford University Press, 2013).

17   Aureli, *Less is Enough*, 8.

18   Aureli, *The Possibility of an Absolute Architecture*, ix–x.

19   Ibid., ix.

20   Ibid., ix.

21   Ibid., x. Emphasis in italics mine.

22   Aureli, *Less is Enough*, 4.

23   Other examples are also considered, however, such as the work of the Israeli artist Absalon, the architecture of Le Corbusier and Hannes Meyer's Co-op Zimmer project.

24   Ibid., 22.

25   Ibid., 7.

26   David Cunningham, 'Architecture, Capitalism and the "Autonomy" of the Political', in *Can Architecture Be an Emancipatory Project? Dialogues on Architecture and the Left*, ed., Nadir Z. Lahiji (London: Zero Books, 2016), 97.

27   Giacomo Todeschini, *Franciscan Wealth: From Voluntary Poverty to Market Society*, trans. Donatella Melucci, eds, Michael F. Cusato, Jean François Godet-Calogeras and Daria Mitchell (Saint Bonaventure, NY: The Franciscan Institute Saint Bonaventure University, 2009), 7–8.

28   Jacques Le Goff, *Money and the Middle Ages: An Essay in Historical Anthropology*, trans. Jean Birrell (Cambridge and Malden, MA: Polity Press, 2012), 76.

29   Caroline Bruzelius, *Preaching, Building, and Burying: Friars in the Medieval City* (New Haven and London: Yale University Press, 2014), 183.

30   Ibid., 183.

31   Caroline Bruzelius, 'The Architecture of the Mendicant Orders in the Middle Ages: An Overview of Recent Literature', in *Perspective 2* (2012), 369.

32   C. H. Lawrence, *Medieval Monasticism: Forms of Religious Life in Western Europe in the Middle Ages* (London and New York: Longman, 1984), 238.

33   Bruzelius, *Preaching, Building, and Burying*, 181.

34   Ibid., 181–182.

35   Bruzelius, 'The Architecture of the Mendicant Orders in the Middle Ages', 378.

36   Ibid., 380.

37   Bruzelius, *Preaching, Building, and Burying*, 151.

38   Le Goff, *Money and the Middle Ages*, 131.

39   Todeschini, *Franciscan Wealth*, 103, 110.

40   Ibid., 134.

41   Nick Dyer-Witheford, *Cyber-Proletariat: Global
     Labour in the Digital Vortex* (London: Pluto Press,
     2015), 8.

5 The Limits of Limits: Schmitt, Aureli and the Geopolitical Ontology of the Island

Models of fluidity, process, self-organization and complexity today enjoy near-hegemonic status in the fields of architectural, landscape and urban design. As against the putatively top-down practices of planning and the authorial mastery of Modernist design, we are led to believe that a progressive turn to more bottom-up, networked, ecologically sensitive and 'new-materialist' principles is under way. The advocates of this turn are, however, in thrall to the same models as are to be found in the history of neoliberal thought and as are frequently employed in the achievement of its political and economic agendas.[1]

The writings of the architect and teacher Pier Vittorio Aureli offer a clear and decisive critique of this development. Perhaps most appealingly, Aureli's account of the architectural archipelago offers a way for architects and architecture to counter the purely economic logic of neoliberal processes of urbanization (particularly where the urban comes to stand, as with Landscape Urbanism, for the purely processual) through the assumption of a political project. He counters the field conditions of urbanism with the self-sufficient autonomy and formal limits of architecture as island.

Aureli's politics of architectural form are, though, questionable in their claim to effectively contest the prevalence of models of the fluid, connective and self-organizing in design, as well as the broader neoliberal conditions in which they operate. The shortcomings of Aureli's archipelago model are rooted in its indebtedness to the thought of the jurist Carl Schmitt, with its agonistic polarizations of land–sea, political–economic, friend–enemy, limited–unlimited, and, especially, in its mythic and fascistic origins.

Landscape Urbanism: from object to field

That the urban has, in recent years, been transformed from a form composed of static architectural objects into a 'field' of processes, networks, mobility and infrastructural connectivity constitutes something like a founding principle for Landscape Urbanism. In his 1999 essay 'Field Conditions,' Stan Allen (a significant figure in the formulation and promotion of Landscape Urbanism) located the emergence of what he identifies as a generalized shift from 'object to field' amid the science, technology and culture of the post Second World War period.[2] Allen defined this 'field condition' as one of 'loosely bound aggregates characterized by porosity and local interconnectivity ... bottom-up phenomena, defined not by overarching geometrical schemas but by intricate local connections'. Employing these insights, Allen recommended, would at last place design 'in contact with the real'.[3]

Contemporary to Allen's essay, Alex Wall's 'Programming the Urban Surface' has been equally significant to the theoretical development of Landscape Urbanism.[4] Here, Wall writes that in contemporary urbanization, 'infrastructures and flows of material have become more significant than static political and spatial boundaries ... The emphasis shifts here from *forms* of urban space to *processes* of urbanization'. Consequently, he continues, we are now experiencing 'a fundamental paradigm shift from viewing cities in formal terms to looking at them in dynamic ways. Hence, familiar urban typologies of square, park, district and so on are of less use or significance than are the infrastructures, network flows, ambiguous spaces and other polymorphous conditions that constitute the contemporary metropolis.'[5]

The paradigms of fluidity, interconnectivity and process promoted by Allen and Wall are echoed in the conception of 'weak urbanism' formulated by Andrea Branzi. This putatively new condition of urbanism, argues Branzi in the essay 'A Strong Century', proceeds according to hermeneutics that is 'more ductile and therefore able to absorb the new and confront the surprises and complexities that this produces'.[6] The ductile and fluid qualities of Branzi's model of urbanism are further elaborated through his adoption of the sociologist Zygmunt Bauman's concept of a 'liquid modernity', of which he writes,

'For Bauman, the term "liquid" positively indicates the idea of a state of material that does not possess its own form (rather, that of its container) and tends to follow a temporal flow of transformations. These conditions converge to describe "the nature of the current, and in many respects, new phase of the history of modernism".'[7]

For Charles Waldheim, landscape is the medium through which urbanism achieves the kind of connective and fluidly interactive performance appropriate to contemporary realities. Landscape, as a 'performative medium', writes Waldheim in his recent *Landscape as Urbanism: A General Theory*, services the Post-Fordist city 'through a unique combination of ecological performance and design culture'.[8] 'Rather than offering an exception to the structure of the city,' he continues, landscape 'aligns with the return to the project of city-making associated with contemporary service, creative and culture economies.'[9] In this fashion, Waldheim argues, landscape succeeds as *the* discipline of urban design, replacing the now hopelessly retrograde one of architecture. The turn to landscape is one in which urbanism is 'unburdened of all that architectural baggage'.[10]

It would be difficult to conceive of anything more diametrically opposed to the position of Aureli than this, invested as it is in the politics of architectural form as the delimited, posed against the connective economies of a landscaped urbanism. Rather than pursuing the economic zeitgeist, or drawing upon ontologies of complexity, he has proposed to redeem what he regards as a foundational politics of architectural form through the geopolitical ontology of Carl Schmitt.[11]

Leviathan and Behemoth

In *The Nomos of the Earth* (1950) and *Land and Sea* (1954), Carl Schmitt argues that a new spatial order has emerged in the aftermath of the Second World War.[12] The great sea powers (England and the United States) have finally established their ascension over the land-based powers of the European continent. For Schmitt, as he posits in *Land and Sea*, 'world history' is a struggle between maritime and land or continental powers that he casts, in mythological terms, as the battle between Leviathan and Behemoth, between sea creature and land animal:

> Behemoth tries to tear Leviathan to pieces with its horns and teeth, while in turn, Leviathan tries hard to stop the land animal's mouth and nostrils with its flaps and fins in order to deprive it of food and air. This is a graphic illustration ... of the blockade to which a sea power subjects a land power by cutting its supplies in order to starve it to death.[13]

The defeat of Germany is made to stand in general for the defeat of the behemoth of Europe by the leviathans of England and America. Noting that in some sense, given the all-encompassing nature of the oceans, all land for Schmitt is effectively an island, this final victory of sea over land brings to a conclusion the 'spatial revolution' initiated when England 'turned her collective existence seawards and centred it on the sea element'.[14] Setting out on this course, transforming itself from 'a nation of sheep herders' into one of 'pirates' in the Elizabethan period, England went on to 'win the first round of the planetary, spatial revolution'.[15] This revolution brings about, for the first time in world history, a truly global order, with the British Empire at its centre. Earlier empires, says Schmitt in *The Nomos of the Earth,* were in some ways interconnected, but these 'lacked a global character': 'Each considered itself to be the *world,* the *cosmos,* the *house.*'[16] Prior to the spatial revolution of modernity there is, then, an effective archipelago of more or less isolated *worlds,* each surrounded by the uncharted and 'malevolent chaos' of the sea.[17] With the coming to hegemony of the new maritime powers, the plurality of *worlds* becomes the singular *world,* a truly global condition.

The ascension of the maritime powers brings to a close a centuries-long struggle between land and sea. Over this period, from the sixteenth to the nineteenth century, the lines of the first planetary order are clearly drawn. They run between the dry land of the European continent (itself clearly divided between sovereign national states) and the sea, ostensibly belonging to no one but ruled in reality by England: 'The dry-land order implies the subdivision into state territories. The high seas, in turn, are free: they know no state and are not subjected to any state or territorial sovereignty.'[18] The turn to the sea, then, marks a rupture in the existing *nomos* of the earth, its literal deterritorialization. The conquest of the sea opens up a new spatial condition in which the old practices of land-based sovereignty (the making of clearly bounded worlds) are undermined. The sovereign order of limits is challenged by new powers that operate through the medium of the unlimited.

In plotting out this dichotomy between the limited and the unlimited, played out between land and sea, Schmitt associates the judicial territory of the land with an established order and the unlimited space of the sea with the practice of commercial trade. He notes, in *Land and Sea,* the popularity among the English for maxims such as those of Sir Walter Raleigh: 'Whoever controls the seas controls the world trade; whoever controls world trade holds all the treasures of the world in his possession, and in fact, the whole world.' 'Slogans about freedom, such as "All world trade is free exchange",' he writes, 'express the zenith of England's maritime and global power.'[19] In constructing these polarities and in the identification of land and island as the 'properly' juridical and political space of man, as opposed to the sea as the chaotic, desacralized and unlimited realm of trade and commerce, Schmitt is rehearsing themes first established in the same ancient world into which he projects the origins of the struggles between land and sea powers.

Anaximander and the *Apeiron*

The profound significance of monetization for the world of ancient Greece, Richard Seaford has argued in his *Money and the Early Greek Mind: Homer, Philosophy, Tragedy* (2004), is registered in the cosmology of Anaximander (610–546 BCE).[20] Seaford suggests that Anaximander's conception of the *apeiron* (the 'unlimited', the primordial, infinite and unendingly productive source from which all things are constituted) is inseparable from the development of monetization in the ancient Greek world of the pre-Socratic philosopher, particularly that of the commercial city of Miletus in which he lived.[21] Just as money serves as a substrate of trade, the *apeiron* serves as the substrate from which all other things come into being. Seaford further pursues this analogy between 'money and *everything* that we know' in Anaximander's conception of the *apeiron*, noting, for instance, that the *apeiron* and money are each said to 'contain all things', to 'steer' and regulate all things, to be in constant movement and circulation, and to be 'undifferentiated, homogeneous'. 'The *apeiron*', writes Seaford, 'is abstract in the sense that (although it surrounds all things and is their source) it is imperceptible. So too money is both concrete and abstract, visible and invisible.' Given the extent of these analogies, Seaford is led to posit that the relationship between the *apeiron* and money is more than simply analogical: we are 'forced to accept [that] Anaximander's cosmos is in some respect a projection of social relations.' His hypothesis is that 'one factor in the genesis of the notion of the *apeiron*, and of philosophical cosmology in general, was money'.[22] Underlying all things is the *apeiron*, and underlying the conception of this is monetization, with its abstract, undifferentiated and impersonal relations, with its fecund and limitless circulation.

The unleashing of the unsettling effects of monetization are played out in what Seaford describes as a 'collision between the unlimit of money and the limit inherent in ritual'. The Athenian poet and legislator Solon (a contemporary of Anaximander), was the first, notes Seaford, 'to believe that there is a hidden *measure* (of intelligence) that holds the limits of all things, and to recommend the principle of moderation'. The notion of limit as figured by Solon in the character of Tellos is, argues Seaford, 'suggestive of *telos*, whose basic sense of *limit* or *completion* qualifies it to refer to ritual'.[23] Likewise in Aristotle's *Politics*, he notes, one can locate the same concern with a wealth that is measured in terms of its adequacy to the 'good life,' as opposed to the unlimited wealth pursued through the buying and selling of commodities.[24] Ritualized orders of limit and moderation, then, are set against the unlimited pursuit of wealth accumulated for its own sake in the collision to which Seaford refers. This struggle follows, logically enough, from the fact that forms of monetized exchange, as Seaford also shows, were developed out of, and historically succeeded, ritual forms of exchange. From ritualized practices of gift-giving, sacrifice and expiation – mediating between men and gods – monetization facilitated an abstract circulation of things and values, endlessly exchanged, as the impersonal relations mediating between men.

Bringing us more tangibly to the theme of the island and the archipelago, Seaford notes that in Aeschylus's *Agamemnon*, 'the sea, as homogeneous and unlimited, evokes the homogeneity and unlimit of money'.[25] As he also remarks, in respect of this figuration of the sea as the unlimited, 'The (potentially alarming and relatively novel) *man-made* inexhaustibility of money is envisaged as in terms of the natural inexhaustibility of the sea.'[26] To envisage this association between two expressions of the unlimited would not be difficult, of course, for people increasingly engaged in commercial trade routed through the waters of the Eastern Mediterranean. The impact of monetization in the world of ancient and classical Greece is registered, in its tragedy and philosophy, in terms of fundamental oppositions. These appear in Aristotle, as Seaford notes, in terms of a polarization 'between community and outsider ... out of which arise the corresponding polarities self-sufficiency–trade, goods–money, limit–unlimit, moral–immoral, natural–unnatural'.[27] Following Seaford's reading of Agamemnon, we can add to this series land–sea; a polarization between the self-sufficient and self-contained limit of the settled territory, as represented by the *island*, and the unsettling commercial space of the unlimited sea of commerce that surrounds and threatens its order.

The discreet charms of Carl Schmitt

The polarities through which Schmitt's geopolitical ontology are performed are then as much ancient as they are contemporary. His arguments, in fact, rehearse an archaic tragedy dressed up as the truth of global modernity. Following Schmitt, Aureli, in turn, is insistent that only clearly bounded, physically and juridically delimited spatial orders can properly sustain the properly political. In adopting Schmitt's geopolitical ontology in this fashion, Aureli revives a definition of the political originally confected to underwrite the appropriation of land and the juridical 'rights' of this appropriation. As the philosopher Bruno Bosteels writes of this ontologizing practice, 'Schmitt first of all presupposes an immediate connection between being and spatiality ... All being is oriented in accord with an immanent principle of justice and right: "Right is the rightfulness of being that is given at the origin." The earth itself, of course, is the primal site for this suturing of being, space, and law as right.'[28] It is this essentializing and archaic foundation of a juridical politics of land appropriation, and its defence, that Aureli takes up as appropriate to the question of contemporary processes of urbanization. The outside, the unlimited 'sea' of urbanism or landscape, is abjured as inescapably economic. 'One can argue,' writes Aureli in *The Possibility of an Absolute Architecture* (2011), 'that the notion of urbanization presupposes the fundamental substitution of politics with economics as a mode of city governance to the point that today it is reasonable – almost banal – to ask not what kind of political power is governing us, but whether we are governed by politics at all'.[29]

Aureli's allegiance to what he terms Schmitt's 'political realism' determines his own definition of the political and the strictness with which it is to be understood as separate and distinct from the economic.[30] Schmitt's account of the political, in turn, is heavily reliant on his infamous friend–enemy distinction, as propounded in *The Concept of the Political*, published in 1932. Here Schmitt proclaims that 'the specific political distinction to which political actions and motives can be reduced is that between friend and enemy'.[31]

For Schmitt the political just *is*, ontologically, the ineluctable struggle between friend and enemy. This struggle marks the perpetual agonism that must exist between sovereign nation states in order that the political exists as such. The necessary and defining expression of this agonism is war: 'A world in which the possibility of war is utterly eliminated,' writes Schmitt, 'a completely pacified globe, would be a world without the distinction of friend and enemy and hence a world without politics.'[32] As opposed to liberal notions of competition that might derive from matters of trade, the properly political is dependent on the possibility of armed conflict between sovereign spatial orders. 'The friend, enemy, and combat concepts receive their real meaning precisely because they refer to the real possibility of physical killing,' Schmitt makes plain in *The Concept of the Political*.[33] As is well known, Schmitt's theories of sovereignty and the political were instrumental to the juridical formulations of National Socialism, particularly during the period of his membership of the Nazi Party. As international relations scholar Benno Gerhard Teschke notes, Schmitt's theory of the political 'inscribed Hitler's "spatial revolution" into a full-scale reinterpretation of Europe's geopolitical history, grounded in land appropriations, which legitimized Nazi Germany's wars of conquest'.[34]

Aureli's reading of Schmitt attempts to abstract this agonistic formulation of what is essentially political from its historically specific political context. Indeed, there appears no reference to Schmitt's fascism, anti-Semitism, or membership of the Nazi party in Aureli's *The Possibility of an Absolute Architecture*. Schmitt is described here simply as a 'German jurist'.[35] For Aureli, it seems, the fascism of Schmitt's politics can be bracketed while its agonism, and its fixation on the appropriation of land, can be repurposed as a universal truth in order to pursue a properly political architectural project.[36]

This project is founded on the formalization of the friend–enemy distinction through an architecture assigned the task of inscribing limits and boundaries upon appropriated land. Aureli argues that the formal 'essentially involves an act of spatial determination, of (de)limitation'.[37] Architecture, as a practice of delimitation, generates the inside–outside binary through which the friend can be distinguished from the enemy. Unlike in Schmitt, however, the purpose of this friend–enemy polarization is not to sanction war but to allow us to know and identify ourselves, as such, through an encounter with what we are not: 'What counters us inevitably constitutes the knowledge of our own limit, our own form.'[38] 'The enemy,' argues Aureli in a quasi-Brechtian formulation, 'estranges us from our familiar self-perception, and gives us back the sharp contour of our own figure.'[39] Since form requires delimitation, architecture, as a formal practice of inscribing limits, achieves a political condition only when it is a 'composition of parts' rather than when it integrates us into the whole of the limitless 'sea'. In the 'composition of parts,' writes Aureli, 'the concept of the formal and the concept of the political coincide and can be posited against notions such as urban space, urban landscape, and network'.[40] Integration with the *apeiron* of urbanism would result in the dissolution of the political and the architectural alike, their disappearance within the sea of a purely economic logic.[41] This dissolution can only be resisted through what Aureli names as the 'metaform of the archipelago'.[42]

In *The Possibility of an Absolute Architecture,* Aureli affirms the architectural archipelago as an essentially political form through an account of its periodic historical appearances. This account ranges across the works of figures such as Andrea Palladio, Giovanni Battista Piranesi, Étienne-Louis Boullée, Ludwig Hilberseimer, Oswald Mathias Ungers and Rem Koolhaas. He praises Koolhaas and Elia Zenghelis's project (as OMA) Exodus, or the Voluntary Prisoners of Architecture, for instance, for its projection of 'an exacerbated version of communitarian citizenship based on self-imposed closure'.[43] In the work of Ungers, Aureli finds a fully developed 'theory of the city as an archipelago'.[44] Ungers, especially in the 1977 project for the shrinking city of Berlin, The City within the City, Berlin as Green Archipelago, produces what Aureli understands to be a politically radical project in its refusal of the megastructural form of architecture prevalent at this time. The megastructure is held to integrate architecture with processes of urbanization, dissolving the possibility of the truly political architecture of the limited enclosure; Ungers' project, in contrast, is 'composed of islands, each of which was conceived as a formally distinct micro-city'.[45]

Aureli also notes the significance of Ungers' earlier research, undertaken with his wife Liselotte, on the history of communitarian (typically Shaker or Anabaptist) settlements in America:

> Religious communities such as the Shakers were characterized by a principle of communal life in which there was no private property; all facilities were for collective use. This resulted in settlements whose form was organized for communal life, with an abundance of common spaces, and in clear contrast to cities, which are shaped by land ownership. Ungers observed that radical communality was possible only within limited settlements.[46]

It is this same possibility for a radically autonomous form of life in common that Aureli also locates in the case of 'Red Vienna' and the 'Hof' superblocks built there in the mid-1930s to accommodate the city's workers.

These superblocks collectively constitute a further historical instance of the archipelago. They are situated 'within the city as self-sufficient islands in pronounced contrast to their surroundings ... an archipelago of places for communitarian life'.[47]

The agonies of the archipelago

As a politics of architecture, Aureli's archipelago is posited against the economics of urbanism; the island against the sea, the limited against the *apeiron*. The decisiveness with which the political is opposed to the economic derives from the equally decisive function of architecture as – essentially and fundamentally – a practice of formal delimitation. This notion of what is essential and fundamental to architecture derives, in turn, from the Schmittian conception of the *nomos,* a word that comes, states Schmitt, from *nemein,* 'a [Greek] word that means both "to divide" and "to pasture". Thus, *nomos* is the immediate form in which the political and social order of a people becomes spatially visible'. Elaborating on the meaning of the *nomos* he continues that it can be 'described as a wall, because, like a wall, it, too, is based on sacred orientations'.[48] The decisive presence of the *nomos* as wall constitutes the foundational act of spatial ordering. It divides inside from outside, friend from enemy.

It is this decisiveness that no doubt endows what Aureli refers to as his 'project' with its appeal for those seeking to challenge the hegemony of the various ecoarchitectures and Parametricisms, all the relational, infrastructural and Landscape Urbanisms and their relentless reassertions of the fluid, flexible and self-organizing. The 'project' offers a clear and concise set of formulations that appear readily translatable into a politics of design thinking and practice. Less often reflected upon, however, are the implications of the politics of agonism on which the archipelago model is premised.

It is seldom noted, for instance, that the political agonism adopted by Aureli is essentially opposed to the possibility of any radical transformation of the social in its totality. The politics of agonism is, by definition, opposed to any form of universalism or internationalism on which any such transformation would depend. It cannot countenance the termination of the friend–enemy distinction, or any movement towards this possibility as a political goal, since its politics are premised on the maintenance of conflict. For Aureli this conflictual condition is essential to our identity, but this forecloses the possibility of identities that are formed not through the appropriation, settlement and delimitation of land, but on relations of solidarity despite of, and across, boundaries, borders and walls. As the philosopher Mark Neocleous writes, 'For Schmitt the vision of a world without the state, without the political friend–enemy distinction and without war is an absurd and impossible dream. It is also of course a communist, but not a fascist one.'[49] While for Aureli the promise of agonism is clearly reoriented to a different agenda from that of Schmitt, the impossibility of even moving towards the overcoming of conflict is, for him, unviable: the overcoming of conflict would annul the political dimension itself (as it is understood here). There can be no dialectical movement.[50] But if this is supposed, somehow, to forestall the universalizing managerialism of life, it serves equally to delegitimize any equally universalizing opposition to this neoliberal agenda.

In its essentializing tendencies, the formalism through which the identities between the political, the architectural and the communal are forged is equally problematic. There are no guarantees that small-scale, architecturally delimited settlements will produce or sustain forms of commonality with any even vaguely radical or progressive orientation. As the cultural historian Fred Turner, among others, has made plain, the communes of America's West Coast counterculture of the 1960s and 1970s, for instance, were largely organized and populated by affluent white men. The organization of these communes tended to exacerbate patriarchal prejudices, sustain class distinctions and produce friend–enemy distinctions of the most racist sort between the communalists and the marginalized indigenous groups they encountered.[51]

It might also be noted that gated communities and securitized apartment blocks, with facilities shared in common, are very much the preferred form of dwelling for the urban rich and super-rich wanting to insulate themselves from the chaos of their immediate surroundings. An archipelago of secured enclaves increasingly defines patterns of urban development. The occupants of these are, precisely, enabled through the decisiveness of walls and boundaries to establish their identities in contradistinction to those of the urban masses that surround them. Need we mention Donald Trump's border wall with Mexico? The formal identity between the archipelago and the political agonism of the friend–enemy distinction appears to work then, but to what end?

Aureli's project appears to challenge the essentially neoliberal turn of contemporary urbanization, as well as the models and practices with which architectural, landscape and urban design have tended to serve it of late. This challenge is, however, in its very definition of the political, absolutely compromised by its Schmittian origins – mythopoetical, archaic and formalist – at its core. In discounting the possibility that the unlimited condition of the urban might itself be a space simultaneously and complexly economic and political, this project effectively concedes the greater part of the territory to the putative enemy. It offers only the possibility of secession from the networks of globalized urbanization that are always already deemed nonpolitical. In doing so, Aureli's politics of form misses what is effectively political in the making fluid, connective and productive of the urban, especially under the contemporary imperatives of neoliberalism.

Marx and Engels, however, already understood the process of urbanization and its economic modes of production in explicitly political terms. This process is understood, dialectically, as the ground of any future universal struggle (antagonistic rather than agonistic) against capital, in their *Communist Manifesto*. Many figures within Western Marxism, perhaps most notably Henri Lefebvre, have since taken up and developed their analysis in attempting to understand the politics of urbanization in the late twentieth and early twenty-first centuries. From a different perspective, but equally concerned with the political, Foucault's concept of the 'biopolitical' understands the production of subjectivity, especially that occurring within neoliberalism, as a political operation achieved through economic means.[52] In addition to the politics of urbanization, there is also a politics of design that is effectively obscured by Aureli's position. By the logic of Schmitt's definition of the political, design that is not concerned with the decisive production of limits and boundaries is not political. The production and articulation of networks, the channelling of subjects according to preferred patterns of movement and association, in fact the very act of dismantling limits and boundaries is, though, a political practice. It is the politics of this practice – and its framing as progressive, natural and ecological, as in the case of Landscape Urbanism – that needs to be contested, rather than discounted *tout court* as a manifestation of the unlimited. The alternative is a politics of regression to an archaically conceived pre-economic condition of autonomy, a monastic politics of retreat that – while now perhaps desirable to some – is evidently attainable only by the most economically privileged.[53] A more ambitious politics would be ready to engage in the no doubt more fraught struggle to understand, and act upon, the spaces of the unlimited as a radically universalizing and collective project.

Notes

1   See Douglas Spencer, *The Architecture of Neoliberalism: How Contemporary Architecture Became an Instrument of Control and Compliance* (London: Bloomsbury, 2016).

2   Stan Allen, 'Field Conditions,' in *Points + Lines* (New York: Princeton Architectural Press, 1999).

3   Ibid., 92.

4   Alex Wall, 'Programming the Urban Surface', in *Recovering Landscape: Essays in Contemporary Landscape Architecture*, James Corner, ed. (New York: Princeton Architectural Press, 1999).

5   Ibid., 234.

6   Andrea Branzi, 'A Strong Century,' in *Weak and Diffuse Modernity: The World of Projects at the Beginning of the 21st Century*, trans. Alta Price (Milan: Skira, 2006), 14–15.

7   Ibid., 20.

8   Charles Waldheim, *Landscape as Urbanism: A General Theory* (Princeton: Princeton University Press, 2016), 5.

9   Ibid., 5.

10 Ibid., 6.

11 I take the term geopolitical ontology as a descriptor for the thought of Schmitt from Bruno Bosteels, 'The Obscure Subject: Sovereignty and Geopolitics in Carl Schmitt's *The Nomos of the Earth*', *South Atlantic Quarterly* 104, No. 2 (2005): 300.

12 Carl Schmitt, *The Nomos of the Earth in the International Law of the Jus Publicum Europaeum*, trans. G. L. Ulmen (1950; rpt. New York: Telos Press, 2006); and Carl Schmitt, *Land and Sea*, trans. Simona Draghici (1954; rpt. Washington, DC: Plutarch Press, 1997).

13 Schmitt, *Land and Sea*, 6.

14 Ibid., 28.

15 Ibid., 49.

16 Schmitt, *The Nomos of the Earth*, 51.

17 Ibid., 51.

18 Schmitt, *Land and Sea*, 46.

19 Ibid., 47.

20 Richard Seaford, *Money and the Early Greek Mind: Homer, Philosophy, Tragedy* (Cambridge: Cambridge University Press, 2004).

21 Miletus was unique, notes Seaford, in being at the centre of a 'commercial network stretching in all directions over much of the known world united ... by that common currency of precious metals (uncoined or coined) that increasingly provided a measure of value and means of exchange, a substrate of all commercial activity'. Ibid., 208.

22 Ibid., 205–8.

23 Ibid., 166.

24 Ibid., 169.

25 Ibid., 169.

26 Ibid., 166.

27 Ibid., 168.

28 Bosteels, 'The Obscure Subject', 300.

29 Pier Vittorio Aureli, *The Possibility of an Absolute Architecture* (Cambridge, MA: MIT Press, 2011), 11, 13.

30 Ibid., 235.

31 Carl Schmitt, *The Concept of the Political*, trans. G. D. Schwab (1932; rpt. Chicago: University of Chicago Press, 1996), 26.

32 Ibid., 35.

33 Ibid., 33.

34 Benno Gerhard Teschke, 'Fatal Attraction: A Critique of Carl Schmitt's International Political and Legal Theory,' *International Theory* 3, No. 2 (2011): 179.

35 Aureli, *Possibility of an Absolute Architecture*, 235.

36 Aureli is, of course, by no means unique in assuming the broad proposition that the politics of Schmitt (despite and not because of his fascism) might offer useful lessons for the political left. For a discussion and critique of this, see Mark Neocleous, 'Friend or Enemy? Reading Schmitt Politically', *Radical Philosophy* 79 (September/October, 1996), 13–23.

37 Aureli, *Possibility of an Absolute Architecture*, 31.

38 Ibid., 29.

39 Ibid., 29.

40 Ibid., 31.

41 Ibid., x.

42 Ibid., xii.

43 Ibid., 196–7

44 Ibid., 178.

45 Ibid. 178.

46 Ibid., 199.

47 Ibid., 201.

48 Schmitt, *The Nomos of the Earth*, 70.

49 Neocleous, 'Friend or Enemy?', 23.

50 Aureli makes clear his rejection of the Hegelian dialectic, at least as is commonly (mis)understood, arguing that 'the political realizes the solution of

conflict not by a synthesis of the confronting parts, but by recognizing the opposition as a composition of parts'. *Possibility of an Absolute Architecture*, 29.

51   Fred Turner, *From Counterculture to Cyberculture: Stewart Brand, the Whole Earth Network, and the Rise of Digital Utopianism* (Chicago: University of Chicago Press, 2006).

52   See Michel Foucault, *The Birth of Biopolitics: Lectures at the Collège de France* 1978– 1979, Michel Senellart, ed., trans. Graham Burchell (Basingstoke, UK: Palgrave Macmillan, 2008).

53   This retreat to the monastic, affirmed as an autonomous form of life that might be recovered as an alternative to the current conditions of urbanization, is presented in Pier Vittorio Aureli's *Less is Enough: On Architecture and Asceticism* (Moscow: Strelka Press, 2013). For a critique of this proposition see, in this collection, the essay 'Less than Enough: A Critique of the Project of Autonomy'.

6 Out of the Loop: Architecture, Automation and Cognitive Disinvestment

Automation, argues Franco 'Bifo' Berardi, is turning us into automata, robot-icized beings made over in the image of our own technologies, now turned against us. '[T]echnology', he writes in the essay 'E-Learning: The Emergence of the Precarious Automaton' for *Volume #45: Learning*, 'is changing the perspective and the format of cognitive activity.'[1] Knowledge, now trans-individual and externalized in the networked 'hyper-cortex' of the internet, effects a 'neurological mutation' that overwrites the singularity of the subject: 'singularity, the mark of conscious experience, is the victim of the hyper-cortex's process of formation in which the individual mind gets more and more automated and inter-connected, more and more uniformatted. When history is replaced by the implementation of a technological model, formatted by the networked machine, then singularity fades, and consciousness is replaced by cognitive formatting of the interaction with the hyper-cortex'.[2] The shift to electronic learning in education, for example, he contends, produces a 'cognitive formatting' of the brain so that it becomes the ready and responsive instrument of neoliberalism's entrepreneurial imperatives. Computational technology robs the human of its own originary autonomy.[3]

Berardi's argument here develops from a position well established within Italian workerism, and later elaborated within its post-autonomist variants according to which, broadly speaking, capitalism is seen to appropriate the innate properties of the worker for its own ends, as opposed to shaping and producing these properties in the first instance. In industrial capitalism muscle power is exploited as manual labour. Post-industrial capitalism subsequently goes further, deeper, into the core of the human to mine its very essence. Capitalism isn't content with our bodies, now it demands our minds, even our souls. As Berardi writes in *The Soul at Work*, '[i]ndustrial exploitation deals with bodies, muscles and arms ... The rise of post-Fordist modes of production … takes the mind, language and creativity as its primary tools for the production of value'.[4] '[E]very fragment of mental activity', he continues, 'must be transformed into capital'.[5] Capitalism captures and exploits what is properly the property of the human worker – 'our' sociability, language, ideas, emotions and desires.

The genealogy of such arguments can, of course, be traced back to the point where Marx, in *Capital: Volume One*, invokes the figure of the vampire to convey how the capitalist imperative to create surplus-value demands it drain and absorb the vital forces of the worker: 'Capital, is dead labour, that, vampire-like, only lives by sucking living labour, and lives the more, the more labour it sucks'.[6] Just as the vampire, after draining the lifeblood from its victims, transforms them into its own inhuman form, so automation appropriates our essence while transforming us, in the process, into its servile automata. Berardi's argument, and the particular Marxian tradition to which it is indebted, however, overlooks what is now especially pertinent, though not entirely novel, about contemporary processes of automation; that rather than causing a mutation in the cognitive capacities of the subject – 'brain-formatting' – capitalism seems disinclined to invest very much at all in these capacities.

Capitalist processes of automation are no longer especially invested in appropriating the muscular or intellectual power of workers because the forms in which these forces are required in its current production processes, especially those of its large-scale enterprises – repetitive and precise performance of sorting and assembly, logistical operations, information management, networked communication etc. – are more cheaply, efficiently and reliably performed by machines. In manufacturing, for example, Adidas opened their first 'sewbot' factory in Germany, 'The Speedway', in 2017, in which the production line was entirely roboticized so as to economically and logistically manage the rapid production of mass-customized trainers.[7] In the service industry, enthusiasts of the 'cognitive automation' of corporate tax and auditing administration promise that relieving humans of this work will bring businesses 'lower costs, smoother workflows, and the ability to scale services rapidly for little or no additional money'.[8]

The production, circulation and instrumentalization of knowledge, in particular, and of the type requisite to the functioning of neoliberal systems of accumulation, increasingly excludes the human subject from its operations. Computational algorithms, for instance – as employed in the much-cited example of high-frequency financial trading – supersede the capacities of the human in the tasks of calculating, circulating and processing the vast quantities of information for which the term 'big data' has come to stand. The issue, then, is not so much that knowledge and the mind are subject to some computational re-formatting or neurological mutation, but that there are few opportunities for the human subject to exercise its reasoning faculties within, let alone against, the planning, organization and orientation of an increasingly automated totality.

The most immediate and obvious concern raised by the disinvestment in the subject, as effected through automation, is that of massively elevated levels of unemployment, with all that this implies socially, economically and politically. But the increasingly ephemeral appearance of the subject, its alienation from the operations of the world it inhabits, is perhaps equally alarming since it contradicts certain deep-seated assumptions regarding human-technological relations. Whatever the twentieth century's periodic anxieties around encroaching forms of technocratic rule, these could at least be balanced by more benign conceptions of technology. 'Man has, as it were, become a kind of prosthetic God', as Sigmund Freud wrote in *Civilization and its Discontents.*[9] Though the civilizing tools now constituting his 'auxiliary organs' might give some cause for discontent they also make man 'magnificent':

> With every tool man is perfecting his own organs, whether motor or sensory, or is removing the limits to their functioning. Motor power places gigantic forces at his disposal, which, like his muscles, he can employ in any direction; thanks to ships and aircraft neither water nor air can hinder his movements; by means of spectacles he corrects defects in the lens of his own eye; by means of the telescope he sees into the far distance; and by means of the microscope he overcomes the limits of visibility set by the structure of his retina.[10]

Marshall McLuhan likewise conceived of the relationship between the human and the technological according to this model of 'extension'. He writes, in his *Report on Project in Understanding New Media* of 1960, that 'any medium whatever is an extension, a projection in space or in time, of our various senses'.[11] McLuhan's seminal *Understanding Media*, of 1964, is subtitled 'The Extensions of Man'.[12]

But the loss of this prosthetic function under contemporary processes of automation, as technology progressively acquires greater degrees of autonomy from the subject, is not all that is at stake here. Not only might technology correct the shortcomings of our existing motor and sensory organs, or facilitate their greater reach, it might also, under certain circumstances, stimulate and enable our faculties of reasoning, and in ways that radically confront existing conceptions of ourselves and our social relations. Copernican and Galilean theories of heliocentrism, to whose formulation astronomical instruments and the development of optical technologies were critical, were central to the establishment of rational and scientific perspectives through which the radical Enlightenment disputed the purportedly irrefutable and eternal truths of the Church.[13] In the 1920s the Soviet filmmaker Dziga Vertov, in his theory of the kino-eye, conceived of the technology of the cinematic apparatus not so much as a means of extending the scope of human vision, but of reorganizing and orchestrating it to revolutionary ends. Where bourgeois traditions and capitalist interests deployed the new technology to turn older narrative and theatrical forms into mass amusements, his montage cinema of facts would be deployed to remake man and his world against its existing order. The path of the kino-eye, the mobilization of its technological optics, declaims Vertov, 'leads to the creation of a fresh perception of the world'.[14]

What is at risk in automation, then, whatever Berardi's arguments against the perils of technological interconnectivity, or its mediation of interpersonal relations, is our disconnection from it, our being taken out of the loop so that any technologically facilitated potential for the exercise of cognitive reasoning, and of deploying this to radical ends, escapes us. We suffer a kind of cognitive disinvestment. Forms of machinic intelligence withdraw the perception and use of information from human experience, rendering it impervious to the dialectic of use and critical reflection. Harvested from personalized mobile technologies, surveillance cameras, web-browsing histories, social media, RFID tracking devices, biometric scanning, banking and shopping activity, big data is the surplus value invisibly produced by and unknowingly extracted from the subject so as to be mobilized by corporate, financial, military and governmental interests. If, as Claudia Aradau argues, big data 'is the new whole', then the role now delegated to the subject within this automated and informatic totality is a largely passive one.[15] We are to be unconsciously and unreflectively productive of the information from which the patterns that will determine our futures will be divined.

This 'new whole' is built, then, on a schism between cognition and sensation, and their operative redistribution within this totality. On one side of the divide stands a machinic perception, its automated cognition sifting through vast quantities of information to glean knowledge of the patterns through which neoliberal capital is able to valorize and secure its operations. On the other, human perception, increasingly directed towards a purely sensory, affective experience of its world. The tendency towards the containment of human perception within conditions of sensuous experience, and its affirmative valorization, are perhaps most readily apparent in the architectural design of the built environment, and most clearly registered in the programmatic positions emanating from architecture's academic culture.

Naive and overly literal materialisms recently adopted in architecture direct our attentions to the authenticity, immediacy and sincerity of matter, or affect a humility before it. Now, pronounces architectural Deleuzian Jeffrey Kipnis, is the 'time of matter', in a tirade against all conceptual thought, in fact against thought itself.[16] Now has always been the 'time of matter', he continues, since at the birth of the universe '[t]here were no signs, no ideas, no concepts, no meanings, no disembodied spirits, no dematerialized abstractions whatsoever around during the first couple of seconds after the Big Bang, nor during the first million or billion years, or, for that matter, even these days'.[17] 'Nothing escapes materiality', writes Kipnis, a fact that guarantees our liberty since '[m]atter is freedom itself'.[18] In the quasi-ontology of Lars Spuybroek, for whom 'meaning' is a 'horrible word', the human subject is refused any special privileges.[19] Humans, he writes, 'are nothing but things among other things'.[20] Ideas, agency and intelligence exist, but these are equalized among things, evenly distributed, rather than centred in any subject exterior to them. 'Matter', he writes, 'can think perfectly well for itself.'[21]

Such assaults on the cognitive and reasoning capacities of the subject appear too in the affirmations of affect now espoused as the proper concern of a post-critical architecture by Alejandro Zaera-Polo, Farshid Moussavi and Sylvia Lavin, among others.[22] This 'affective turn' owes much to the thought of Deleuze, in particular to his *Francis Bacon: The Logic of Sensation,* in which he affirms the immediacy of sensation. Sensation 'acts immediately', he claims, upon the nervous system, bypassing the 'intermediary of the brain'.[23] Sylvia Lavin's *Kissing Architecture* typifies the affective turn's denigration of the linguistic and interpretive mediation of experience: 'No one can speak when kissing ... kissing interrupts how faces and facades communicate, substituting affect and force for representation and meaning.'[24] Dispensing with the cold and cognitive logics of Modernism, and following the lead of Deleuze towards feeling and sensation, architecture should make its newly pliant surfaces 'kissable'. This practice is already exemplified, for Lavin, in architectural projects by FOA, UNStudio, Preston Scott Cohen and Diller Scofidio + Renfro.

These, and other similarly fluid, elegantly warped and parametric architectures – a shopping mall by Thomas Heatherwick, a port terminal by Reiser + Umemoto – enjoin the eye's confluence with the forms and patterns articulated by their exposed walkways and lighting strips, by the panels and grilles ribboned around their surfaces. Successive layers of torqued forms and meshes obscure any vanishing point, inviting a continuously mobilized appreciation of form, surface and materiality. The eye is not invited to apprehend, calculate or interpret anything from its experience of such environments. In constant motion it is afforded no point of rest, no space from which to gain perspective or to pause and reflect. As Peter Hallward has written 'to think means to break with sensible immediacy'.[25] In these experiences of architecture the subject is offered, and rewarded, instead, with the simple pleasures of immediate affect, a revelling in the newly sensuous freedoms offered up to it. Architecture assists us in the 'bypassing of the intermediary of the brain'. This is taken up as its work by some, now, in acculturating the subject to the position delegated to it by the schism between cognition and sensation through which an autonomously machinic intelligence can proceed, unperturbed by the intrusions of critical reasoning.

Notes

1   Franco 'Bifo' Berardi, 'E-Learning: The Emergence of the Precarious Automaton', *Volume #45: Learning*, 2015, 136–42.

2   Ibid., 138.

3   Ibid., 138.

4   Franco 'Bifo' Berardi, *The Soul at Work: From Alienation to Autonomy*, trans. Francesca Cadel and Giuseppina Mecchia (Los Angeles, CA: Semiotext(e), 2009), 21.

5   Ibid., 24.

6   Karl Marx, *Capital, Volume I*, trans. Ben Fowkes (London: Penguin, 1976), 342.

7   Tansy Hoskins, 'Robot Factories could Threaten Jobs of Millions of Garment Workers', *The Guardian*, 16 July 2016, <https://www.theguardian.com/sustainable-business/2016/jul/16/robot-factories-threaten-jobs-millions-garment-workers-southeast-asia-women>.

8   Shamus Rae, 'Thinking Exponentially', KPMG, <https://home.kpmg/uk/en/home/insights/2016/06/thinking-exponentially.html>.

9   Sigmund Freud, *Civilization and its Discontents*, trans. Joan Riviere (New York: Dover Publications, 1994), 43.

10 Ibid., 41.

11 Marshall McLuhan, 'Report on Project in Understanding New Media: A Report to the United States Office of Education. National Association of Educational Broadcasters', 1960, <https://mcluhangalaxy.wordpress.com/2014/11/19/report-on-project-in-understanding-new-media-1960-available-online/>.

12 Marshall McLuhan, *Understanding Media: The Extensions of Man* (London: Routledge & Kegan Paul, 1964).

13 For an insightful analysis of the place of heliocentrism within the Enlightenment see Jonathan I. Israel, *Radical Enlightenment: Philosophy and the Making of Modernity 1650–1750* (Oxford: Oxford University Press, 2001), 26–8.

14 Dziga Vertov, 'Kinoks: A Revolution', in *Kino-eye: The Writings of Dziga Vertov*, trans. Kevin O'Brien (Berkeley, LA: University of California Press, 1984), 18.

15 Claudia Aradau, 'The Signature of Security: Big Data, Anticipation, Surveillance', *Radical Philosophy*, Vol. 191, May/June 2015, 25.

16 Jeffrey Kipnis, 'On the Wild Side', in Farshid Moussavi, Alejandro Zaera-Polo and Sanford Kwinter, eds, *Phylogenesis: FOA's Ark* (Barcelona: Actar, 2004), 578.

17 Ibid., 571.

18 Ibid., 573.

19 Lars Spuybroek, *The Sympathy of Things: Ruskin and the Ecology of Design* (Rotterdam: V2_Publishing, 2011), 174.

20 Ibid., 74.

21 Ibid., 96.

22 See, Alejandro Zaera-Polo, 'The Politics of the Envelope', *Volume* #17 (Fall 2008); Farshid Moussavi, *The Function of Form* (Barcelona and New York: Actar/Harvard University Graduate School of Design, 2009); Sylvia Lavin, *Kissing Architecture* (Princeton and Oxford: Princeton University Press, 2011).

23 Gilles Deleuze, *Francis Bacon: The Logic of Sensation*, trans. Daniel W. Smith (London and New York: Continuum, 2003), 36.

24 Lavin, *Kissing Architecture*, 14.

25 Peter Hallward, *Badiou: A Subject to Truth* (Minneapolis and London: University of Minnesota Press, 2003), 6.

7 Architecture after California

Karl Marx famously observed that revolutionaries, seemingly engaged in 'creating something that did not exist before', will 'anxiously conjure up the spirits of the past to their service, borrowing from them names, battle slogans, and costumes in order to present this new scene in world history in time-honored disguise and borrowed language'.[1] Written in the aftermath of France's failed revolution of 1848, Marx notes in *The Eighteenth Brumaire of Louis Bonaparte* that 'the tradition of all dead generations weighs like a nightmare on the brains of the living'.[2] Those seeking to create 'something that did not exist before' are now more likely the protagonists than the enemies of capital, but they too tend to outfit themselves, if more knowingly than anxiously, in the costumes and language of the past.

The Californian counterculture of the 1960s and 1970s, the enterprises, technologies and mentalities it spawned, are a case in point. The subject of an exhibition at the Design Museum in London in 2017, *California: Designing Freedom,* the counterculture sought out new ways of life while invoking those drawn from history. Those organizing its ex-urban communes and forging its new technologies drew consciously on the mythology of the Wild West, fashioning themselves as pioneers, settlers, boom-time prospectors and frontiersmen. The book of the exhibition replays this mythos, drawing a direct line of inheritance from the *Sears, Roebuck Catalog* to Stewart Brand's *Whole Earth Catalog,* each equipping the pioneer with supplies for new forms of enterprise.[3]

Architects and designers inspired by and associated with the counterculture were equally ready to claim kinship with the frontier spirit. Architectural practice Ant Farm, whose work featured in Brand's *Whole Earth Catalog,* produced a 'Cowboy Nomad Manifesto' declaring 'There are cowboy nomads today, living another lifestyle, and waiting for the electronic media … to blow the minds of the middle-class American suburbanite. While they wait the cowboy nomads (outlaws) smoke loco weed around electric campfires.'[4] Reyner

Banham, settled in Los Angeles and sharing in the counterculture's enthusiasms for Buckminster Fuller and life lived on the road, staged his own performance of the technologically equipped 'cowboy nomad'. Full-bearded and costumed in Stetson, bolo tie and aviator sunglasses, Banham had himself photographed as he rode his Bickerton bicycle across a Californian salt flat. Reflecting on the experience, he adopted the kind of transcendental tones favoured within the counterculture, invoking the rapturous experience of 'sheer' space, sensory 'intoxication' and a revelatory feeling of 'freedom'.[5]

While in retrospect such play acting might be easily enough derided, the dispositions animating it are a more serious matter. Rather than amusingly outmoded, the beliefs and values of this period, if not the precise costumes and language, substantially shape and inform the present. As the curators of *California: Designing Freedom* note 'Californian products have affected our lives to such an extent that in some ways we are all now Californians'.[6] For McGuirk the freedoms offered to us in the 'Californian Mode', the 'tools of personal liberation', are distinctly double-edged. The devices served up by Silicon Valley – Google Maps, iPhones, self-driving cars – create a world 'in which the individual can express himself or herself to a hyper-connected world', yet these same tools 'also turn you into information'.[7] 'One cannot', writes McGuirk 'celebrate the influence of California on design without acknowledging what, especially from a European perspective, is its dark side.'[8] This 'dark side' consists, for McGuirk, in the capacity for tools of individual liberation to serve simultaneously as tools of domination, as instruments of 'mass-surveillance' and private monopoly.[9] But it is also the very notion of the 'individual', as such – one conceived in terms of natural freedoms and concerned with the elimination of any and all threats to these – that deserves critical reflection, particularly as it bears upon notions of freedom in design and architecture, and the part now played by these within neoliberalism.

The counterculture of California historically coincides and is effectively aligned with the rise of neoliberalism in its conceptions of freedom and the individual. For neoliberalism's most significant theorist and advocate, Friedrich Hayek, liberty is defined as the freedom of the individual to pursue their economic interests unimpeded by any endeavour to consciously plan or direct the social order. In this essentially entrepreneurial account of freedom, the liberty of the individual is necessarily threatened by any programme aimed at directing the economic system, including those geared towards the eradication or easing of social inequality. All planning, writes Hayek, 'leads to dictatorship'.[10] Neoliberalism, instead, aims to have the economic market and its 'natural laws' direct society so as to ensure the liberty of the individual as a fundamentally economic being, a *homo economicus*. Any common or collective pursuit of liberty, alongside the practices of critical reasoning that might inform this, are proscribed in advance since, Hayek claims, human beings are always dangerously deluded in presuming to change the world for the better. It is a 'fact', he writes, that there is a 'necessary and irremediable ignorance on everyone's part of most of the particular facts which determine the actions of all the several members of human society'.[11] The freedom of the individual, then, is only assured when everyone sticks to their own business, when there is no presumption on anyone's part to seek any larger perspective, or to collectively pursue liberty on the basis of this.

This definition of freedom is not newly invented in neoliberalism. The freedom of the entrepreneurial individual is essentially that of the free labourer described by Marx in *Capital;* the proletarianized subject of capitalism free in the 'double sense' of being free to sell their labour as a commodity on the market, and free of any determination over its social use.[12] These are also the senses of freedom with which Hegel wrestled in his *Philosophy of Right;* freedom as the merely abstract capacity to make choices, as against the freedom to realize the very conditions in which such choices are made. As Jason Read argues, Hegel sought to redefine freedom 'not as the abstract capacity to will this or that, to make a choice or to own property, but as the capacity to posit its presuppositions, to choose its conditions, including structures and norms'.[13]

Neoliberalism revives this conception of liberty in its 'double sense'. Freedom is to be expressed through choices made within the economic market, but without choice or determination over the norms structuring this condition. Neoliberalism is not, however, simply a return to older market-based notions of freedom but a concerted intellectual mobilization against all forms of planning, welfare, reform and socialism, particularly as these gained ground in the aftermath of the Second World War. Neoliberalism presents its project as premised on the need for liberation from these, and claims that this can only be achieved on condition of the absolute depoliticization of its subjects. Rather than as a species of political animal, an Aristotelian *zoon politikon,* neoliberalism conceives of the individual subject as the bearer of its own 'human capital'.[14] As essentially economic actors, we are free to take our labour to market and at liberty to invest in and realize our very being within it. This investment of the self as capital takes place now in conditions where divisions between labour and its reproduction, between production and consumption, are progressively dissolved.

The 'tools of personal liberation' gifted to us from Silicon Valley not only equip us for this world but enable and reproduce it. The hyper-connected, informationally dense world of neoliberal capitalism demands constant availability, innovation, interaction. We are obligated to intensively fashion, display, communicate about and market ourselves. While the apps, maps and devices of Apple, Google, Facebook, Hewlett Packard afford us the liberty to continuously, and competitively, represent and reinvent ourselves, any freedom to individually or collectively reimagine or remake this world's structures and norms is placed permanently beyond our grasp. The very function of these norms and structures, argues Jonathan Crary, is to place us in a position permanently lagging behind the technological advances that determine the temporality of late capitalism. Exhausted by the struggle to keep pace with the relentless rate of technological innovation, barraged with endless requirements to update and upgrade, we are unable even to find the time to critically reflect upon these conditions, let alone to act upon them.[15] As Crary observes in *24/7: Late Capitalism and the Ends of Sleep:*

> There will never be a 'catching up' on either a social or individual basis in relation to continually changing technological requirements. For the vast majority of people, our perceptual and cognitive relationship to communication and information technology will continue to be estranged and disempowered because of the velocity at which new products emerge and at which arbitrary reconfigurations of entire systems take place.[16]

Neoliberalism delegitimates participation in the political on the ethical grounds that all planning leads to dictatorship, and on the ontological ones of the 'necessary ignorance' of human beings. California's 'tools of personal liberation' further the depoliticizing ends of neoliberalism, both in the conditions of temporality they impose, and in their tendency to atomize the social into an aggregate of hyper-connected individuals constituted, as such, by their investments in capital and its technological apparatus. Depoliticization, rather than some unfortunate and unforeseen outcome of an originally radical counterculture, is inherent to it.[17] Though McGuirk might lament that the original 'spirit of the counterculture' was *latterly* 'recast as a techno-utopian entrepreneurialism', Stewart Brand, the author of this movement's bible, the *Whole Earth Catalog,* was always clear enough in his disavowal of the political.[18] As Felicity D. Scott observes, in her *Outlaw Territories: Environments of Insecurity/Architectures of Counterinsurgency,* Brand notably refused to protest against the US bombing of Vietnam and campaigned on a platform of 'environment yes, politics no'.[19] The *Whole Earth Catalog* also provided the counterculture with the slogan perhaps best capturing its antithetical relationship to any politics of collective solidarity when, as McGuirk notes, *Catalog* editor Fred Richardson declaimed 'Workers of the world, disperse', reversing Marx and Engels' 'Workers of the world, unite!'[20]

In this respect at least, the counterculture was justified in conjuring up the spirit of the prospectors and pioneers of the Wild West. For Marx the Californian Gold Rush, commencing in the very same year of 1848 as that of France's failed revolution, was symbolic of the victory of capital in its capacity to disperse proletarian solidarities through promises of individual reward. In *The Eighteenth Brumaire of Louis Bonaparte,* discussing the rigged lottery designed, in the wake of 1848, to entice French workers to leave their political struggles and depart for California so as to make their fortunes, he writes 'golden dreams were to supplant the socialist dreams of the Paris proletariat, the seductive prospect of the first prize the doctrinaire right to work. Naturally the Paris workers did not recognize in the glitter of the California gold bars the inconspicuous francs that were enticed out of their pockets'.[21] Calls to disperse – nineteenth-century, twentieth-century or twenty-first – are calls to abandon the political sweetened with the promise of individual fulfilment.

The disavowal of the political in neoliberalism also features in the design and architecture of the counterculture. Design comes in some sense here to displace the political just as, in a parallel and complementary turn, 'environments' come to displace the social as the object of architecture. Technologically facilitated and cybernetically modelled, design and architecture are reconceptualized as essentially innovative practices of managerialism. As Scott notes, Buckminster Fuller 'quite literally argued that communications technology and management techniques could replace political discourse'.[22] Much as technologies and techniques of management might replace the political, these might also, as Reyner Banham proposed, serve to displace older conceptions of 'civilized' architecture in the cause of individual freedom. The bounded and contained architecture of the city, an architecture of 'walls, floors and ceilings', could, through projects such as his 'standard of living package' or 'unhouse', now be abandoned by nomadic and territorially dispersed individuals, each managing their personalized environment so as to enjoy 'free' space.[23] Some sense of how design was to acquire a broader meaning and scope, displacing older conceptions of the political in the process, is also brought to light by Scott. The declaration of Habitat: The United Nations Conference on Human Settlements held in Vancouver in 1976, she notes, proposed in its official declaration 'a revolution not by violence but by design'.[24] Such reconfigurations of revolution and design, and of the relationship between the two, are of course also at the core of Robert Venturi and Denise Scott Brown's *Learning from Las Vegas*, whose opening lines read 'Learning from the existing landscape is a way of being revolutionary for an architect. Not the obvious way, which is to tear down Paris and begin again, as Le Corbusier suggested in the 1920s, but another, more tolerant way; that is, to question how we look at things.'[25] Where the Modernist architect would question the existing state of things with a view to changing them, the contemporary architect would question only their own perception of this state of things – here the 'vernacular' of commerce – with a view to learning from them. The forms through which the commodified landscape of capital are expressed are presented as pedagogical for the advance of an architecture that can still, somehow, regard itself as revolutionary.

Such reconfigured conceptions of architecture and design, premised on the disavowal of the political, the affirmation of individual freedoms, and the utilization of technologies and techniques drawn from within capitalist development, originate in significant part from California and the beliefs and mentalities cultivated within its counterculture. Their legacy is readily discernible in much contemporary design and architecture. 'Design', specifically 'design thinking', has come to be conceived as a kind of universal panacea for all the ailments of the social, a discipline now operating in an 'expanded field' encompassing 'service design, system design and strategy', and operating across 'education, health, government, technology, the social sector and business', to quote from the website of 'global design company' IDEO.[26] This company, with roots going back to working with Apple in designing their first mass-manufactured mouse, typifies the ways in which design now trades in post-political practices of consultation, innovation and creative solutions, and whose reach now extends to the design of government itself.[27]

Where the avant-garde of the early to mid-twentieth century premised its practice on the inseparability of the formal and the social, of the aesthetic and the political, the contemporary architect can content themselves with being recognized for the achievement of purely formal innovation, this now valued as the expression of individual freedom and deemed sufficiently radical as such. Through Frank Gehry's use of the CATIA CAD software system, writes McGuirk, the architect was able to 'express himself more freely'.[28] In the process, he goes on to argue, Gehry 'arguably did more than any living architect to liberate architecture from the right angle'.[29] Social 'content' set aside, architecture is read as a formal condition now serving as the object and focus of the architect's creative capacities. Every break with disciplinary or formal convention, regardless of the larger interests it may or may not serve, is always an act of liberation. Likewise, the jargon of 'blurring boundaries' and 'traversing borders' in architecture – owing its origins in part to figures such as Banham, and further elaborated in the spatial 'smoothing' and 'folding' of architectural Deleuzism – confers on its agents the status of the radically transgressive without obligation to reflect on the social or political implications of their practice.[30]

The figure of the 'hacker' constitutes a further legacy of the Californian counterculture. 'The myth of the lone hacker', writes Crary, 'perpetuates the fantasy that the asymmetrical relation of individual to network can be creatively played to the former's advantage.'[31] Whatever its origins in the field of computer coding, 'hacking' has now become a kind of second order myth of subversion, where the smart operator learns the rules of the game so as to creatively inhabit, redirect or refashion them. The practice Gensler style their re-purposing of buildings as an architecture of 'hacking', the existing structure taken as the 'code' to be creatively adapted through the removal of floors or the addition of programs.[32] Other architects and designers 'hack' symbols of uniformity – IKEA and the shipping container – appropriating the products of standardization as their medium of self-expression.

Largely absent of any political motivation, where not explicitly proscribing this from the concerns of the discipline, our most well-regarded architects are typically content with surfing the waves of what exists. Scoring points for flexibility and efficiency, the innovation they bring to each manoeuvre is marked for individual performance. Lack of political motivation does not, though, necessarily equate to lack of political effectivity. The individual freedoms exercised and embodied in the architect exemplify neoliberal ideals of the entrepreneur of the self. Their works are valorized for the ways in which they open up space to the free use of the individual, thus liberated, in turn, to pursue their own entrepreneurial performance.

Notes

1   Karl Marx, *The Eighteenth Brumaire of Louis Bonaparte* (New York: International Publishers, 1963), 15.

2   Ibid., 15.

3   Justin McGuirk, 'Selling Freedom: Tools of Personal Liberation,' in *California: Designing Freedom*, Justin McGuirk and Brendan McGetrick, eds (London and New York: Phaidon, 2017), 10.

4   Ant Farm, 'The Cowboy Nomad Manifesto,' 1969. Reproduced in Felicity D. Scott, *Living Archive 7: Ant Farm. Allegorical Time Warp: The Media Fallout of July 21, 1969* (Actar: Barcelona and New York, 2008), 21.

5   Reyner Banham, *Scenes in America Deserta* (London: Thames and Hudson, 1982), 99.

6   Ibid., McGuirk and McGetrick, inside cover.

7   Ibid., McGuirk, 9.

8   Ibid., 15.

9   Ibid., 15.

10 Friedrich A. Hayek, *The Road to Serfdom* (Abingdon, Oxford and New York: Routledge, 2001), 74.

11 Friedrich A. Hayek, *Law, Legislation and Liberty: A New Statement of the Liberal Principles of Justice and Political Economy* (Abingdon, Oxford and New York: Routledge, 2013), 13.

12 Karl Marx, *Capital, Volume 1*, trans. B. Fowkes (London: Penguin, 1976), 272.

13 Jason Read, *The Politics of Transindividuality* (Chicago: Haymarket Books, 2016), 51.

14 Gary S. Becker, 'Human Capital', *The Concise Encyclopedia of Economics*, (Carmel, IN: Library of Economics and Liberty, 1975).

15 Jonathan Crary, *24/7: Late Capitalism and the Ends of Sleep* (London and New York: Verso, 2013). As Crary notes, 'Billions of dollars are spent every year researching how to reduce decision-making time, how to eliminate the useless time of reflection and contemplation. This is the form of contemporary progress – the relentless capture and control of time and experience.'

16 Ibid., 37.

17 On the relationship between the counterculture and new modes of power see Fred Turner, *From Counterculture to Cyberculture: Stewart Brand, the Whole Earth Network, and the Rise of Digital Utopianism* (Chicago and London: University of Chicago Press, 2008); Felicity D. Scott, *Outlaw Territories: Environments of Insecurity/Architectures of Counterinsurgency* (New York: Zone Books, 2016).

18 Ibid., McGuirk, 14.

19 Ibid., Scott, 2016, 372, 19.

20 Attributed to Fred Richardson 'Production in the Desert,' *Whole Earth Catalog*, 1971, cited in Felicity D. Scott, *Living Archive 7: Ant Farm. Allegorical Time Warp: The Media Fallout of July 21, 1969* (Barcelona and New York: Actar, 2008), 81.

21 Ibid., Marx, 1963, 84–5.

22 Ibid., Scott, 2016, 256.

23 Reyner Banham, *The Architecture of the Well-tempered Environment* (Chicago: University of Chicago Press, 1984), 19–21.

24 Ibid., Scott, 2016, 247.

25 Robert Venturi, Denise Scott Brown, Steven Izenour, *Learning from Las Vegas* (Cambridge, MA: MIT Press, 1972), 3.

26 Tim Brown, 'Hello I'm Tim Brown, Chair, <https://www.ideo.com/people/tim-brown>.

27 Peter Hall, 'IDEO Takes on the Government: The Nimble Consultancy Brings Design Thinking to Political Structures in Desperate Need of Reinvention', *Metropolis* (June 2011), 100–23.

28 Ibid., McGuirk, 14

29 Ibid., 14.

30 Douglas Spencer, 'Architectural Deleuzism: Neoliberal Space, Control and the "Univer-City"', *Radical Philosophy* 168 (July/August 2011).

31 Ibid., Crary, 46.

32 Alex Garkavenko, 'Meet the New Class of Architecture Hackers', *Architizer* (12 March, 2014), <https://architizer.com/blog/inspiration/industry/gensler-hackable-building/>.

Fulton Center Metro, Manhattan, New York, USA, Grimshaw Architects, 2014

Section 3.
Reckoning with Theory

8 Going to Ground: Agency, Design and the Problem of Bruno Latour

Letting the object speak

We are obliged now, it seems, to give objects and things their due. Their agency must be recognized. We must ask them what they want and allow them their say. This may not be entirely new. It might be recalled, for instance, that Louis Kahn asked a brick what it wanted to be, and that the brick replied that it wanted to be an arch, and from this that the architect noted it important that one 'honor the brick and glorify the brick instead of short-changing it'.[1] Current imperatives to acknowledge and respect the nonhuman speak, though, to a specifically contemporary desire to escape the supposedly anthropocentric perspective of modernity, and with it the environmental, social and even philosophical problems for which it is held responsible.[2] At the same time, such recognition promises to enrich the practice of design, and its discourse, through the novelty of its perspective. Less available to recognition, however, are the problematic implications for design of the various flat and object-oriented ontologies, alongside the new varieties of materialism, through which this desire is articulated. Presiding over design as normative principles, these stricture its scope, conception and practice. Seemingly radical in their extension of agency to nonhuman actors, they effectively mirror capitalism in their fetishization of the object. Supposedly progressive in their denouncement of human hubris, they align with neoliberal ideologies in refusing the human subject any agency other than that of accommodating themselves to things as they already are. Unable to countenance contradiction or hierarchy, they seek out the reassuringly even ground from which all difference has been smoothed out. Subject collapsed into object, attempts to grasp the totality of capital damned as 'totalizing', what remains for the designer is a restricted and post-political outlook on their praxis and its possibilities.

Central to this normative turn towards the perspective of the thing is the thought of Bruno Latour. The Actor-Network Theory (ANT) through which this is inflected refuses any special significance to human action. Agency, in ANT, is equally redistributed between human and nonhuman actors. This apparently more equitable arrangement of things comes, however, at the cost of obscuring the actually existing inequalities of agency through which power operates. It effectively depoliticizes, in the process, the field of design.

Down to earth

Latour first directly engages with design in his keynote address, 'A Cautious Prometheus? A Few Steps Toward a Philosophy of Design (with Special Attention to Peter Sloterdijk', to the 2008 Design History Society conference *Networks of Design*.[3] He observes here that 'the typically modernist divide between materiality on the one hand and design on the other is slowly being dissolved away'.[4] Where design used to consist in the addition of a superficial aesthetic veneer to material things it is now materialized in the making of those things. Design, argues Latour, 'increasingly matters to the very substance of production'.[5] The current immanence of design to matter is considered positive since it marks a transition from the shaping and mastery of things from the outside, from a wilful and hubristic impulse identified as both modernizing and revolutionary, to a more sensitive and modest engagement with them on their own terms. 'The present historical situation', Latour writes, 'is defined by a complete disconnect between two great alternatives – one of emancipation, detachment, modernization, progress and mastery, and the other, completely different, of attachment, precaution, entanglement, dependence and care.'[6] 'Design' stands in this account as the antithesis of modernization and revolution. Being possessed of a 'non- or a post-Promethean's sense of what it means to act', of 'humility' and 'modesty', it is, for Latour, eminently qualified to address our 'ecological crisis'.[7]

What Latour is forging here, under the guise of merely finding it already in existence, is a morality of design founded on its purported immanence to matter; 'materiality and morality', he writes, are 'finally coalescing'.[8] While design is held up as the vehicle through which our ecological crises will be remediated, the terms under which it will carry out this mission are to be contained within prescribed moral bounds. Where a wealth of existing critical reflection on this crisis has sought to understand its causes and their origins within industrial capitalism,[9] Latour points his finger, instead, at the moral failings and radicalism of Modernist design in its servicing of modernization. Modernism is charged with 'hubris', reprimanded for its 'search for absolute certainty, absolute beginnings, and radical departures'.[10] The argument derived from this moral perspective is that design lower its horizons without becoming radical, that it ground itself in a humility before matter without being tempted to reflect on, or tamper with, the roots of our crises while it is down there. Indeed, 'going to ground' in this fashion so as to evade or delegitimize the political, at least as is conventionally conceived, appears a recurrent trope in Latour's oeuvre. In his recent essay collection, *Down to Earth: Politics in the New Climate Regime,* he argues that the existential need to rediscover the ground beneath our feet, to feel our attachment to the land, is a more pressing concern even than of 'ecological crisis' or 'environmental problems'.[11] In Latour's voyage to rediscover our foundational ground, the old political markers – 'Right' and 'Left', 'Liberation', 'emancipation', and 'market forces' – must be cast aside.[12] 'Everything', he argues (breaching his own embargo on 'absolute beginnings'), 'has to be mapped out anew.'[13]

In the process of this new existential grounding 'critique' – Latour's long-avowed foe – must likewise be wiped off the map.[14] 'Critique', he says in his address to the Design History Society, 'will simply not do the job of finding an alternative design.'[15] The 'simple', and therefore unelaborated reasoning at work here is that critique will not do this job because its practice is premised on the now delegitimated capacities of a cognitively reflective subject. Where critique is classically concerned with reflection on the conditions of possibility of its object, Latour's ontology cannot countenance the subject's capacity to extricate itself, however momentarily, from the immediate world of things in which it is imbricated in order to effect this reflection. Not, at least, without being judged guilty of a will to mastery. The designer must instead abide by a moral code of humility whose basis is itself placed beyond critical reflection, bound by moral imperatives and existential necessities. These are the conditions of possibility for Latour's discounting of and hostility towards critique.

Latour's desire to relieve design of its supposed will to mastery is not entirely novel. In some sense he is just very late in arriving to the party of Postmodernism. His anti-Modernist and environmental stance echoes a long-standing agenda in architecture first articulated in the 1960s and 70s. Buckminster Fuller is its godfather, Reyner Banham its proselytizer-in-chief, the geodesic domes of the countercultural commune and the inflatable structures of Ant Farm among its concrete manifestations.[16] In the seemingly new-found respect for 'things' as they are, rather than as they might be bent to the will of the architect, it is not so difficult to discern, either, an echo of the new pragmatism announced in the opening sentence of Venturi, Scott Brown and Izenour's *Learning from Las Vegas:* 'Learning from the existing landscape is a way of being revolutionary for an architect.'[17] But Latour nonetheless adds something novel to the established formula. Where Postmodernism famously disavows all 'grand narratives', he provides the basis for a new one (without owning up to it as such) in his account of agency, which now appears to be everywhere and in everything. Extended to and evenly distributed between humans and nonhumans, equally the property of everybody and everything, all are included and implicated within agency's effectively totalizing network of actors.

The seemingly democratic gesture at the heart of Latour's projection of an all-inclusive network of agents comes, though, with terms and conditions. The costs of these, already alluded to, are worth elaborating. As Andreas Malm remarks in his *The Progress of this Storm,* Latour's flat ontology, and its various kindred new materialisms, refuse to allow of any real difference in the agency of human actors as distinct from that of nonhuman ones.[18] These refuse to register, for instance, that there is 'anything qualitatively different between UN climate negotiations and the process of photosynthesis'.[19] Spelling out the consequences of this, Malm notes that 'not only is there an evident difference – one constructed by humans, the other not – denial of it also whisks away the significance of the combination. For the problem of climate change is constituted precisely by how social relations combine with natural ones that are not of their making'.[20]

It might be added that in Latour's network of actors, for all its inclusiveness, there is no place available for those forms of agency that might interrupt its essentially horizontal perspective. The agency of human subjects, for instance, exercising their cognitive capacities to arrive at reflective forms of knowledge, being especially unwelcome at his 'parliament of things'. The flatness of Latour's ontology is in fact premised on smoothing over any difference between subjects and objects to the point where it makes no sense to employ such terms. While objects are liberated from their subservience to subjects, elevated to the status of things, the status of the subject is diminished, admonished for its hubris. It is brought down to size and required to assume the requisite moral dispositions of humility and modesty towards the thing.

The poverty of the new materialism

There is no room in Latour's flat ontology, either, for the agency of the 'automatic subject' that is capital; for Marx the 'all-dominating economic power of bourgeois society'.[21] Overlooked in not qualifying as a thing, slipping beneath the horizon of visibility, the agency of the biggest actor of them all is rendered obscure in Latour's schema. While offering up the promise of releasing us from the grip of mastery, flat ontologies only make the kind of mastery that matters most ungraspable.

Latour's materialism, and its other new varieties, are, then, of a peculiar sort. At odds with the 'old' and Marxian materialisms they discredit, they refuse to recognize the dialectics of subject and object as played out through the exchange relations produced within capitalism. So, while Latour can claim that design 'increasingly matters to the very substance of production', questions of what that production is conditioned by, and of what conditions it is geared to bring forth – socially, economically, politically, subjectively – are bypassed so as to focus on the explicitation of 'substance', conceived of in the most literal and one-dimensional fashion. The following passage from the essay '"Give Me a Gun and I Will Make All Buildings Move": An ANT's View of Architecture', written by Latour and Albena Yaneva, makes plain the implications of this for the agency of design, and the limits therefore prescribed of its theoretical practices:

> Instead of explaining the assembly building in Chandigarh with economic constraints or with the trivial conceptual repertoire of Le Corbusier's modernist style and his unique non-European experience in master planning, we should better witness the multifarious manifestations of recalcitrance of this building, resisting breezes, intense sunlight and the microclimate of the Himalayas, etc. Only by generating earthly accounts of buildings and design processes, tracing pluralities of concrete entities in the specific spaces and times of their co-existence, instead of referring to abstract theoretical frameworks outside architecture, will architectural theory become a relevant field for architects, for end users, for promoters, and for builders.[22]

All that is abstract, conceptual, subjective, theoretical, anything that cannot be grounded and brought to 'earthly account', is to be excised from consideration. In the impoverished version of materialism offered up by Latour and Yaneva, production is made to appear self-evident in its immediate substantiality. There is nothing to reflect on, to contest, or to challenge. No scope for resistance other than in such literally material forms as that of a wall blocking the passage of the breeze. The same impoverished materialism, accompanied by the same kind of normative commentary on how design should be thought, practised and experienced, also mark Yaneva's application of ANT to design in her essay, 'Making the Social Hold: Toward an Actor-Network Theory of Design'.[23] 'Design', she writes here, 'is a mode of connection that cannot be explained by other economical, social, political means. It has its own ... objectivity, its own solidity.'[24] 'An ANT approach', she clarifies, 'does not try to unveil the "hidden meaning" of a design.'[25] In the introduction to her *The Making of a Building: A Pragmatist Approach to Architecture*, Yaneva opens her account of OMA's design for the NEWhitney project stating her reliance 'on the assumption that buildings are pragmatically knowable not symbolic'.[26] Warding off the 'wrong' forms of interpretation or analysis, the experience of design is to be conducted, for Yaneva, strictly in terms of an attentiveness to its performative qualities. In the account of her daily trajectory through her university building from which the ANT-based analysis of 'Making the Social Hold' draws, she experiences the staircase, the elevator and the security-coded door lock as 'affordances', agents of shared social enjoyments. These are encountered happily performing their role as actors in the construction of a network held to be immediately social. Designed objects may, of course, perform in such non-discursive ways, and regardless of if, or how, they are interpreted. Yaneva dogmatically insists, however, that the analysis of this performance can only be conducted in opposition to, and in place of, other modes of analysis.

In the case of that security lock, for instance, she writes that 'the implications of the particular design … cannot be conferred on the symbolic relationships between departments, disciplines, hierarchies, divisions of labor, the university building design or the psychological need of university fellows to double the number of locking mechanism and key devices that would guide them to their mail boxes and their copy machines'.[27] This is a revealing remark, intimating at once Yaneva's recognition that such concerns *are* suggested by, and pertinent to, the encounter with the security lock, and that these must, at the same time, be immediately discounted in accord with the strictly grounded perspective of ANT. In fact, the wider issue of the securitization of higher education precisely *does* become amenable to critical reflection through its particular concrete manifestations, and we are shortchanged here out of an analysis that might move *between* the abstract and the concrete, the ideological and the material, by the 'earthly' accounting methods of ANT.

ANT's insistence on restricting its scope of enquiry to the pure immediacy of things and their actions also succeeds in occluding the question of labour from its perspective. The work of mining, manufacturing or cultivating materials, their extraction, treatment and circulation as resources for production, the conditions of labour under which this production takes place, the labour of the designer, the means by which all of this is valorized and exploited, are all obscured by ANT's prohibition on any 'unveiling' of immediate appearances. They are discounted as a 'matter of concern' in Yaneva's account of the built and designed environment. Again, the point is not that any such unveiling is necessarily and unquestionably enough in itself, that the old ways of critical theory are themselves beyond critique, but that ANT sets such strictures on the scope of the analysis of design that these severely limit our understanding of its agency. Absent any account of the backstory of the things arrayed before us, acting out their roles in 'making the social hold', their appearance will tend to reinforce an unquestioning acceptance of the given as such, a conditioning to *what is*. For critical theory, taking Marx's critique of commodity fetishism as its starting point, this conditioning is a kind of special effect – for Theodor Adorno or Walter Benjamin a 'phantasmagoria' – whose hidden workings must be revealed.[28] As Tafuri put it, 'it will never be repeated too often that, when wishing to discover the secret of a magician's tricks, it is far better to observe him from backstage than to continue to stare at him from a seat in the orchestra'.[29] Barring access to such observations, under the injunction that there is, after all, nothing to unveil or disclose, effectively reinforces the account of things already offered to us in capital's conditions of production and consumption. As the philosopher Andrew Cole has noted of such schools of interpretation as the new materialism and ANT, 'for Marx, at least, this way of thinking about objects is what keeps capitalism ticking. To adopt such a philosophy, no questions asked, is fantasy – commodity fetishism in academic form'.[30]

Obscured objects of design

What might be further elaborated from Cole's remarks is that if the flat ontologies of new materialism and ANT reproduce the fantastical quality of the commodity in academic form, then this is because of the work they undertake in focusing attention exclusively on things in themselves and their immediate appearance as social actors. As Marx noted, the 'mysterious character' of the commodity form lies 'simply in the fact that the commodity reflects the social characteristics of men's own labour as objective characteristics of the products of labour themselves, as the 'socio-natural' properties of these things'.[31] We do not need Latour or Yaneva to remind us that 'things' are performative. We can read this in *Capital*. For Marx 'things', in capitalism, perform the naturalization of a social relationship by rendering the practices of alienated labour obscure. Yes, 'things' are 'holding the social together', but they are holding it together in a particular form; that of the exchange relations on which capitalism is founded. It is this detail, crucially, that is withheld from view in ANT. Also crucial is that what Marx is pointing to as fantastical and mysterious in capitalism is that its objects, in the form of commodities, exert a power over its subjects. As he writes in the *Grundrisse:* 'Production thus not only creates an object for the subject, but also a subject for the object.'[32] The objects of consumption, commodities, are not only *produced,* but are themselves *productive.* They produce the tastes, needs and desires on which their consumption is contingent.

The kind of conceptual work being undertaken by Latour and his followers withdraws this dialectic of subject and object from analysis. As Latour notes in the glossary of his *Pandora's Hope: Essays on the Reality of Science Studies,* he has replaced the 'subject-object dichotomy' with the pairing 'human-nonhuman' and this not so as to '"overcome" the subject-object distinction but [as] a way to bypass it entirely'.[33] This 'bypassing' of the subject-object pairing, supposed to overturn the mastery of the subject over the object, is premised, though, on a reductive understanding of the relations between subjects and objects, especially as these operate in late capitalism. Rather than a one-way deterministic relationship in which subjects rule over objects, objects produce subjects as much as subjects produce objects. And subjects are themselves subjected and subjectified, even objectified, often by other subjects, as well as by objects. Fairly obviously, as well, not all subjects are afforded equal powers to subjectify or to objectify. The nature of these relations, the forms of power through which they are enacted and reproduced, escape consideration when the subject-object dialectic (it is not a 'dichotomy') is bypassed for that of the human-nonhuman pairing.

In place of accounting for the differentiated powers of agency relayed back and forth between subjects and objects, these are levelled out in the syntax of

Latour's notorious litanies; concatenations of actors assembled around 'matters of concern', lined up as equal partners in their performance of the social. Yaneva offers her own version of this performative levelling in *The Making of a Building*, describing the architectural studio of OMA, Rem Koolhaas's Office for Metropolitan Architecture, as assembled from 'objects and architects, foam cutters, sketches and maps'.[34] Is the agency of the foam cutter really equivalent to that of the architect? Is the agency of every architect working at OMA of the same order as that of Rem Koolhaas? Such lines of questioning are ruled out in advance within the analytical framework presented as 'pragmatic' by Yaneva.[35]

Recovering agency

The refusal to countenance inequalities of agency does not amount to making them go away. Likewise, the refusal to address anything beyond that which is immediately apparent does not mean that everything that counts *is* immediately apparent. Questions of power, inequality and exploitation, of the political and the economic, cannot be sidelined or conjured out of existence by theoretical manoeuvres such as are addressed here. They require, among other things, recognizing and critically reflecting on the forms of agency involved in maintaining or challenging their current configurations, and on the development of a critical praxis through which to achieve this. These requirements are pertinent both to the often precarious and exploitative conditions of labour under which the teaching and practice of design is undertaken, and to the sites and conditions to which its projects are addressed. As Latour himself notes, 'everything has to be designed and redesigned (including nature)', and the scope of design extends now to 'cities, landscapes, natural parks, societies, as well as genes, brains and chips'.[36] This is the very context, however, in which the dichotomy he has manufactured between Modernist mastery and modest humility is so problematic. As an account of the agency of the designer, it is both disempowering and ineffectual. It results in a prescription for the good moral conduct of the designer – humble, modest, cautious – confining their agency to the gentle modulation of things as they already are. The agency of the designer need not, however, necessarily be circumscribed by Latour's cautionary warnings against Promethean mastery. One can attempt to grasp the workings of mastery, however imperfectly, without assuming a position of mastery itself. Being equal to the ecological and other crises in which the designer is implicated in fact requires a willingness to comprehend and challenge the conditions and mechanisms of mastery through which these are produced.

Notes

1 Louis Kahn, transcribed from the 2003 documentary *My Architect: A Son's Journey by Nathaniel Kahn*, Master class at Penn, 1971.

2 The 'nonhuman' is defined by Bruno Latour in the glossary of *Pandora's Hope: Essays on the Reality of Science Studies* (Cambridge, MA: Harvard University Press, 1999): 'This concept has meaning only in the difference between the pair "human-nonhuman" and the subject-object dichotomy. Associations of humans and nonhumans refer to a different political regime from the war forced upon us by the distinction between subject and object. A nonhuman is thus the peacetime version of the object: what the object would look like if it were not engaged in the war to shortcut due political process. The pair human-nonhuman is not a way to "overcome" the subject-object distinction but a way to bypass it entirely.' 308.

3 Bruno Latour, 'A Cautious Prometheus? A Few Steps Toward a Philosophy of Design (with Special Attention to Peter Sloterdijk)', keynote lecture for the *Networks of Design* meeting of the Design History Society Falmouth, Cornwall, 3 September, 2008 <http://www.bruno-latour.fr/sites/default/files/112-DESIGN-CORNWALL-GB.pdf.>.

4 Ibid., 2.

5 Ibid.

6 Ibid.

7 Ibid., 3,7.

8 Ibid., 5.

9 See, for instance; Lewis Mumford, *Technics and Civilization* (London and Chicago: Chicago University Press, 2010); Murray Bookchin, *The Ecology of Freedom: The Emergence and Dissolution of Hierarchy* (Palo Alto, CA: Cheshire Books, 1982); Rachel Carson, *Silent Spring* (Boston and New York: Mariner Books, 2002), and, of more recent publication, Andreas Malm, *Fossil Capital: The Rise of Steam Power and the Roots of Global Warming* (London and New York: Verso, 2016).

10 Latour, 'Prometheus', 5.

11 Bruno Latour, *Down to Earth: Politics in the New Climate Regime*, trans. Catherine Porter (Cambridge, UK, and Medford, MA, 2018), 8.

12 Ibid., 33.

13 Ibid.

14 See, for example, Bruno Latour, 'Why has Critique Run out of Steam? From Matters of Fact to Matters of Concern', *Critical Inquiry*, Vol. 30, No. 2, 2004, 225–248.

15 Latour, 'Prometheus', 13.

16 For an extensive critique of anti-Modernist and environmentalist architecture and design of this period, see Douglas Spencer, *The Architecture of Neoliberalism: How Contemporary Architecture Became an Instrument of Control and Compliance* (London: Bloomsbury Academic, 2016). See too, Felicity Scott, *Outlaw Territories: Environments of Insecurity/Architectures of Counterinsurgency* (New York: Zone Books, 2016).

17 Robert Venturi, Denise Scott Brown, Steven Izenour, *Learning from Las Vegas* (Cambridge, MA: MIT Press, 1972), 3.

18 Andreas Malm, *The Progress of this Storm: Nature and Society in a Warming World* (London and New York: Verso, 2018).

19 Ibid., 74.

20 Ibid.

21 Karl Marx, *Grundrisse: Foundations of the Critique of Political Economy*, trans, Martin Nicolaus (Harmondsworth: Penguin Books in association with New Left Review, 1973),

22 Bruno Latour and Albena Yaneva, '"Give me a Gun and I Will Make All Buildings Move": An ANT's View of Architecture', in *Explorations in Architecture: Teaching, Design, Research*, Reto Geiser, ed., (Basel: Birkhäuser, 2008), 88.

23 Albena Yaneva, 'Making the Social Hold: Toward an Actor-Network Theory of Design', *Design and Culture*, 1(3) (2009), 273–88.

24 Ibid., 9.

25 Ibid., 6.

26 Albena Yaneva, *The Making of a Building: A Pragmatist Approach to Architecture* (Oxford: Peter Lang, 2009), 6.

27 Ibid.

28 For recent analyses of the concept of 'phantasmagoria' in the writings of Theodor Adorno and Walter Benjamin in relation to architecture and design, see Spencer, *Neoliberalism;* and Libero Andreotti and Nadir Lahiji, *The Architecture of Phantasmagoria: Specters of the City* (London and New York: Routledge, 2017).

29   Manfredo Tafuri, *The Sphere and the Labyrinth: Avant-Gardes and Architecture from Piranesi to the 1970s* (Cambridge, MA: MIT Press), 288.

30   Andrew Cole, 'Those Obscure Objects of Desire: The Uses and Abuses of Object-Oriented Ontology and Speculative Realism', *Artforum,* Summer, 2015 < https://www.artforum.com/print/201506/the-uses-and-abuses-of-object-oriented-ontology-and-speculative-realism-andrew-cole-52280>.

31   Karl Marx, *Capital, Volume I*, trans. Ben Fowkes (London: Penguin, 1976), 164.

32   Karl Marx, *Grundrisse: Foundations of the Critique of Political Economy,* trans. Martin Nicolaus (Harmondsworth: Penguin Books in association with New Left Review, 1973),, 92.

33   Latour, *Pandora's Hope*, 308

34   Yaneva, *Making of a Building*, 116.

35   I am grateful to Helen Runting for sharing with me her own critique of ANT, and this example of its limitations she recalled from her reading of Yaneva's *The Making of a Building*.

36   Latour, 'Prometheus', 2, 5.

9 Returns on the City: Detroit and the Design of Late Fordism

Fordism is said to have reached its mature phase in the decades following the Second World War, only to have collapsed, sometime in the early 1970s, under the combined weight of its various crises and contradictions.[1] Detroit, the city in which Ford, alongside Chrysler, General Motors and others, had established their industries earlier in the century, did not, though, get to share in the fortunes of this maturation. By the middle of the century automobile manufacture had already begun to leave the Motor City behind. After testing the capacity of its workers to the limits with the accelerating pace of its assembly line, and in the face of the unionization that Ford had done everything in its powers – sometimes in the most brutal fashion – to forestall, the company pushed ahead with the decentralization and automation of its production facilities, decamping these from the city to its regional hinterlands.[2]

The stakes of decentralization were clear to workers and managers alike. As Thomas J. Sugrue records in his *The Origins of the Urban Crisis: Race and Inequality in Postwar Detroit,* 'In August 1951, Ford went so far as to haul machines out of the Rouge under the cover of darkness because they feared "action by Ford workers to protect their jobs".'[3] The new mobility of capital – facilitated by advances in transportation and telecommunications, and fostered by the policies of federal government – enabled companies such as Ford to expand and prosper in the postwar era, but at the expense of those unable to access such mobility for themselves. While the rapid populational decline of Detroit in this period is often noted, less so is the fact that Detroit's African American citizens, just as in the Depression, were especially disadvantaged in the wake of the city's industrial evacuation. 'Persistent racial discrimination', writes Sugrue, 'magnified the effects of deindustrialization on blacks.'[4] 'As Detroit's population shrank', he notes, 'it also grew poorer and blacker. Increasingly the city became the home for the dispossessed.'[5] We can hardly be unaware, in our own supposedly 'Post-Fordist' times, of how our cities remain at the mercy of the mobility of capital, or of how the consequences of these arrangements exacerbate existing inequalities. Today the lures of corporate investment are baited with promises of jobs and revitalized urban economies. Cities, in turn, compete with one another for such offerings – the location of a corporate campus, headquarters or manufacturing facility – advancing promises of easy terms and flexibilized workforces. In such circumstances corporate investment in the city acquires the status of an act of benefaction rather than one of, say, opportunism or exploitation. The recently announced return of Ford to Detroit is a case in point.

The long-standing crisis of Detroit's urban economy culminated, in 2013, in the city filing for bankruptcy to the tune of an estimated $18–20 billion.[6] Despite the subsequent, and questionable, talking up of its recovery, the city's economic prospects suffered a further blow, when in January 2018 Amazon turned down its tax-incentivized bid to locate the company's second headquarters, alongside 30,000 new jobs, in Detroit.[7] Into this fraught urban scenario the much trumpeted return of Ford to Detroit, announced in June 2018, appears endowed with something of the salvational. 'We are planting a special piece of our company's future in one of the city's great neighborhoods, because we believe in Detroit, its people and what we can build together,' announced Bill Ford (the company's executive chair and great-grandson of Henry Ford) at the event staged to publicize Ford's purchase of Detroit's long abandoned Michigan Central Station.[8] With the reopening of the station – a building latterly renowned as emblematic of the city's much aestheticized urban decay – as the hub for its revived Corktown campus, Ford declared 'Detroit is open for business for good.'[9] The terms under which Ford intends to make a return on this investment are shaped and envisioned through its architecture. The analysis of this, in turn, affords an opportunity to revisit and rethink the periodizing designations 'Fordism' and 'Post-Fordism', as typically subscribed to in architectural history and theory.

Fig. 9.1: Michigan Central Station, Detroit, USA, Warren and Wetmore, and Reed and Stern, 1914

Reimagining Detroit

For the design of its corporate campuses in Dearborn and Corktown and their workspaces, as well as the redesign of Michigan Central Station as their 'anchor' building, Ford have employed the services of Snøhetta. The practice, with its track record in forging publicly accessible spaces from the landscaping of architectural form, seems a logical choice. As Craig Dykers conveyed in an interview published in the *Detroit Free Press,* in relation to his practice's work for Ford, 'We don't just design a building for you to look at; we create new pathways, new walkways, new landscapes, new gathering places in and around the building that we also have to create.'[10] Snøhetta's designs for Ford exist as yet only at a formative stage of development. It is not difficult to imagine, though, how the landscaped forms of their Oslo Opera House, or the civic agenda of their recently completed Times Square reconstruction project in Manhattan, might have appealed to the current ambitions of Ford to reimagine and rebrand themselves as a civically responsible, sustainability conscious, and (of course) innovative 'mobility company'.

This reimagining is focused on connectivity; on the making of an integrated ecology of work, business, leisure and transportation set against a backdrop of reanimated urban life and publicly accessible park space. Begun in 2016, the Snøhetta-designed transformation of the company's Dearborn campus and headquarters to the west of Detroit, for instance, will involve the substantial reduction of the number of existing buildings on the site. This so as to open the fabric of the campus to 'reflect Ford's commitment to sustainability' in making space for a 'central green area that will link buildings with walking trails [and] bike paths'.[11] The flythroughs present a familiar picture; architectural forms – seemingly skewed by the pull of some unseen force field – arrayed across a park space patterned with a connective tissue of undulating pathways.

The now standardized design tropes of the fluid and the connected, working here at the scale of the campus, also operate at that of the interior. At Dearborn, and in the converted factory buildings of the Corktown campus, office layouts are designed to facilitate productive interactions and exchanges between workers. Sight-lines will be opened up above lowered workstation partitions. There will be more cafés and informal drop-in spaces. Donna Inch, CEO of Ford Land, conveys in a promotional film that the 'new workspaces will give our employees the power to choose where and how they want to work'.[12] Ford is committed to the creation of 'workspaces that foster collaboration and spark innovation', intones the film's narrator.[13]

As in the Japanese 'Toyotist' model, such managerial strategies are designed to build team mentalities and to elicit the production and sharing of knowledge between workers, the end goal of which is to achieve 'continuous improvement' in production. As with existing precedents, such as the Zaha Hadid Architects'-designed BMW Central Building in Leipzig, however, other benefits – though for obvious reasons ones not publicized – might also accrue to Ford from their adoption. At the Leipzig plant, for instance, the team-building and integrative agenda facilitated through Hadid's architecture can also be seen to work at easing tensions between managers and managed at BMW, particularly those caused through the conditions of precarious and flexibilized labour endured by the latter.[14]

The proposed refurbishment of Michigan Central Station might be seen in a similar light, here smoothing over long-standing antagonisms between Ford Motor Company and the City of Detroit. Remodelled as a mixed-use development, housing the company's offices and research centre at its upper levels, the station's Beaux-Arts ticket hall is envisaged as a Main Street-themed pedestrian promenade. Reanimated by the footfall of visitors attracted to its new shops and restaurants, the civic life once accommodated in this now derelict space appears rescued by Ford, now generously hosting the public within the space of the corporate. Liberally populated with figures of diversity, the renderings of Detroit's positive transformation under Ford effectively gloss over the impact of its historical dereliction of Detroit. Ford's promotional apparatus proclaims 'just like they did over a hundred years ago, Ford and Detroit will look forward together'.[15] What occurred in the interim, however, is passed over in silence.

Ford have staged other returns to Detroit. In the 1970s Henry Ford II commissioned the Renaissance Center for the city. Here Ford invested in finance and spectacle, in the Late Modernist architecture of John Portman's mirror-faced skyscrapers clustered into an island fortress of banks, restaurants and hotels. The company's current projects for Detroit, in contrast, eschew the citadel in favour of the campus, the monumental in favour of the landscaped. The terms and conditions of Ford's current investments in Detroit appear governed by a logic of integration, driven by an imperative to overcome and erase all antagonisms. The campuses coordinate relations between the company and its partners in business and industry. Open-spaced offices network relations between workers. Main Street style promenades combine business with leisure, the corporate with the civic. The positive conditions of Detroit's transformation under such terms are persuasively rendered in a scenography of environmentally conscious and public-minded free enterprise. Following the conventions of periodization to which architectural theory has tended to subscribe, this latest turn in the architecture of Ford might logically, if somewhat paradoxically, be defined as Post-Fordist.

The architecture of Post-Fordism

Originally formulated in the 1970s, the concept of Post-Fordism has been accessed in architectural discourse principally via its treatment in David Harvey's *The Condition of Postmodernity,* and in Fredric Jameson's *Postmodernism, or, the Cultural Logic of Late Capitalism.*[16] Fordism is understood on this model as based upon standardization, mass production and the scientific management of industrial labour, as epitomized by the factories of Ford. The cracks in this 'regime of accumulation' had, according to Harvey, begun to appear as early as the 1960s: 'Technological change, automation, the search for new product lines and market niches, geographical dispersal to zones of easier labour control, mergers, and steps to accelerate the turnover time of their capital surged to the fore of corporate strategies for survival under general conditions of deflation.'[17] Pressured to escape the compromises forced by labour unionization, and drawn to the opportunities for capturing new markets through product differentiation, capital turns, in the 1970s, to a new regime of accumulation based upon diversity, mobility and flexibility: Post-Fordism.

Fig. 9.2 Renaissance Center, Detroit, USA, Portman Architects, 1977

Corresponding to this turn in what we might designate – employing the Marxian vulgate – the 'economic base' of capital from Fordism to Post-Fordism, there is a turn in the 'ideological superstructure' from Modernism to Postmodern. The cultural, and specifically architectural dimensions, of this Postmodern turn are famously addressed by Jameson in his reading of the disorienting experience of the Westin Bonaventure Hotel in downtown Los Angeles.[18] Harvey, too, attends to the ways in which the logic of Post-Fordism is registered in the architecture of Postmodernism.

Drawing upon Harvey, Patrik Schumacher and Christian Rogner's 2001 essay 'After Ford' offers a reading of contemporary Detroit as symptomatic of the urban and architectural implications of the above-described formulation.[19] But where Harvey understands the turn to Post-Fordism critically, Schumacher and Rogner have it appear progressive, even radical. Harvey identifies Post-Fordism with the agency of capital in resolving its own crises and contradictions, and maximizing its accumulative capacities. Schumacher and Rogner, though, tend to couch their account of Post-Fordism in the naturalizing language of 'evolution' and 'self-organization'. The turn to Post-Fordism, in their account, appears largely as the outcome of some spontaneous process of 'emergence'. The naturalizing connotations of Schumacher and Rogner's discourse are given a further twist, towards the progressive, by way of association with the philosophy of Gilles Deleuze and Félix Guattari. The 'radical organizational paradigms' elaborated by the philosophers 'seem to foreshadow the paradigms of today's corporate restructuring. The arborescent command pyramid of Fordist arrangement is mutating towards the rhizomatic plateau upon which leadership (and all other social functions) is distributed in a permanently shifting multiplicity'.[20] The new organizational paradigms of the Post-Fordist corporation are, for the authors, essentially radical, rooted in the horizontality of the rhizome as opposed to the hierarchy of the tree. Constituting nothing less than a 'revolution', these new paradigms 'render corporate organization non-hierarchical and replace command and control mechanisms with participatory and open structures'.[21] Although currently compromised by the lingering presence of capitalism, these paradigms should be adopted as the basis of a new agenda for architecture, aligning itself with the 'thrust of development [that] tears and shakes the corporate edifice of Fordism'.[22]

The new architecture affirmed as progressive by Schumacher and Rogner will be for Post-Fordism what Modernism was for Fordism. If not Postmodern in terms of its semiotic playfulness or architectural self-referentiality, it will be so at least in its 'rejection of homogeneity, coherence, and completeness'.[23] The architecture of Post-Fordism will be radical in its rejection of 'The totalizing notion of Fordism [that] became instrumental to the underlying rationality of modern architecture and urbanism'.[24] Where Modernist architecture followed Fordism in its functionality, hierarchy and standardization, the architecture of Post-Fordism advocated by Schumacher and Rogner will be flexible, anti-hierarchical and differentiated. Where the Modernism of Le Corbusier and Ludwig Hilberseimer followed the productive logic of Ford's factories in conceiving of architecture as a machine, the new architecture will be aligned with Post-Fordist principles of evolutionary and co-operative self-organization.

Following Schumacher and Rogner's reasoning, the architecture of Ford's latest return to Detroit counts as progressively Post-Fordist, a triumphal victory over the Modernist edifice of Fordism. But their argument – and they are by no means alone in its articulation – is, constructed on some dubious foundations, the examination of which might give us cause to reject not just the claims staked for the progressive character of this architecture, but also the very distinction between Fordism and Post-Fordism on which it rests.

Mr Ford makes men

Fordism is typically thought of as a matter of making things, of the industrial and mass production of standardized commodities. But as Greg Grandin argues in his *Fordlandia*, Henry Ford had wider ambitions for his business, as made plain in the statement by one of Ford's representatives he cites in support of this: '"The impression has somehow got around … that Henry Ford is in the automobile business. It isn't true. Mr Ford shoots about fifteen hundred cars out of the back door of his factory every day just to get rid of them. They are the by-products of his real business, which is the making of men.'"[25] Nor was this larger perspective lost on Ford's contemporary critics. As Antonio Gramsci remarked in his *Prison Notebooks*, Ford's production system constituted a project whose 'consciousness of purpose [was] unmatched in history', a project focused on the production of 'a new type of worker and of man'.[26]

The means for 'making men' at Ford's disposal were various; the famous $5 a day wages ensuring workers could afford to purchase the products of their labour; the company's sociological department studying and surveilling the lives of employees, families and communities; the 'service men' employed to administer intimidation and physical violence to dissenting workers. Especially pertinent among these means was Ford's interest in the design and production of spatial environments for his employees, and his antipathy towards the modern industrial city motivating his pursuit of alternatives to mitigate its deleterious effects on their physical and moral wellbeing.

Likely influenced by the linear city proposals of the architect Edgar Chambless, Ford was possessed of the same communitarian and anti-urban ethos as directed similar early-twentieth-century explorations of alternatives to the city, such as those of the Soviet disurbanists.[27] 'Ford', argues John R. Mullin, 'wanted to create an environment in which technology, modern production, and agriculture could coexist', and he pursued this ambition in his 'village industries' programme.[28] Determined to insulate his workers from the ill effects – moral, political, physical – of the city, he experimented in locating them in rurally situated sites of production. In the 1920s, more ambitiously, Ford established his own settlement, 'Fordlandia', in the Amazon rainforest. Though designed to secure the supply and processing of rubber supplies at source, Fordlandia also functioned as an entire environment made after and designed to realize Ford's particular vision of an ideal world. In this respect Ford's projects are precursors to those of Disney (whom Ford had met); 'imagineered' lands and worlds shaped by often anti-modern and typically anti-metropolitan impulses.

While not without certain idiosyncratic qualities, these projects of Ford's hardly represent an isolated case peculiar to the Ford Motor Company. Other corporations, and not just those involved in automobile manufacture, followed Ford in automating production and fleeing the city to locate their plants and headquarters in more rural settings, particular after the Second World War. There is something seriously amiss, then, in straightforwardly identifying Fordism with the Heroic phase of Modernist architecture, the locus for which is ideally the modern metropolis. Architectural Modernism might have been inspired by mass production methods and standardization, but Ford, and other companies, were quite capable of designing and realizing their own spaces of work, recreation and consumption.

Rather than looking for the decisive and neatly correlated breaks suggested by prefixing Fordism and Modernism with their respective 'posts', attending to the continuities might prove a more usefully critical practice. The models of Ford's current investments in Detroit might then be seen, like those of its corporate contemporaries in other cities, within the playing out of a longer story arc, one in which the self-exiled corporation hones its skills in the wilderness, before then returning to the city to exercise these in a final act of victory. With the ground now more or less clear from other alternatives, the corporation can resume its place in the city, making this over in its own image and according to its own agenda. While the means and the situations may change, the concern to 'make men' as much as making things has not. Call it Late Fordism.

Notes

1   See, for instance, David Harvey, who notes in *The Condition of Postmodernity: An Enquiry into the Origins of Cultural Change* (Malden, MA and Oxford: Blackwell, 1990), that 'The problem of the proper configuration and deployment of state powers was resolved only after 1945. This brought Fordism to maturity as a fully fledged and distinctive regime of accumulation. As such, it then formed the basis for a long postwar boom that stayed broadly intact until 1973.' 129.

2   As Greg Grandin notes, Henry Ford was also known to his employees as the 'despot of Dearborn' whose 'service men' were happy to mete out the harshest punishment for dissenters to his workplace regime, including the shooting dead of protesting workers in the infamous 'Dearborn massacre' of 1932. *Fordlandia: The Rise & Fall Of Henry Ford's Forgotten Jungle City* (New York: Metropolitan Books, 1989), 243.

3   Thomas J. Sugrue, *The Origins of the Urban Crisis: Race and Inequality in Postwar Detroit* (Princeton and Oxford: Princeton University Press. 2014), 157.

4   Ibid., 144.

5   Ibid., 149.

6   Brad Plumer, 'Detroit Just Filed for Bankruptcy. Here's How it Got There', *The Washington Post*, 18 July 2013, accessed 27 August 2018, https://www.washingtonpost.com/news/wonk/wp/2013/07/18/detroit-just-filed-for-bankruptcy-heres-how-it-got-there/?noredirect=on&utm_term=.877e2763b488.

7   Candice Williams, Christine Ferretti and Charles E. Ramirez, 'Why Amazon didn't Pick Detroit', *The Detroit News*, 18 January 2018, accessed 27 August 2018, https://www.detroitnews.com/story/news/local/detroit-city/2018/01/18/amazon-passes-over-detroit-2nd-hq/1043515001/.

8   John Gallagher, 'Here's What You Might Not Know about Corktown's History', *Detroit Free Press*, 9 July 2018, accessed 27 August 2018, https://www.freep.com/story/money/business/john-gallagher/2018/07/09/detroit-corktown-history/745668002/.

9   Daniel Howes, 'Ford Depot Move Signals "Detroit is Open for Business"', The Detroit News, 19 June 2018, accessed 27 August 2018, https://www.detroitnews.com/story/business/columnists/daniel-howes/2018/06/19/ford-depot-bid-backs-regional-case-mobility-hub-detroit-revival/715195002/.

10 Craig Dykers, in Allie Gross 'Architect Behind Corktown Revival Gives First Glimpse of its Future', *Detroit Free Press*, 22 June 2018, accessed 27 August 2018, https://eu.freep.com/story/news/local/michigan/detroit/2018/06/22/craig-dykers-snohetta-ford-corktown/717906002/.

11 Ford Motor Company, 'Dearborn Campus Transformation', 2016, accessed 27 August 2018, https://www.youtube.com/watch?v=KVo5WhpI9hl.

12 Ibid.

13 Ibid.

14 See Douglas Spencer, *The Architecture of Neoliberalism: How Contemporary Architecture Became an Instrument of Control and Compliance* (London and New York: Bloomsbury Academic, 2016), 84–93.

15 Ford Motor Company, 'Ford's Vision for Michigan Central Station and Corktown', accessed 27 August 2018, http://www.crainsdetroit.com/article/20180624/news/664541/video-fords-vision-for-michigan-central-station-and-corktown.

16 David Harvey, *The Condition of Postmodernity: An Enquiry into the Origins of Cultural Change* (Malden, MA: Blackwell, 1990); Fredric Jameson, *Postmodernism, or, the Cultural Logic of Late Capitalism* (Durham: Duke University Press, 1991). The term 'Post-Fordism' originates in the thought of the 'Regulation' school of political economy. See, for example, Michel Aglietta, *A Theory of Capitalist Regulation: The US Experience*, trans. David Fernbach (London: New Left Books, 1979).

17 Harvey, *Postmodernity*, 142, 145.

18 Jameson, *Postmodernism*, 47–50.

19 Patrik Schumacher & Christian Rogner, 'After Ford', 2001, accessed 27 August 2018, https://www.patrikschumacher.com/Texts/AfterFord.htm.

20 Ibid.

21 Ibid.

22 Ibid.

23 Ibid.

24 Ibid.

25 Grandin, *Fordlandia*, 34

26 Antonio Gramsci, *Selections from the Prison Notebooks of Antonio Gramsci*, ed. and trans. Quintin Hoare and Geoffrey Nowell Smith (New York: International Publishers, 1971), 302.

27   John R. Mullin, 'Henry Ford and Field and Factory:
     An Analysis of the Ford Sponsored Village Indus-
     tries – Experiment in Michigan, 1918–1941', *Jour-
     nal of the American Planning Association* 41, 1982,
     accessed 28 August 2018, https://scholarworks.
     umass.edu/larp_faculty_pubs/41.

28   Ibid.

10 Enjoy the Silence: On the Consolations of the Post-political

Architecture appears at times strangely withdrawn, reluctant to speak of anything much other than its own bare existence. In the spaces of contemporary mass transit, for instance, materials are presented as is, raw and unadorned. Restricted palettes patterned into grids, grilles and meshes enveloping entire structures with their austere geometries. In the old 'dreamworlds' of West and East, capitalist and state socialist alike, the styling of transit architectures was designed to consciously register on the perceptions of its users.[1] Today meaning is withdrawn, appearance reduced to the disinterested indexing of operational logistics and structural efficiencies.

In 1980 London Transport commissioned artist Eduardo Paolozzi to furnish the interiors of its Underground station at Tottenham Court Road with a series of mosaics. The work, undertaken over several years by the Scottish Pop Artist and his assistants, covered 950 square metres of the station. Adorning platforms and passageways, the mosaics featured the imagery of 'mechanisation, urbanisation, popular culture and everyday life' that typified Paolozzi's work.[2] They also address the station's locale. The saxophones and cameras pictured in the mosaics refer, respectively, to nearby Denmark Street's musical stores and to the electronic equipment shops that used to line Tottenham Court Road to the north of the station. Egyptian iconography signals the station's proximity to the British Museum.

In 2015, Paolozzi's mosaics were removed during the station's remodelling for the city's Crossrail redevelopment. A few of them, including the rotunda, were restored and re-installed, but most have been permanently relocated to Edinburgh, where they will be displayed as museum exhibits. In their place, lengthy stretches of pedestrian tunnels are clad in uninterrupted swathes of white tiling. In concession to the need for some form of embellishment, French conceptual/Minimalist artist Daniel Buren's abstract, striped geometries now feature in the entrances and ticket halls of the station.

Fig. 10.1: Mosaic mural, Tottenham Court Road Underground Station, London, UK, Eduardo Paolozzi, 1984

Other metro systems have assumed a similarly laconic aesthetic. Iidabashi Station, on the Toei Ōedo Line of the Tokyo metro, was designed by Makoto Sei Watanabe so as 'to make visible the physical fabric of the framework used in the construction of the subway tube'.[3] Its interior features unrelieved expanses of concrete, corrugated steel panelling and exposed fluorescent lighting. In Manhattan the metro station designed by Grimshaw Architects for the Fulton Center offers a more self-consciously engineered take on this theme, but makes similar play of its lighting, like some work by Dan Flavin repurposed for commuter consumption. The Tube stations designed for London's Jubilee Line Extension in the 1990s exemplify the uses found for 'High-Tech' architects such as Norman Foster, and Hopkins Architects, in summoning from the machinery and structure of Underground transport an aesthetic of trustworthy matter-of-fact efficiency. These particular instances indicate a broader tendency in the architecture of public transit; a shift from

Fig. 10.2: Tottenham Court Road Underground Station, London, Hawkins\Brown, 2017

Fig. 10.3: Tottenham Court Road Underground Station, London, UK, Daniel Buren, 2017

signification to silence, from the marking of place and meaning to an atopic atmospherics.

How to grapple with the significance, if any, of this? How to make sense of an aesthetic situated somewhere between a residual High-Tech and a repurposed Minimalism?[4] Not from a normative or nostalgic perspective, prescribing some proper relation between architecture and its public, or lamenting the disappearance of this. The point, rather, is to ask what the change from one form of appearance to another might signify, both in terms of the relationship between architecture and the subject, and in terms of the larger historical and material conditions in which any such change is situated. Our existing and default modes of architectural critique, however, leave us ill-equipped for this task. We are, after all, not dealing with an architecture of 'spectacle' that dazzles and distracts, but with one likely experienced as

Fig. 10.4: Iidabashi Station, Tokyo, Japan, Makoto Sei Watanabe, 2000

a merely ambient condition, something hovering at the periphery of attention. Neither is the space of mass transit necessarily a hostile or disorienting experience, such as Fredric Jameson famously, and influentially, found LA's Westin Bonaventure Hotel to be.[5] The spaces of the contemporary subway and the metro are more than adequately mapped out for us, fine-tuned to the capacities of our existing sensory apparatus, designed to steer users through structures with maximal efficiency. And, given the absence of explicit signification, how to practise our skills in 'decoding'?

We are confronted with an architecture that deflects sustained attention from itself and confounds existing modes of analysis. Accompanying this phenomenon in the experience of architecture there is, in its discourse, an anti-theory or post-theory insisting that there is, anyway, nothing to look at here, at least not through the lenses of theory or critique. Representative of this discourse are two recently published books; *The Building*, a collection edited by José Aragüez, and Valerio Olgiati and Markus Breitschmid's *Non-Referential Architecture*.[6]

Aragüez, in the introductory chapter to *The Building*, remarks on the way in which the architectural object came to be displaced by 'High Theory':

> The production of knowledge – mainly in the most advanced segment of architecture, but also elsewhere – started to undergo a major transformation in the 1960s … That transformation occurred in an opening up to various other systems of thought (such as semiotics, psychoanalysis, Marxism, and structuralism) and a consequent rewriting of some of those systems' key concepts … into architecture's idiolect.[7]

These remarks are lifted, near verbatim, from K. Michael Hays' introductory chapter to his anthology *Architecture Theory Since 1968:*

> From Marxism and semiotics to psychoanalysis and rhizomatics, architecture theory has freely and contentiously set about opening up architecture to what is thinkable and sayable in other codes, and, in turn, rewriting systems of thought assumed to be properly extrinsic or irrelevant into architecture's own idiolect.[8]

Hays positively valorized this incursion of theory into architecture, but for Aragüez it detracts from the proper focus for thinking about architecture, which should be that of the 'architectural object'. Aragüez's disagreement with Hays appears (he is not explicit about this) to centre on the issue of mediation, on how thinking about architecture is made to pass through theoretical models extrinsic to the discipline. For Hays – here obviously influenced by Fredric Jameson – theory allows us to place and think about architecture in relation to the world as a 'totality'. 'It is an essential and essentially practical problem of theory', he writes, 'to rearticulate that totality, to produce the concepts that relate the architectural fact with the social, historical, and ideological subtexts from which it was never really separate to begin with.'[9] Hays argues that neither the socio-historical contexts of architectural production, nor the objects it produces, can be approached as 'things-in-themselves', but Aragüez, conversely, would have theory re-centred on these 'things-in-themselves', sparing us the detour through 'high theory' by imposing a ban on the import of *mediatory concepts*.[10] The architectural object, displaced from its proper position at the centre of things, suffering at the hands, or minds, of 'high theory', is to be restored to its rightful position as the locus and source of all 'architectural thinking'.

Aragüez's is not opposed to theory as such. His concern is with how it is conducted. His complaint against the deployment of 'high theory' is that it is 'unidirectional', that it deals only in ready-made concepts, subsequently applied to architecture only so as to prove the validity of the theory.[11] Our understanding of architecture is impoverished in such practices, according to Aragüez, since it is obstructed by the imposition of outside concepts foreign to the 'thinking' of architecture itself.[12]

In attempting to escape conceptual mediation, the thinking of architecture nevertheless burdens itself with a concept through which it thinks itself: the *metaphysical* conception of the architectural object. In seeking out as a foundation for thinking architecture that which is 'irreducibly architectural',[13] and in the proposition that architecture be thought of outside mediating concepts, knowledge and thought are imputed to the architectural object in and of itself, to the *'ontological primacy'*[14] of the building, to 'what buildings know', and to the building as 'a form of knowledge in its own right'.[15] To invoke Marx, in trying to make architecture stand on its own two feet, the danger is that it is allowed also to stand on its head, so that it starts to spout 'grotesque ideas'.[16] Against this personification of the object – the defining mark of fetishization – critical theory is concerned with grasping how the object mediates, and is mediated by, the larger totality in which it exists. This is not a unidirectional process but a dialectical one. Theory, as a labour of the concept, the *Arbeit des Begriffs*, is mediated by the object of its theorization, in all its concrete specificity, as much as its object is mediated by the process of being theorized.[17] Theory and object are each transformed in the encounter with one another. This is the immanent process and practice of critique, rather than its mere application. The proposition that we trust in architecture to provide for its own immediate theory of itself, in its own terms, and allowing it to simply speak for itself as a thing-in-itself, only brings us to the standstill of the self-evident, bypassing in the process the whole question of how this self-evidence is produced, and to what effect.

Olgiati and Breitschmid's line of argument is similar to that of Aragüez. 'Instead of taking recourse to the extra-architectural to imbue buildings with sense', they write in *Non-Referential Architecture*, 'buildings themselves can be sense-making.'[18] But they go further than Aragüez in prescribing that this sense-making be purged of reference to anything that is not directly a matter of the architectonic. Architecture should not only speak *for* itself, it should speak only *of* itself. Olgiati and Breitschmid arrive at this proposition by asserting that ours is a time of conceptual exhaustion. This circumstance, moreover, is not to be lamented, but celebrated, embraced as the proper foundation for architecture today: 'We live in a non-referential world. Therefore architecture must be non-referential.'[19]

Those who still labour under the misapprehension that architecture might address and engage with common societal concerns, taking the 'economic, the ecological, and the political as the chief bases for making architecture', are mistaken, their efforts futile, according to Olgiati and Breitschmid.[20] Following the failed projects of modernity and postmodernity, with their outdated utopian and multicultural aspirations, there are, they argue, no longer any

Fig. 10.5: Fulton Center Metro, Manhattan, New York, USA, Grimshaw Architects, 2014

Fig. 10.6: Westminster Underground Station, London, UK, Hopkins Architects, 1999

common social ideals, and therefore nothing extra-architectural for architecture to concern itself with representing. 'Non-referential architecture has no other choice' than to produce meaning through the 'purely architectonic', they write, 'because for the first time in history, our society functions quite well without a fundamental comprehension of cultural and historical relationships … the world does not seem to be worse than before.'[21] Absent the obligation to address social, political, economic or ecological matters, relieved of the burden of extra-architectural representation, the architect is free to focus on what is supposed to be properly architectural, namely 'the conception, construction, and building of rooms'.[22] This is not a practice, argue Olgiati and Breitschmid, to be inflected through ideological concerns, but is rather a 'mind-generative act of conceiving, the "throwing forth" of buildings'.[23] The authors clarify that they are not opposed to meaning or sense-making as such, but specifically to the notion that there can be any common, ideological or intellectually based experience of this sense-making in architecture. The building, insist Olgiati and Breitschmid, 'is its own sense-making thing'.[24] The building, which 'exists only for itself', provides meaning for the subject outside any mediation, outside discourse, outside ideology: 'Non-referential architecture must speak to the unbounded and non-ideological mental agility of people who live in that non-referential world of today.'[25] The ideological 'no longer exists',[26] and the part played by architecture is to be, exclusively, that of allowing each individual to build their own world from its experience.[27]

The historical narrative of the post-political and post-ideological to which Olgiati and Breitschmid subscribe, however, seems plainly to recall, rather than to contest, the period of postmodernity whose failures they castigate and claim we have now surpassed. The waning of belief in the social and the political, the ending of history, the celebration of individually differentiated experience, all seem overly familiar as characterizations of the recent historical past, rather than of our particular moment. What marks our own time is in fact, and rather obviously, the re-emergence of the political, and the eruption of a renewed historical consciousness around contested and competing systems of shared belief; an urgent intensification of efforts to comprehend 'cultural and historical relationships', not least in relation to the 'economic, the ecological, and the political'. Olgiati and Breitschmid however, charge that engaging with such issues amounts to 'moral righteousness', and that architecture can only 'make sense for the people of the twenty-first century' by 'liberating itself from the vessel of non-architectural meanings'.[28]

Olgiati and Breitschmid posit a post-ideological architecture as that which is proper to a post-ideological 'people'. In doing so they point, inadvertently, to the ideological nature of their own proposition. If 'the people' and our times are, as outlined above, not in the least done with history and politics, then a non-referential architecture would be one that withholds from view its own status as inevitably implicated in the ecological, the economic and the political. A non-referential architecture, under these conditions, is an architecture of dissimulation, presenting its refusal to speak about the conditions in which it is implicated under the guise of there being nothing to say about them, and in which no one would be interested anyway. Nothing to see here.

As with its discursive counterpart, the laconic, muted and matter-of-fact appearance of so much contemporary architecture, especially that of transit systems, might then be critically conceived as one designed to condition us to accept that *what is* simply *is;* not to be subject to scrutiny, but consigned to the background of experience where it serves, like some architectonic equivalent to the ambient works of Brian Eno, as reassuringly uninvolved. Architecture as frozen music for airports. Achille Mbembe's characterization of neoliberalism in his *Critique of Black Reason* seems apposite here: 'The process is ... characterized by the production of indifference; the frenzied codification of social life according to norms, categories, and numbers; and various operations of abstraction that claim to rationalize the world on the basis of corporate logic.'[29] In its reassuring patterning of experience, its gesturing towards the efficiency and benevolence of the systems that subtend its operations, the contemporary architecture of public transit is an exercise in the cultivation of this indifference, of a disposition in which we happily accept that there is nothing more to be said, or done.

Notes

1   Susan Buck-Morss, *Dreamworld and Catastrophe: The Passing of Mass Utopia in East and West* (Cambridge, MA: MIT Press, 2000). As Buck-Morss observes of Stalin's 1930s Moscow metro, 'This was, indeed, interior decoration for the masses. And if in the last years of glasnost you asked the residents of Moscow about their childhood experiences of this extraordinary metro, they would tell you that it was a magical place, comparable to a Disney theme park, except that it cost only a few kopecks to enter, and that its multiple phantasmagorias intervened habitually into their daily life – comparable, also, to a cathedral, except that you traversed it in a distracted state, always moving with, through, or against the crowd, on your way to somewhere else.' 208.

2   'Paolozzi Restoration at Tottenham Court Road Station', February 2017, <https://art.tfl.gov.uk/projects/paolozzi-restoration-at-tottenham-court-road-station/>.

3   Makoto Sei Watanabe, 'Algorithmic Design/Induction Design, Iidabashi Station 2000',<https://www.makoto-architect.com/iidabashi.html>.

4   I am indebted to Tony Fretton for suggesting to me the term 'residual High-Tech' to describe the type of architecture addressed here.

5   Fredric Jameson, *Postmodernism, or, the Cultural Logic of Late Capitalism* (Durham: Duke University Press, 1991), 38–45.

6   José Aragüez, ed. *The Building*, (Baden, Switzerland: Lars Müller Publishers, 2016); Valerio Olgiati and Markus Breitschmid, *Non-Referential Architecture* (Zurich, Switzerland: Park Books, 2019).

7   Ibid., 11.

8   K. Michael Hays, ed., *Architecture Theory Since 1968* (Cambridge, MA: MIT Press, 1998), xi.

9   Ibid., xii.

10   Aragüez, *The Building*, 12. Emphasis in original.

11   Ibid., 12.

12   Ibid., 14.

13   Ibid., 17.

14   Ibid., 11.

15   Ibid., 18.

16   Speaking of the metaphysics of the commodity, Marx writes that 'The form of wood, for instance, is altered if a table is made out of it. Nevertheless the table continues to be wood, an ordinary, sensuous thing. But as soon as it emerges as a commodity, it changes into a thing which transcends sensuousness. It not only stands with its feet on the ground, but, in relation to all other commodities, it stands on its head, and evolves out of its wooden brain grotesque ideas, far more wonderful than if it were to begin dancing of its own free will.' Karl Marx, *Capital, Volume I*. trans. Ben Fowkes (London: Penguin, 1976), p. 163–4.

17   As Steven Helmling has written, this term – a 'Hegelian chestnut' – 'suggests both the work that concepts do, and the labor that making ourselves conscious of the problematics of the concept ... imposes upon us'. Steven Helmling, *Adorno's Poetics of Critique* (London: Continuum, 2009), 19.

18   Olgiati and Breitschmid, *Non-Referential Architecture*,16–17.

19   Ibid., 14.

20   Ibid., 18.

21   Ibid., 15–16.

22   Ibid. 15.

23   Ibid., 19.

24   Ibid., 19.

25   Ibid., 26.

26   Ibid., 16.

27   Ibid., 24.

28   Ibid., 18–19.

29   Achille Mbembe, *Critique of Black Reason*, trans. Laurent Dubois (Durham and London: Duke University Press, 2017), 3.

11 Architecture's Abode of Production: Beyond Base and Superstructure

The 'critique of capitalism', argued the Marxist historian Ellen Meiksins Wood in *Democracy Against Capitalism: Renewing Historical Materialism*:

> requires not only adaptations to every transformation of the system but a constantly renewed critique of the analytic instruments designed to understand it. There can never have been a time since Marx's day when such a task needed doing more urgently, as more and more branches of knowledge, both in cultural studies and in the social sciences, are absorbed into the self-validating assumptions of capitalism or at least into a defeatist conviction that nothing else is possible.[1]

The analytic instruments employed in the critique of architecture likewise require constant renewal and should themselves be subject to immanent and institutional critique. Opposing the post-critical with the critical, just as it existed before being challenged, when made the foil for all the progressive claims issued by the turns to affect, new materialism, to the object-oriented and the actor-networked, is hardly in the dialectical spirit of critique itself. Critique has to move with its targets.

The institution of critique

On this subject Marko Jobst, reviewing my *The Architecture of Neoliberalism*, alongside Nadir Lahiji's *Adventures with the Theory of the Baroque and French Philosophy*,[2] takes these as symptomatic of current 'crude swings between the "critical" and the "post-critical"'. He finds this situation regrettable, not least in terms of what he claims is a failure to properly read Deleuze and Guattari on our parts.[3] Jobst suggests that the path through this stalemate lies in the use of 'more complex conceptual tools'.[4] On the contrary, what is needed is not some sublimation of the opposition between critical and post-critical into one between the 'crude' and the 'sophisticated', at least not for those of us for whom the critique of architecture is necessarily part and parcel of the critique of capitalism. The goal in renewing the analytic instruments of the critique of architecture is a partisan one, its object being to render these more effective against the 'defeatist conviction that nothing else is possible'. To this end, William Hutchins Orr's recent remarks on the conditions of possibility for what is now referred to as 'architecture theory', and the institutionalization of critique from which it was formed, are apposite.[5]

Orr argues, in his thesis *Counterrealisation: Architectural Ideology from Plan to Project*, that the post-critical and the depoliticization of architecture occurred not in the late 1990s, as is usually assumed, but in the 1970s:

> the periodisation ... that opposed post-critical architecture to the heyday of critical architecture in the 1970s, already misses the true post-critical turn, which for architectural discourse, occurs precisely in the moment in which criticality becomes a self-conscious value *for architectural discourse,* which ... sublimates and transfigures the critique of architecture as bourgeois institution.[6]

Where Manfredo Tafuri's 1969 essay 'Toward a Critique of Architectural Ideology' is a critique of architecture *as* ideology, Orr claims, much of what follows in its wake marks out architectural theory as itself ideological. As architecture theory passes through a succession of post-Marxian models drawn from semiotics, structuralism, post-structuralism and deconstruction, it becomes progressively and effectively more anti-Marxian, long before its more recent Deleuzian, affective or object-oriented turns. Architecture theory, from the 70s onwards, becomes a 'self-reflexive Project', institutionalized within capital 'A' Architecture, that serves to validate its own institutional discourse. Furthermore, architecture effects this pivotal turn – from the critique of its own institution to the institutionalization of criticality – at precisely the same historical juncture as it withdraws from its engagement with the Plan, turning instead to the promise of autonomy offered in the Project. As architecture attempts to distance itself from being assimilated into urban planning, as well as from the 'plan of capital' itself in the era of the welfare state, it seeks refuge in the establishment of its formal autonomy from the economic institutions of capital. Orr's charge is that theory's critical edge is blunted, made effectively 'post-critical' *avant la lettre,* in being used to ideologically valorize the institution of architecture in its academic context.

As Orr also notes, the institutionalization – and thus the defanging – of critique and theory within architecture is indicative of a more widespread tendency towards what he describes as its 'sublimation'.[7] He defers to Christoph Henning's *Philosophy after Marx: 100 Years of Misreadings and the Normative Turn in Political Philosophy* to argue this point, but something akin to this has also been addressed at length by both Perry Anderson and E.P. Thompson. Each of these have also pointed to how critique's institutionalization has gone hand in hand with its culturalization.[8]

In his *In the Tracks of Historical Materialism,* Anderson argues that semiotics, structuralism and post-structuralism are incapable of adequately accounting for the historical and material dynamics at work in capitalism.[9] These models, he argues, represent nothing less than the defeat of Marxism 'on *the very terrain* of Marxism itself'; that of addressing the relations between structure and subject.[10] In place of a Marxist account of these relations, concerned with understanding them in terms of a process of ongoing struggle occurring within particular historic and material conditions, structuralism, argues Anderson, proposes an ahistorical and 'unbridgeable gulf between the general rules of syntax', i.e. structure, 'and the utterance of particular sentences', i.e. subject. In the preceding work of Anderson's 'unpremeditated trilogy', *Considerations on Western Marxism,* he had set his sights on accounting for the separation of theory and practice that had already been set in motion, as early as the 1920s, with the advent of 'Western Marxism'.[11] Early generations of Marxist intellectuals – Rosa Luxembourg, Rudolf Hilferding, Karl Kautsky – had insisted on the unity of theory and political practice and 'had been united in their scorn for *Kathedersozialisten* [professorial socialists]'.[12] They had served as active members of communist and socialist parties, and taught within the programmes of workers' education organized by these. The so-called 'Frankfurt School' of critical theory, however, became progressively more detached from any overt political or party organizations, and increasingly embedded in the setting of the university. Rather than a straightforward betrayal, Anderson understands this shift as to some degree determined by the 'sombre' historical circumstances of the 1930s, not least those of Stalinism and Fascism, and the related conditions of exile and refuge to which intellectuals became subject at this time.[13] Yet, as he also notes, there is an element of choice at work on the part of the thinkers of Western Marxism, such as Theodor Adorno and Max Horkheimer, in deciding to focus their attentions on philosophical and cultural concerns, as opposed to those of political economy. As Anderson remarks of this turn, 'Not merely did Marxist philosophy achieve a general plateau of sophistication far beyond its median levels of the past; but the major exponents of Western Marxism also typically pioneered studies of *cultural* processes – in the higher ranges of the superstructures – as if in glittering compensation for their neglect of the structures and infrastructures of politics and economics.'[14] From Anderson's perspective, at least, it might then be said that the post-political can be further backdated, now from the 1970s to the 1930s, this being the critical juncture at which theory takes academic refuge from direct political engagement.

E.P. Thompson's extended essay 'The Poverty of Theory', whose object of critique is the theory of Louis Althusser, presents arguments similar to those to be found in Anderson's *In the Tracks of Historical Materialism*.[15] The triumph in academia of theory over history, as represented in Althusser's structural Marxism, stands for nothing less than an 'extraordinary fracture … in the Marxist tradition'.[16] Actively opposed to the practice of history, which finds itself condemned as mere 'empiricism', 'Althusser's structuralism is a structuralism of *stasis,* departing from Marx's own historical method.'[17] Where for Anderson the problem of structuralism lies in its failure to account for the relations between structure and subject as a historical process, for Thompson the subject, under the terms of this theoretical model, disappears, other than as a functional effect of structure. The result, in any case, is similar to that remarked upon by Anderson, that of the 'eviction from history of human agency'.[18] Thompson is especially forthright in his critical assault on

Althusser as the figurehead for theory, calling him out for pedalling idealism as materialism. Firmly lodged in the academic world of the *'lumpen-intelligentsia'*, Althusser is held to be representative of an 'elitist division between theory and practice'.[19] Whatever one makes of Thompson's vituperative tone, his central argument bears decisively upon the whole question of the problematic of theory, in general, as well as in its specifically architectural guises: the 'conjuncture' from which theory emerged 'has broken the circuits between intellectuality and practical experience (both in real political movements, and in the actual segregation imposed by contemporary institutional structures)'.[20]

In architecture theory this rift between intellectuality and practical experience has been upheld and furthered, at least until recently. Its focus has fallen principally, if not exclusively, on architecture as superstructure, as a realm of signs and meanings. Even where it has sought to address the relations between capital and architecture, this has more often than not assumed the form of a moral condemnation of the fetishization of appearance, as in the discourse of 'spectacle' and 'starchitecture', without questioning its own fixation on the appearance of things, or the fact that this fixation circumscribes its understanding of what is political in architecture. Typically, architecture theory has focused on the 'higher ranges' of its superstructure, on a given canon of architects and architecture deemed worthy of endless discussion and debate. Little attention has been paid to the political and economic infrastructures of this architecture, and even less to the vastly greater quantity of architecture built and experienced outside it.

Symptom and spectacle

Fredric Jameson's 'symptomatic' reading of the Westin Bonaventure Hotel in Los Angeles occupies a canonical position within architecture theory. Presented in his *Postmodernism, or, the Cultural Logic of Late Capitalism,* his account of the spatial experience of the hotel is especially marked by the influence of Althusserian structuralism.[21]

Inside the hotel, Jameson finds in architectural form the 'suppression of depth' he has identified as characteristic of postmodernism in art and cinema. The 'bewildering immersion' of the Bonaventure produces an experience of profound spatial disorientation.[22] '[T]his latest mutation in space – postmodern hyperspace,' he writes, 'has finally succeeded in transcending the capacities of the individual human body to locate itself ... cognitively to map its position in a mappable external world.'[23] While Jameson describes in detail his personal experience of this 'postmodern hyperspace' – not unproblematically universalizing this experience as that of the 'individual human' in the process – his larger quarry is the underlying condition for which the bewildering and disorientating experience presented by the hotel is merely symptomatic: the 'mutation' of capital into its latest, postmodern, 'stage' of development. This new stage represents, for Jameson, the Althusserian 'structure in dominance'; that which determines from the economic base – even if only in the famous 'last instance' – the ideological superstructure. This mode of theorizing is premised on the conviction that we cannot stare directly into the face of the economic, and that since it cannot be approached directly, its workings must somehow be fathomed through this superstructural register alone. More specifically, and as Jameson understands his own method, the essentially abstract nature of the economic, and of the historical, can only be grasped in being translated into representational terms through the operation of *transcoding:* 'The invention of a set of terms, the strategic choice of a particular code or language, such that the same terminology can be used to analyze and articulate two quite distinct types of object or "texts", or two very different structural levels of reality.'[24]

Jameson employs architecture as the cultural code through which to represent the otherwise unrepresentable realms of the economic and the historical. He claims in *The Political Unconscious* that through transcoding 'the separation ... of the ideological from the political, the religious from the economic, the gap between daily life and the practice of the academic disciplines' can be mediated, 'at least locally overcome'.[25] Yet in the process of shifting between codes, Jameson passes over more direct relations of mediation between the economic and the cultural in which architecture is implicated here.

The more immediate relations between John Portman's hotel and the economic and political infrastructure of Los Angeles, or the financing of the project itself, for instance, are unremarked upon. Issues of class and race, highly pertinent to this type of project, likewise remain unconsidered. Even where Jameson remarks on the rupture between the hotel's vast interior world and that of the city outside, and of its mirrored facade, this is taken as point from which to embark on further transcoding, so as to point to the larger meaning revealed by these surface-level observations. In the process, the more 'local' questions of class, race and social exclusion – in which architecture is implicated in such projects – are glossed over, reduced to a brief aside about how the hotel's facade serves to repel the 'Other'.[26] When Jameson comes, finally, to the 'principal point' derived from his experience of the Bonaventure, it is that the bewildering experience of the hotel 'can itself stand as the symbol and analogue of that even sharper dilemma which is the incapacity of our minds, at least at present, to map the great global multinational and decentered communicational network in which we find ourselves caught as individual subjects'.[27] Here the 'symbol' and the 'analogue' effectively serve to maintain – rather than to close – the gap between lived experience and economic infrastructure by presupposing that these exist as 'different structural levels of reality'. Absent any account of the more direct points of communication between these supposedly separate levels, then it is difficult to see, either, any points of friction, contestation or struggle that might take place between them, and through which historical change may result. Jameson's transcoding, premised on the articulation of points of confirmation and correspondence, therefore, tends to reproduce the kind of stasis for which Thompson condemns Althusser. While Jameson is, very evidently, concerned with the history of capitalism, this is for him primarily a matter of recognizing the appearance of and designating its successive 'stages'. Despite his well-known call to 'always historicize' it may be more accurate to say that Jameson's larger concern is to always *periodize*.[28]

Where Jameson's transcoding takes architecture, and its experience, as a mode of representation through which to reveal capitalism's otherwise unapproachable foundation, for Guy Debord capitalism has simply *become* its own representation. 'Everything that was directly lived has receded into a representation', he writes in *Society of the Spectacle*.[29] 'In societies dominated by modern conditions of production', he declares, 'life is presented as an immense accumulation of spectacles.'[30] For Debord it appears that the goal and the end of capitalism is now that of the production of appearances. The spectacle, he writes, 'is capital accumulated to the point where it becomes images'.[31]

Insisting on the absolute identity of spectacle and capital, Debord's Situationist critique mistakes manifestation for essence. As Gilles Dauvé wrote in 1977, 'Debord's theorisation ... gives the impression of a fundamental analysis, when in fact the method, and the subject being studied, remain always at the level of social appearances.'[32] Dauvé further argues that '[t]he S.I. [The Situationist International] had no analysis of capital: it understood it, but through its effects. It criticized the commodity, not capital – or rather, it criticized capital as commodity, and not as a system of valuation which includes production as well as exchange'.[33] For Dauvé, the Situationists had no critique of political economy. Their analysis – principally derived from an avant-garde perspective – is fixated at the level of cultural expression, hung up on appearances, misread and mistaken for the sum total of capital.

The notion of spectacle, while often thought to be developed from and complementary to Marx's notion of the commodity fetish, is in practice an impoverishment of Marx's theory, in that it removes labour, and its place in political economy, from consideration. The fetishism of the commodity derives, for Marx, from the 'social character' of labour as a 'mode of production' which it conceals through its form of appearance.[34] Approached and understood critically, however, the concept of the fetish also presents an opportunity to *reverse* this perspective so as to reveal the mode of production, and the conditions of labour though which it is reproduced, via the very means of their concealment. The fetish becomes, for Marx, a 'social hieroglyphic' through which one can approach 'the secret of our own social products'; it opens up a passage, in other words, through which we can move between appearance and essence, abstract and concrete.[35] Marx does not argue that capitalism *is* commodity fetishism, in the way that Debord argues that capitalism *is* spectacle.

Commodity fetishism is, rather, a concept through which one can grasp the relations of production and appearance in capitalism dialectically, whereas the notion of spectacle collapses this dialectic into a one-sided picture.

The critique of spectacle therefore has us remain at the level of the image, captured in its surface expression, as if this really were all that mattered and all that existed. Trying to understand capitalism only through what it makes appear to be its essence would be like trying to understand to Fordist industrial mass production only through the appearance of the Model T.

Tafuri and the architect as producer

Roland Barthes, in fact, undertook an exercise of this sort in his 1957 essay 'The New Citroën', in which he wrote 'it is obvious that the new Citroën has fallen from the sky inasmuch as it appears at first sight as a superlative object'.[36] Barthes is, of course, presenting a critique of the mythological language in which design speaks through the commodity, and of how this appears 'at first sight'. But as with the critique of spectacle, the scope of this type of analysis is restricted to the surface appearance of things – even if so as to question this appearance – and therefore to saying nothing, for instance, of the conditions of labour in Citroën's factories. This is, broadly speaking, the criticism Manfredo Tafuri made of Barthes' semiological methods in 'L'Architecture dans le Boudoir'.[37] Tafuri argued in this essay that the problem with the criticism of signs and language, when applied in architecture, is that it becomes trapped in the terms of what it proposes to critique; the magic circle of language that excludes and eludes any grasp of the circuits of production.[38] Criticism will then necessarily be confined to the critique of representation. The critique, not only of architecture, but of capital itself, will be caught in this magic circle, unable to grasp the place of architecture within circuits of production other than those concerned with appearances. Critique will, at best, be confined to an account of production as only and always the production of architecture as image. The legacy of this perspective, all too evidently, is the substitution of liberal criticism for critique as such; a normative condemnation of architecture as 'spectacle' and architecture as 'iconic' that, to paraphrase Dauvé, is a criticism of architecture's commodification, a criticism that architecture is reduced to appearance, and not a critique of its role in the reproduction of capitalist social relations. Implicit in this liberal criticism is the unquestioned assumption that architecture should properly be somehow above the vulgarity of commercial display. This criticism of architecture's commodification, though too often assumed to be effectively radical, is, though, concerned with the cultural status of architecture, and is a world away from the kind of class critique of architecture called for by Tafuri: 'just as there can be no such thing as a political economics of class, but only a class critique of political economics, likewise there can never be an aesthetics, art or architecture of class, but only a class critique of aesthetics, art, architecture and the city'.[39]

In 'L'Architecture dans le Boudoir' Tafuri proposes a way out from the impasse of the magic circle of language: 'we abandon the object itself and move into the *system* which, in itself, gives meaning ... criticism thereby explicitly moves its inquest from a specific task to the structure that conditions the total meaning of the object'.[40] The focus of criticism should, in other words, shift from individual products as forms of cultural expression to the relations of production; from the ideological superstructure to the 'dynamics of the entire economic cycle'.[41] Tafuri, then, concurs with Barthes' diagnosis but parts company with him over the remedy. While he finds the notion of 'mythological' second-order sign systems applicable to the language games evident in 'recent architectural trends' – works by James Stirling, Aldo Rossi, Peter Eisenman, Michael Graves, Richard Meier – he is unable to follow Barthes onward towards the 'pleasure of the text', to the consoling moments of 'jouissance' to be found in the free play of the signifier.[42] As Tafuri notes, 'it will be ridiculous to ask in which way a linguistic choice will express or anticipate more free ways of life'.[43] Instead, he heads in the opposite direction, against the structuralist – soon to be post-structuralist and postmodern – currents of the later twentieth century, and back to earlier approaches to critical analysis; those of Walter Benjamin, Bertolt Brecht and Theodor Adorno.[44] Tafuri's move is also one from the surface to the depths, following Marx's descent in

Capital from 'this sphere of simple circulation or of exchange of commodities' to the 'hidden abode of production, on whose threshold there stares us in the face "No admittance except on business"'.[45]

In order to effect this exit from the magic circle of language Tafuri turns to the propositions set out by Walter Benjamin in the essay 'The Author as Producer'.[46] Arguing in favour of Benjamin's radical viewpoint Tafuri writes:

> Among the questions posed in 'The Author as Producer,' there are no con-
> cessions to proposals for salvation by means of an 'alternative' use of lin-
> guistic elements, no ideology beyond a 'communist' art as opposed to a
> 'fascist' art. There is only a structural consideration – authentically struc-
> tural – of the productive role of intellectual activities, and therefore cer-
> tain questions regarding their possible contribution to the development of
> the relations of production.[47]

Anticipating the charge that this turn to the relations of production will reduce the criticism of architecture to an analysis of building production and
construction, a crudely deterministic and vulgar form of Marxism unwor-
thy of the critic, Tafuri answers that 'we can only reply that it will never be
repeated too often that, when wishing to discover the secret of a magician's
tricks, it is far better to observe him from backstage than to continue to stare
at him from a seat in the orchestra'.[48]

In its reference to laying bare the mechanisms of the magician's tricks, Tafuri's resort to Benjamin's 'The Author as Producer' also calls to mind Theodor
Adorno's analysis of the staging of Wagner's opera *Der Ring des Nibelungen*.[49]
In his *In Search of Wagner*, Adorno argues that Wagner's opera is an essentially 'phantasmagorical' work, here drawing upon Marx's analysis of the fantastical appearance of the commodity-form to define it as such.[50] In concealing
from the audience the presence of the orchestra, and the stagehands working
the devices through which the Rhine Maidens appear to float in the air above
the stage, for example, Wagner masks the means of production involved in the
performance of his opera. For Adorno this is an 'occultation of production by
means of the outward appearance of the product'.[51] The effect of this phantasmagorical mode of appearance is that the end product, as experienced by the

audience, 'presents itself as self-producing ... In the absence of any glimpse of the underlying forces or conditions of its production, this outer appearance can lay claim to the status of being'.[52]

Much recent architecture, in assuming landscaped, biomorphic and fluid forms, has laid claim to something like this 'status of being' and, in the process, concealed the 'underlying forces of conditions of its production'. I have elsewhere criticized architects both for concealing the mode of construction of their projects in the outer form of their appearance, and, relatedly, for their seeming ignorance towards the sometimes inhumane conditions of labour implicated in construction work.[53] Others have, in recent years, turned to similar (if not precisely the same) issues. The group Who Builds Your Architecture? are concerned with examining and exposing 'the links between labor, architecture and the global networks that form around building buildings'.[54] The Architecture Lobby, likewise concerned with issues of architecture and labour, was established in 2013 as 'an organization of architectural workers advocating for the value of architecture in the general public and for architectural work within the discipline'.[55] In her contribution to the collectively produced work *Can Architecture Be an Emancipatory Project?*, the Lobby's founder, Peggy Deamer, argues for the continued and contemporary importance of Tafuri for his 'emphasis on production'.[56] After quoting, with approval, the passage from 'L'Architecture dans le Boudoir' recommending that we attend to the backstage mechanisms of the magician, she writes:

> Contemporary architecture's typical attention to consumption instead of production can and should be seen in the context of capitalism's own historical development, from nineteenth century concentration on production to twentieth century focus on consumption and service. Indeed, one could say that this is neo-liberalism's particular ideological success: it deflects our attention away from labour ... Whatever one might think about theories that foreground labor over consumption – old or crude Marxism? – one cannot deny that this vital aspect of architecture ... has been overlooked.[57]

The recent turn, or return, to this 'emphasis on production' is indeed significant in directing our attention to the conditions and practices of labour implicated in both architectural design and building construction. While Deamer's remarks appear here to challenge the perspective of consumption for its superficial enthusiasms for architecture's appearance – 'let's talk about how great architecture looks!', she writes, mocking this position[58] – this holds too for the *critique* of the spectacular and the iconic in architecture, whose perspective is similarly confined to the appearance of things: 'let's talk about how we don't like this architecture because it looks spectacular!' Tafuri's seemingly retrograde move, against the tides of structuralism and the postmodern, also, in effect, already offers something in advance of Jameson's method of analysis. In attending to the conditions of labour implicated in architectural design and construction, and in undertaking the painstaking work of researching the 'global networks that form around building buildings', architecture no longer appears simply as an analogue, or allegory, for the otherwise obscure and deeper workings of capitalism; it can be approached as regards its immediate relations to and place within these.

In proposing that labour and production in architecture always and only take place in these otherwise hidden abodes, however, we are working with somewhat limited, and limiting, conceptions of labour and production for our understanding of architecture, and of capitalism, and indeed of the relations between them. Working within these limits, and failing to recognize them as such, the tendency is for the critique of architecture to fall back on practices of 'unveiling' and 'unmasking' alone, and to the model of 'economic base' and 'ideological superstructure' which subtends and authorizes these.

Beyond base and superstructure

As many have argued, the base and superstructure model is a somewhat crude and ineffective means through which to model the relations between modes of production and forms of consciousness within capitalism. The very terms through which it structures its problematic are themselves held by some to obscure the real complexity of the relations they are supposed to explain. However much the relations of determination between base and superstructure might be qualified, corrected or rethought, what remains, and remains a problem, is the underlying conception of separate and distinct realms of reality, each possessed of its own particular properties. As Meiksins Wood notes in *Democracy Against Capitalism: Renewing Historical Materialism:*

> In one form or another and in varying degrees, Marxists have generally adopted modes of analysis which, explicitly or implicitly, treat the economic 'base' and the legal, political, and ideological 'superstructures' that 'reflect' or 'correspond' to it as qualitatively different, more or less enclosed and 'regionally' separated spheres. This is most obviously true of orthodox base-superstructure theories. It is also true of their variants which speak of economic, political and ideological 'factors,' 'levels' or 'instances', no matter how insistent they may be about the interaction of factors or instances, or about the remoteness of the 'last instance' in which the economic sphere finally determines the rest. If anything, these formulations merely reinforce the spatial separation of spheres.[59]

For E. P. Thompson, base and superstructure is nothing more than an analogy that has, through overuse, 'been petrified into a concept'. This concept, in turn, effectively obscures the true scope of production in capital.[60] Contrary to this, he writes,

> Theoretical practitioners are familiar with a central concept of Marx: that a given productive system not only produces commodities, it also reproduces itself, its productive relations and its ideological forms and legitimations. These, in their turn, become a necessary condition for the process of reproduction.[61]

Moishe Postone, in *Time, Labor, and Social Domination: A Reinterpretation of Marx's Critical Theory,* argues that 'if social meaning and social structure are to be related, the categories that grasp them must be related intrinsically', and not 'on the basis of concepts that already contain within them that opposition'.[62] For Postone, as for Meiksins Wood, the categorical opposition between base and superstructure presents an obstacle to the effective analysis of the relations between the economic and the ideological as these operate within capitalism. And with Thompson, Postone argues that the model of base and superstructure obstructs the understanding of capitalism's productive and re-productive relations. Postone elaborates on these arguments by pointing to the limitations of a Marxian critique that understands its essential task to be that of 'unmasking' labour as 'the source of wealth' in society.[63] In arguing that la-bour – properly recognized as the real source from which the production of wealth issues – can then, and as it already exists, form the basis of a social-ist society, this critique overlooks the historically specific means and condi-tions through which labour is produced in and for capitalism. In place of this traditional critique, rooted in the model of base and superstructure, Postone proposes that we attend to the 'constitution of consciousness', to a 'social and historical theory of subjectivity' through which we could apprehend not only what is produced by labour, but how labour, as it exists within capitalism, is itself produced.[64]

Postone, in his reinterpretation of Marx's critical theory, is not breaking with Marx himself here, but rather with what he understands as the traditions of twentieth-century critical theory. Marx himself, after all, in the first volume of *Capital,* identified in the chapter on 'primitive accumulation' the historical conditions through which the proletariat were *produced* as subjects of and for capitalism: the 'bloody legislation', the forced expropriation of the people from the soil, the making of the 'free' proletariat as wage earners, the introduction of the factory system of labour. In the *Grundrisse* Marx provides a succinct statement on the dialectical relations obtaining between the production of ob-jects and the production of subjects: 'Production thus not only creates an ob-ject for the subject, but also a subject for the object.'[65] Here, and in this sense, production is not an activity that takes place in a *hidden* abode, apart and dis-tinct from the ideological world of consumption. The two are immanently re-lated, co-constituted. Each is understood as participating in production, on the basis that production also includes the production of the producers them-selves. The production of subjectivity also extends to the realm of consump-tion, to the cultural, and the ideological. Commodities are produced not only so as to be consumed, to realize economic value, but also because they be-come productive in the act of their consumption; producing the very tastes, needs and desires on which their consumption is premised. As Marx notes, '[t]he need which consumption feels for the object is created by the perception of it. The object of art – like every other product – creates a public which is sensitive to art and enjoys beauty'. 'Production', in fact, 'creates the consumer.'[66] These remarks, taken together with the preceding critical assessment of the existing analytical instruments available to architecture theory, suggest the possibility of a renewed critique of architecture in its relationship to capitalism. It is not just the architect who is, following Tafuri, a producer, but architecture itself that *produces* – in the circumstances, conditions and experience its use. This, in turn, is only possible because the subject is not 'given' outside historically and materially specific conditions of production and consumption. Architecture, in its production and its consumption, is thoroughly implicated in the 'social and historical theory of subjectivity' to which Postone refers.

The labour of design occurs under conditions in which workers are required to acquire not only disciplinary knowledge and skills – becoming subject to indebtedness in the process – but the dispositions, mentalities and tolerances requisite to rendering themselves employable. The architecture produced from this labour, in turn, goes to work on its users, contributing to the means through which subjectivity is produced. Architecture is distinctive, if not unique, in this regard. Its sites of production are everywhere, producing its own producers, producing the imaginary of capital, producing conduct, habits and perceptions, producing affects and meanings. The production and reproduction of capital through architecture is not so much confined to a hidden abode as it is hiding in plain sight. Fashioning the analytic tools capable of grasping the significance of these multiple sites of production, and their interrelatedness – itself an ongoing work – will better equip us to recognize, and contribute to, the struggles occurring through and within these.

Notes

1   Ellen Meiksins Wood, *Democracy Against Capital-*
    ism: Renewing Historical Materialism (Cambridge,
    UK: Cambridge University Press, 1995), 4.

2   Nadir Lahiji, *Adventures with the Theory of the*
    Baroque and French Philosophy (London and New
    York: Bloomsbury Academic, 2016).

3   Marko Jobst, 'Deleuze, Space and the Architectural
    Fragment' in Constantin V. Boundas and Vana
    Tentokali, eds, *Architectural and Urban Reflections*
    After Deleuze and Guattari (London and New York:
    Rowman and Littlefield, 2018), 58.

4   Ibid., 58.

5   William Hutchins Orr, *Counterrealisation: Architec-*
    tural Ideology from Plan to Project (PhD thesis, The
    Open University, 2019), http://oro.open.
    ac.uk/61433/.

6   Ibid., 38. Emphasis in original.

7   Ibid., 38. 'Architecture theory exists as the sub-
    limation of a critical theorisation of architecture's
    institutional character within bourgeois society, and
    an internalisation of that critique as a self-reflexive
    Project.'

8   Christoph Henning, *Philosophy After Marx: 100*
    Years of Misreadings and the Normative Turn in Po-
    litical Philosophy, trans. Max Henninger (Chicago:
    Haymarket, 2015).

9   Perry Anderson, *In the Tracks of Historical Material-*
    ism (London: Verso, 1983).

10 Ibid., 33. Emphasis in original.

11 Perry Anderson, *Considerations on Western Marx-*
    ism (London: Verso, 1979), ix. The third work in this
    trilogy being *Arguments Within English Marxism*
    (London: Verso, 1980).

12 Ibid., 49.

13 Ibid., 50.

14 Ibid., 17. Emphasis in original.

15 E.P. Thompson, 'The Poverty of Theory' in *The Pov-*
    erty of Theory and Other Essays (New York: Monthly
    Review Press, 1978).

16 Ibid., 5.

17 Ibid., 5. Emphasis in original.

18 Ibid., 79.

19 Ibid., 3.

20 Ibid., 3.

21 Fredric Jameson, *Postmodernism, or, the Cultural*
    Logic of Late Capitalism (London and New York:
    Verso, 1991).

22 Ibid., 43.

23 Ibid., 44.

24 Fredric Jameson, *The Political Unconscious: Narra-*
    tive as a Socially Symbolic Act (London and New
    York: Routledge, 1983) 25. Elsewhere, Jameson has
    offered some analysis on the more direct, as opposed
    to merely analogous, relations between architecture
    and its economic infrastructure. See, for example,
    'The Brick and the Balloon', in *The Cultural Turn:*
    Selected Writings on the Postmodern, 1983–1998
    (London and New York: Verso, 1998), 162–89.
    My point, however, concerns the influence of the
    Bonaventure analysis upon what too often passes for
    theory in architecture; the attempt to read off some in-
    sight into the deeper workings of capitalism from the
    observation of architecture's formal qualities alone.

25 Jameson, *The Political Unconscious*, 25.

26 Ibid., 42

27 Ibid., 44.

28 Jameson, *The Political Unconscious*, 9.

29 Guy Debord, *Society of the Spectacle*, trans. Ken
    Knabb (Detroit: Black & Red Books, 1977), 7.

30 Ibid., 7.

31 Ibid., 17.

32 Gilles Dauvé, 'Critique of the Situationist Interna-
    tional', *Red Eye*, No. 1 (1979): https://libcom.org/li-
    brary/critique-situationist-internation-
    al-gilles-dauve.

33 Ibid.

34 Karl Marx, *Capital, Volume I*. trans. Ben Fowkes
    (London: Penguin, 1976), 165.

35 Marx, *Capital*, 167.

36 Roland Barthes, *Mythologies*, trans. Annette Lavers
    (New York: Hill and Wang, 1972), 88.

37 Manfredo Tafuri, 'L'Architecture dans le Boudoir:
    The Language of Criticism and the Criticism of Lan-
    guage', *Oppositions* 3 (May 1974), 38–62.

38 Ibid., 53. 'The simple linguistic analysis of architec-
    ture that confines itself to speaking only of the
    work's status as language laid bare would result in
    mere description. Such an analysis would be unable
    to break the magic circle that the work has drawn
    around itself, and, consequently, it would only be
    able to manipulate the very process by which the text
    produces itself, thereby repeating the laws of this
    productivity.'

39   Manfredo Tafuri, 'Toward a Critique of Architectural Ideology' in *Architecture Theory Since 1968,* K. Michael Hays, ed. (Cambridge, MA: MIT Press, 2000), 32.

40   Tafuri, 'L'Architecture dans le Boudoir', 53.

41   Ibid., 57.

42   Roland Barthes, *The Pleasure of the Text,* trans. Richard Miller (New York: Hill and Wang, 1975).

43   Ibid., 57.

44   On the significance of Brecht for Tafuri, see María González Pendás, 'Realism under Construction. Manfredo Tafuri's Other Road to Criticism', *Conference Proceedings for Where do you Stand? 2011 ACSA* (Washington: ACSA Press, 2011), 11–20. On the significance of Adorno and Benjamin for Tafuri, see Hilde Heynen, *Architecture and Modernity: A Critique* (Cambridge, MA: MIT Press, 1999).

45   Karl Marx, *Capital : A Critique of Political Economy, Volume 1,* trans. Ben Fowkes (London: Penguin, 1976), 279–80.

46   Walter Benjamin, 'The Author as Producer', in *Benjamin, Reflections: Essays, Aphorisms, Autobiographical Writings* (New York: Schocken, 1986).

47   Tafuri, 'L'Architecture dans le Boudoir', 57.

48   Ibid., 57.

49   Theodor Adorno, *In Search of Wagner,* trans. Rodney Livingstone (London and New York: Verso, 2005).

50   'The mysterious character of the commodity-form consists therefore simply in the fact that the commodity reflects the social characteristics of men's own labour as objective characteristics of the products of labour themselves, as the socio-natural properties of these things ... It is nothing but the definite social relation between men themselves which assumes here, for them, the fantastic ['phantasmagorisch' (phantasmagorical) in the original] form of a relation between things. (Marx, 1976, 164–5.)

51   Adorno, *In Search of Wagner,* 74. See too Susan Buck-Morss, 'Aesthetics and Anaesthetics: Walter Benjamin's Artwork Essay Reconsidered', in *October,* Vol. 62 (Cambridge, MA: MIT Press, 1992).

52   Ibid., 74.

53   Douglas Spencer, *The Architecture of Neoliberalism: How Contemporary Architecture Became an Instrument of Control and Compliance* (Bloomsbury Academic: London and New York, 2016).

54   Who Builds Your Architecture? <http://whobuilds.org/about/>.

55   The Architecture Lobby <http://architecture-lobby.org/wp-content/uploads/2016/11/2014_Tactics_Pamphlet_01b.pdf>.

56   Nadir Z. Lahiji, ed., *Can Architecture Be an Emancipatory Project?: Dialogues on Architecture and the Left* (Alresford, UK: Zero Books, 2016), 120.

57   Ibid., 121.

58   Ibid., 121.

59   Meiksins Wood, *Democracy Against Capitalism,* 21.

60   Thompson, 'The Poverty of Theory', 140.

61   Ibid., 190.

62   Moishe Postone, *Time, Labor, and Social Domination: A Reinterpretation of Marx's Critical Theory* (Cambridge and New York: Cambridge University Press, 1993), 225.

63   Ibid., 82–3.

64   Ibid., 224.

65   Karl Marx, *Grundrisse: Foundations of the Critique of Political Economy,* trans. Martin Nicolaus (Harmondsworth: Penguin Books in association with New Left Review, 1973), 92. Marx continues: 'Thus production produces consumption (1) by creating the material for it ; (2) by determining the manner of consumption ; and (3) by creating the products, initially posited by it as objects, in the form of a need felt by the consumer. It thus produces the object of consumption, the manner of consumption and the motive of consumption. Consumption likewise produces the producer's inclination by beckoning to him as aim-determining need.'

66   Ibid. 92.

Library of Birmingham, Birmingham, UK, Mecanoo Architects, 2013

12 On Allegory, the Architectural Imagination and Radical Disillusionment: In Conversation with Miloš Kosec

Miloš Kosec: One of the things I've always appreciated about your work is that it addresses the physical matter of architecture, not merely as a built allegory or an illustration of a theoretical point, but as a field of theoretical inquiry, as fruitful as the written discourse. I think that for many decades there hasn't been such a disconnection between what is built and what is thought and written about in architecture as there is now, and I read your work as the re-initiating of a critical reading of the visual, material and temporal existence of architecture. How do you think your way of reading and thematizing buildings and space in the forthcoming book has changed from *The Architecture of Neoliberalism?*

Douglas Spencer: I think that the allegorical reading of architecture is something of a default approach to analysis, and needs to be questioned. This is something I've been trying to do in my more recent writing, including this book. The most influential example of the allegorical reading is, of course, Fredric Jameson's analysis of the Westin Bonaventure Hotel in LA, in his *Postmodernism, or, the Cultural Logic of Late Capitalism.* For Jameson, the disorientating personal experience of losing one's bearings in the hotel is presented as an allegory of a new and 'postmodern' form of capitalism, one whose operations are beyond our grasp. But projects like the Bonaventure are directly economic and political interventions within the city, not just vehicles through which the critic might gesture towards some claim to an insight into the transformation of capitalism as whole.

The idea that architecture, or anything supposed to be purely in the realm of culture, can be taken as a sign of something deeper and more substantial going on in the 'economic base' is not exclusively or originally Jameson's own, however. He's drawing – though through a specifically structuralist and Althusserian approach – on a much deeper tradition of critical theory. It was

Theodor Adorno who, notoriously, criticized Walter Benjamin for missing the mediation between deep structures and their surface appearance, effectively charging him for settling, instead, for the presentation of 'magical' correspondences. Even Adorno, much as I'm sympathetic to so much of his thinking, falls into the same trap himself, working by means of analogies, metaphors and allegories to leap between the phenomenal world of tangible experience and the more abstract substrata supposed to be lurking mysteriously behind it. Likewise the concepts of the commodity fetish, the spectacle and the phantasmagoria are perhaps somewhat exhausted, or at least of limited use now in understanding architecture in relation to capital. The idea that architecture is just about creating visual illusions that can be peeled back, unveiled, to show what is *really* happening is itself somewhat superficial.

I haven't entirely avoided using those default models of analysis in my own work, including *The Architecture of Neoliberalism,* but there are parts of that book where I also try and do the more painstaking work of seeing architecture as a form of mediation between, for instance, neoliberal models of higher education, on the one hand, and the making of 'student-entrepreneurs', on the other.

This book, *Critique of Architecture,* is in places more self-conscious about these issues and includes reflections on the methods used in the critical analysis of architecture, as well as efforts to practise this analysis differently. I think Moishe Postone's work on the limitations of Frankfurt School critical theory is really pertinent to this task, as are some of the writings of Perry Anderson and E.P. Thompson on the practice of theory.

MK: There seems to be a basic dilemma when discussing a built piece of architecture. Should the text address the intentions of its architect, the wishes of the client, or the way the building actually develops and changes, often quite in contrast to the initial expectations of both? There is naturally a certain connection between the conditions of production of architecture and its effect in society and space; but how to account for the many other contingent factors in this equation?

DS: This is also an important methodological question. The issues you raise are, again, things I had not perhaps always consciously reflected on while writing *The Architecture of Neoliberalism*. Certain ways of operating become kind of intuitive after a while – which can be a problem in itself – and it seems obvious to me that discussing a building as if it were the product of a single figure is just a form of mystification. Addressing architecture in order to validate the genius of its 'author', looking for signs of the 'master's touch', etc., is hagiographical, not analytical. That said, individual and prominent architects do wield some power and influence, and this can usefully be analyzed in terms of the part they play in transforming architectural discourse, practice and pedagogy.

Looking at the role of the client is important too, so long as you see their goals and ambitions as situated within the larger conditions of political economy. Manfredo Tafuri was exemplary in this respect, for example in his analysis of the early company towns. This is something I was influenced by in my analysis of the BMW building in Leipzig by Zaha Hadid Architects, for example.

There are other approaches, some of them developed more recently, and by younger researchers, historians and theorists, especially around issues of labour and construction. I'm thinking, for instance, of Jane Hutton's work on 'Reciprocal Landscapes', analyzing the connections between the sites of material extraction, productive labour, and landscape and architectural construction. Then there's the Who Builds Your Architecture? group, researching issues like the plight of construction workers. I think the work of Jessica Garcia Fritz on material and construction specification, as a political act, is also really important and original in this regard.

For myself, I suppose the real goal of the analysis of any building is not the architecture itself, but the part it plays in producing certain types of subjects. In that sense I sit, maybe uncomfortably, somewhere between a Marxist and a Foucauldian approach. And I'm still exploring other sources that provide for significant accounts of subjectivity and the processes of subjectification, such as the decolonial thought and work of Sylvia Wynter.

MK: Architecture as production not only of space and materials but also of subject types is a fascinating field. Not only in the case of the subjects understood as clients and users of architecture, but also as subjects that produce architecture: the builders, engineers and architects. Notions of underpaid precarious employment and compensation in the form of professional self-fulfillment, unpaid apprenticeships, class prejudice, snobbery and professional pride as economic and not merely psychological factors, have been crucial elements of the architectural office for more than a hundred years, and seem to have foretold some of the crucial elements of the neoliberal service-economy. Should we reorient from researching the product of the architectural office, the building, to researching the architectural office itself?

DS: The short answer is yes. The longer version is that in researching the architectural office, as a space which produces its own particular kind of subject formation, one could grasp the way in which it demands the development of certain tolerances and accommodations – survival mechanisms. I've witnessed the kind of verbal abuse some of the most respected names in architecture dish out to their employees, for example, and I suppose one has to develop an ability to cope with that in order to keep one's job. And then there's expectation in some, if not all, firms of putting in extremely long hours without further financial remuneration. The architectural office seems like it thrives on a mentality of self-sacrifice. Additionally, there are issues of class, gender and ethnicity that play out in particular, if not entirely unique ways, for the architectural worker. The Architecture Lobby have been instrumental in raising and working to address some of the issues.

MK: Sven-Olov Wallenstein at the end of his book *The Silences of Mies*, a historiography of twentieth-century reception of the defining Modernist architect Mies van der Rohe, calls for a reinvention of critical theory for the contemporary context. I think most theorists today agree that the critical recipes of the mid-twentieth century don't work any more, and I see in your work one of the strands to take on the vastly changed conditions of architectural production and governance of space. But the academic environment, the basic condition of production of theory, has vastly changed as well. How do outsourcing, zero-hour contracts, the symbolic capital of academia and precarious working conditions, affect the (in)ability to reinvent critical theory today?

DS: I certainly concur with Wallenstein's call. If critical theory is to be both dialectical and immanent to its object, it can't simply occupy an entrenched position, standing its ground against the post-critical. In fact the post-critical, and all the subsequent varieties of non- or anti-critical theory that have followed on from it in recent years, give critical theory something to work on that should provide it with an opportunity to sharpen its practice, shake it out of its old habits and certainties. In terms of the old 'recipes' of critical theory, the problem is precisely that they have become recipes, default modes of operating that are, in some ways, inherently problematic – I'm thinking here for instance of 'spectacle', and Fredric Jameson's 'transcoding', which I tackle and take issue with in this collection – and they are ill-equipped to tackle the way that architecture exists and operates now. It is of course true that 'iconic' and 'spectacular' architectures are still being built, but much of what we experience is designed to operate as a kind of background structuring, or staging, of social interaction.

It's worthwhile reflecting, as well, on how the changed conditions of academia might be implicated in the possibility, or otherwise, of 'reinventing' critical theory. The predicament of precarious employment, of short- and fixed-term contracts, of working multiple jobs across a number of institutions (at least that is what happens in the UK), and in the US the demands of the tenure system, all place terrible burdens on younger academics, especially. It's easy to see the negative consequences in terms of the practice of theory. Increasingly 'research' takes precedence over theory, becoming the chief metric of achievement, and one is obliged to perform as a researcher and bring in research funding to one's institution. This type of research is often structured around the production of measurable 'outcomes', which is hardly compatible with theorizing as an open-ended and non-productive undertaking. Joan Ockman has written a persuasive critique of this turn to research, by the way. Another negative aspect of this, though it may not be especially new, is that academics, especially in the US, can be very territorial and competitive about what they consider 'their' areas of research. The tenure system, in particular, is practically a machine designed to structure the practice of thought into an entrepreneurial, individualistic and competitive exercise. Sometimes theory, on the contrary, requires the capacity to be adventurous with thought, to not be tied to the archive, to information, to results. Theory also requires intellectual exchange, generosity and camaraderie to flourish, as well as situations in which this can happen.

The positive side of the current predicament, though, is the consequent radical politicization of some in academia. I'm thinking of faculty and students expressing solidarity with the struggles of cleaning staff over the terms of their contracts, for instance, in UK universities. And I think, in terms of the question of the reinvention of critical theory, that because of the situation that many find themselves in, where exploitation and inequality is so much part of everyday lived experience, that this mobilizes academics to undertake work relevant to challenging these conditions.

MK: In relation to the previous question: what, through your many years in academia, is your personal experience of difficulties in trying to sustain a critical reflection in today's academia? It seems that a retreat into privileged solitude or contemplative autonomy that you criticize in your texts is also a half-hearted reaction to a changed landscape of academia. What would in your mind constitute a more measured and truly critical theoretical response?

DS: The whole question of withdrawal from, or engagement with, networked systems of interaction and communication is, as your question suggests, fraught with many difficulties. I've argued that there is, effectively, a compulsion to network, to fashion oneself as a kind of commodity through this activity. My argument was informed by certain post-autonomist thinkers in this regard. I think withdrawal from these systems, to the extent that it is even really possible, presupposes that there is some authentic or true self that can be insulated from the frenzy of communicative interaction in which we are otherwise situated. But I just don't believe that, seeing as how I believe subjectivity is always produced, rather than given. I think that the idea of the autonomous self-sufficient intellectual is as much a fabrication as that of the entrepreneur of the self, and that the best way to sustain critical reflection in academia today is to have an openness to the thought of others, to cultivate intellectual generosity, to not territorialize an area of expertise. It's not easy, because the conditions of academic labour are structured around individual competitiveness. At the same time, there has to be some space apart from continual interruption for solitary work, as this is necessarily part of critical reflection and practice too. In other words, I think that rather than dealing in absolutes, the key consideration is of *how* one communicates, makes use of networks, etc., and of maintaining the opportunity for certain strategic moments of solitude and withdrawal.

MK: In general you seem to be critical of the New Materialism, Object-Oriented Ontology and other post-anthropocenic strands of theory, and some of these certainly fit nicely within the 'naturalization' and 'de-anthropization' principles of neoliberalism, but do you think there is room within these intellectual strands for critical theory to be restructured and updated to resolve some of its paralysis as well?

DS: I really find it hard to think of much, if anything, that can be salvaged – if I can put it that way – from these strands of theory. They are, mostly, opposed to criticality. This is logical enough, given that they are based on staking out ontological claims rather than conducting epistemological enquiry, and since they effectively return us to a pre-critical position of dogmatic assertion, philosophically, as if Kant, Hegel and Marx had never existed, or shouldn't have. I might yet be proven wrong, but find it difficult to imagine what New Materialism, or OOO, might usefully have to say to us about the relationship between architecture, settler colonialism and white supremacy, for instance. The decolonial theory of figures like Walter D. Mignolo or Sylvia Wynter, on the other hand, seems absolutely vital right now as a further elaboration of a critical project, and I'm deeply impressed by how this has been taken up with reference to architecture in recent research and writing by Mabel O. Wilson and Irene Cheng, for instance.

MK: You say that 'the enemy of my enemy is not my friend'. In an age where the most decisive result of the proliferation of information seems to be self-contained feedback loops and the predetermination of discourse, I very much support this position. On the other hand, how to prevent the relative novelty of this position itself being commodified into another exception on the market of ideas?

DS: I don't think anyone has ever yet found a way to make anything, or any idea, immune to marketization of some sort! 'The enemy of my enemy is not my friend' refers to the fact that I find some currents of anti-neoliberal thought, especially in architecture, to be problematic in themselves. Most obviously this refers to the current of theory and architectural practice centred around Pier Vittorio Aureli. I should say, because it might not be clear, but is very important, that I don't see Aureli's position or work as equally problematic as that of Patrik Schumacher, whose absolute embrace of neoliberalism and all its values is completely egregious. My issues with Aureli, to crudely summarize these, are twofold. Firstly, I think that he overestimates the formal capacity of architecture, conceived as its political essence, to act against the economic impact of capitalist urbanization. Secondly, I don't believe that there is any authentic or true way of being for human subjects. I see his work as premised on the notion that architecture can insulate a certain idea, or ideal, of the self from outside interference, or can sustain certain idealized models of community. I think that a universal humanity is something that has yet to be created, rather than something to be recovered, and that this, in the broadest political terms, is the work that radical politics has to be engaged with.

MK: You write about the changed relation between architecture and landscape design and about the defining shift from the singular object to a field as thematized by Stan Allen. While the stress on the 'field' might suggest an increasing interest in interdependency and critical reading of relations of different conflicting forces, it seems that in most of architectural discourse it had the effect of blurring power relations, a certain phantasmagorical 'naturalization' of the status quo. Supplanting socially based vocabulary with a nature-based one suggests this very literally. How did the theoretical frame built on relations and metabolisms manage to such an extent to overlook the predominant carnivorous and even cannibalistic metabolism of architectural production of today, namely the socio-economic relations in the age of global neoliberalism?

DS: I think you frame this question in a really insightful way, in asking how the turn to 'metabolism', for instance, could, in theory, become a means to situate architectural production in relation to any number of extra-architectural concerns. The desire to make architecture somehow akin to landscape, and where landscape is conceived of only in terms of metabolic, ecological and geological processes, as in Stan Allen's promotion of 'landform building', is a project of 'naturalization' in the worst possible sense. Landscape, is of course not nature itself (and even 'nature' is a perhaps peculiarly Western/colonial concept), but a certain symbolic representation of nature that serves social and ideological ends. This doesn't make landscape inherently bad or suspicious. It is only when you can't or don't acknowledge the artifice, fabrication and symbolic work involved in the making of landscape that invoking it as a somehow progressive agenda for architecture becomes suspect. So yes, you're right, if we pursued the notion of metabolic relations all the way it would reveal how socio-economic relations are naturalized, and how nature is always already implicated in these socio-economic relations. This is, after all, something that Marx addresses, deriving from Hegel this model of our metabolic relations with the natural world. Urban political ecology (UPE) has engaged in understanding these relationships for some time, and the work of critical landscape scholars like Jane Hutton and Elise Misao Hunchuck is significant in showing how the symbolic, the natural, the historical and the material are mutually implicated. Architecture, sadly, remains too much attached to formalism in design and to the promotion of trends in its discourse.

MK: Coming from a former socialist, although perhaps not a typical socialist, country (Yugoslavia), I notice that despite the same prevalence as elsewhere, the neoliberal order does have certain difficulties in establishing its 'ahistorical naturalness' here, not least in the spatial realm, where much of the public infrastructure and public space is inherited from the socialist era.

Do you think that such 'counter-narratives' could be simply subsumed within the 'production of difference', becoming exotic fetishes, or is there a chance of them presenting a truly pluralistic wedge in the homogeneity of the global order?

DS: Well of course I can't speak from the same experience as you in this regard, but the question, I think, raises the issues of temporality and historicity, and their representation, which I can try and speak to. I think that neoliberalism is a profoundly ahistorical ideology, and this is because its advocates do not think that people should make history, under any circumstances. For them society is and should be governed through and mediated by the extra-human processing powers of the market. The only notion of historical movement acceptable to neoliberalism is that of 'progress', by which is meant that everyone and everything is eventually encompassed/liberated within its ultimately vacuous logic of consumer choice. I think this is the reason why the abstract patterning, the a-signifying appearance of what I call the architecture of neoliberalism, appears as it does. It seems to speak only of the fact that it has nothing that it needs to say to us.

Your question though is not just about the appearance of architecture, but about the architectural structuring of urban space, and the provision of infrastructure as a historical achievement, rather than an overt monument to history. These are perhaps the more difficult legacies for neoliberalism to deal with, where they are the product of societies that were once oriented to realizing certain social, political and economic objectives. The possibility of demonstrating that history is still in motion – rather than history as a repository in which the past can be confined – is always open, and might be activated through the radical reimagining of how they can be used as collective spaces in which a politics can be articulated. I'm thinking of the movements of the squares, and more recently of the Black Lives Matter protests of 2020 that took place on highways and intersections that were originally designed to break up Black and working-class communities in the US. I take these as examples of people grasping the historical significance of built space, and seeking somehow to reanimate that history.

MK: In reading some of your essays, one gets the distinct feeling that architecture isn't merely one among a number of fields where the project of 'cognitive disinvestment' takes place, but that space has become perhaps the central and foundational education, surveillance and disciplining arena for the new human mind: the mind that unquestioningly acknowledges the neoliberal world as the natural substrate on which to operate. You link this to its apparent opposite, where the human mind is understood as the substrate itself, as Franco 'Bifo' Berardi writes about post-industrial capitalism mining the human mind. Could you say more about architecture as a re-education and mining tool? I remember hearing you talk about the London Tube as one of the quintessential infrastructures of the 'new type', not exuberant but quiet, automated and discreet. Is this new type of infrastructure an example of the 'mining tool' of the human mind?

DS: OK, so what I mean by 'cognitive disinvestment' is that capital, as the kind of self-moving and automatic subject that Marx understood it to be, is interested in producing value as an end in and for itself. Historically, of course, it has extracted this value from human labour – manual and intellectual – but it doesn't necessarily have to rely on human capacities to sustain its need for value, at least not entirely. For Bifo Berardi it seems like his concern – and this is broadly in line with the post-autonomist current of thought from which he comes – is that technology is penetrating deeper into our very minds and souls, and not just our bodies, in order to shape us and extract value from us. While I think there might be some instances in which this is true, we should not overlook the fact that our intellectual and sensory capacities are also now somewhat surplus to requirements, as is our physical labour, and often superseded by technology. For the lucky and affluent few, this means we are treated and governed more as affectively oriented beings than intellectual, symbol-making, meaning-making ones. We can zone out, go with the flow, sit back and let happy feelings wash over us. So that's the 'cognitive disinvestment' that I'm thinking about, and my reference to the changed appearance of the spaces of mass public transit is suggesting that we can register this phenomenon there. Largely stripped of anything explicitly symbolic or iconic, and reduced to bare surfaces or simple geometric patterning, the spaces of

Underground transport operate through affect, are designed to induce feelings of security, of confidence in the system, and not thoughts about place or meaning. It makes me think of that Beatles song written by George Harrison, *Tomorrow Never Knows:* 'Lay down all thoughts, surrender to the void'. Only with the void being the empty heart of neoliberalism.

MK: In creating these voids through gentrification, standardization, privatization of public spaces as well as 'redevelopment' and destruction of unwanted remnants of the welfare state such as social housing, much of the existing social and spatial ties are being destroyed. Haussmann in nineteenth-century Paris proudly proclaimed himself as an *artiste-démolisseur* – today such a designation might be a bad PR move, but at the same time it becomes a more truthful designation of the state of the profession as it was 150 years before. With the crucial help of the uncritical architectural profession, the great void you speak of, a field of oblivion, one could almost say spatial dementia, spreads through cities and landscapes. Isn't this a void produced more for the erasure of the past than of the present, deleting the memory of a different kind of normality that is still in the living memory, but this memory has fewer and fewer spaces to hold on to and resist becoming forgotten?

DS: Yes, I agree. I would only add that I've always found this issue of how our architectural environment evokes a certain temporality intriguing. I remember as a child somehow sensing that the Brutalist shopping centre and council offices of my hometown – Aylesbury, near London – envisioned a future that was here already for us to enjoy. The erasure of this type of architecture is, in this sense, not an erasure of the past but of the future, of its promise. I think maybe that's what this void we're talking about is, the emptying out of promise.

MK: We started this discussion at the time the crisis of the Covid-19 pandemic struck. In my personal experience this has become the one truly perceivable global event that has rapidly and tangibly changed the way we function and perceive space: especially the dividing line between personal/private and public spaces that have started to blur and intersect. The world we're concluding our discussion in might not be a completely different to the one we started our discussion in in March 2020, but it does seem to have been 'accelerated' and has brought to the fore usually hidden conflicts and contradictions. On the other hand I'm sure that the title of Philip Mirowski's book *Never Let a Serious Crisis Go to Waste* resonates as much as in the 2008 Financial Crisis. How does the Covid-19 crisis affect your work and your thinking about architecture post the pandemic?

DS: I agree that the pandemic has changed the way we perceive, use and think about space, but in all sorts of unexpected ways. I'm not sure, for example, that the Black Lives Matter-led mass protests we've seen this summer in the US, and beyond, could have happened under 'normal' circumstances. Not least of the exceptional circumstances is the disproportionate impact of Covid-19 on BIPOC communities; the rapid loss of tens of millions of jobs, the terrible handling of the crisis by the Trump administration, and, of course, the police killings of George Floyd, Breonna Taylor, and others. This just underlines that for capitalism huge swathes of the population are considered utterly expendable.

It's too soon to know exactly how this will affect my work, but I do think that we will be seeing the further exacerbation of inequalities, that these will now play out even more than before in terms of the environmental conditions in which people live and work, and that architecture will play some part in that. That might sound cynical or pessimistic, but without some larger and fundamental societal change, architecture will remain in its current position of solving the problems of those who can afford to have their problems solved by the profession.

MK: Would you then say that architecture is always merely a subordinate of the prevailing social order? I can't overlook the fact that the principles of architectural production and rational planning in general are often in direct conflict with laissez-faire economic and social principles. I mean to say that architecture retains at least the potential (even if it does not always enact it) of planning and articulating spaces and projects along the lines of a prescribed anthropocentric plan. Isn't there a structural glitch between the way architecture understands and orders space, and the neoliberal ideal of deregulation and laissez-faire? Or to put it another way – isn't the specifically architectural imagination one of the few remaining intellectual systems that hasn't yet succumbed to the imperatives of neoliberal restructuring, even if the vast majority of the architectural offices and schools did just that?

DS: Let me just deal with this by responding to the idea of the 'architectural imagination' that you mention. I think this is double-edged, at least. What concerns me about the 'architectural imagination' is how, as a disciplinary disposition cultivated in architectural education and culture, it imagines that all sorts of problems, issues and crises can be resolved by the powers of architecture. I don't find fault with the ambition as such. In fact, it's one of the main reasons that I teach students of architecture – so many of them are ethically and politically motivated to make the world a better, more equitable place. But one can't simply 'imagine' a better world into being through envisioning its architecture alone. When one does this, in the form of rendering beautiful images of environmentally sustainable scenarios, the danger is that it bypasses the question of exactly how we get from here to there, and of who gets to decide how this future is imagined. So, even when well-motivated, the 'architectural imagination' has to be integrated with questions of political allegiance, social alliances and solidarity.

MK: In the age of border fences, migrations, anti-terrorist weaponized cities, protests, police violence and Covid-19 quarantine and social distancing measures, the awareness of the government of space seems to come to the forefront of public dissent and resistance. A number of architectural initiatives, such as Forensic Architecture, revealed the potential of architectural imagination not only to help build but also to help deconstruct and destroy the oppressive spatial structures, intellectual constructions and organizational principles. Do you think architectural education in the future will experience a division between pragmatic practitioners and critical activists, or is there perhaps still enough room to incorporate specifically architectural and spatial criticality within the practice of architecture?

DS: I really think that the ideal would be to incorporate both the 'pragmatic practitioners' and the 'critical activists', as you refer to these. There's a danger that the more 'critical', experimental and research-oriented side of contemporary architectural culture is confined to the more renowned, and often more economically exclusive, schools and departments of architecture. There's certainly more cultural capital in this side of things, and as we know, this is inseparable from economic capital. The division you're addressing suggests a division of labour between intellectual/critical/academic and skills-based/pragmatic/practice-based. This division already exists, and I don't think it should be furthered in the future. Surely it's important that a practising architect, working, say, on a housing project, can think critically? Some of the studios on the Green New Deal that I've seen in different schools recently exemplify what I'm thinking of; students engaging in research, speculation, aligning themselves with larger political and environmental projects, and trying to come up with pragmatic architectural responses.

MK: In analyzing the contemporary condition and neoliberal hegemony in particular, you often thematize the work of the economic historian Philip Mirowski and his understanding of the 'neoliberal thought collective' he writes about extensively. For me, his work engages with the crucial elements the left has disengaged from in the past decades: strategy and tactics of the rational long-reaching intellectual project that first constructs the field on which it then distributes its ideas and instils them into society. You also fascinatingly write about Ford's goal of 'making men' through producing cars and industrial plants, not the other way around. When I feel optimistic, I sometimes think architectural thinking is structurally ideal for refashioning a long-term and ongoing intellectual project for the critical left out of the present dispersed and short-term eruptions of dissent as well. What do you think about the potential of such a project of dissent?

DS: Well, its good to be optimistic, but I'm not so sure I would place my bets on architectural thinking like this. We're still at the point where the 'architectural imagination' imagines it can subvert Trump's border wall with Mexico through some form of creative intervention, rather than just refusing to have any part in designing it. The same goes for the architectures of incarceration designed for the prison-industrial complex. Structurally, institutionally and historically, architecture is a terribly opportunist practice. I'm going over ground I've already touched on earlier here, but I think that architecture can only be useful to the left by organically connecting, somehow, with various left-based and 'progressive' struggles. This would involve, among other things, addressing questions of the class position of the architect, and unsettling long-standing attachments to middle-class professionalism. I think architecture will only be ready to be of use in the way you suggest if it can countenance working through its own process of radical disillusionment.

*   Miloš Kosec is an architect, editor and publicist living and working in Ljubljana, Slovenia. He graduated from the Faculty of Architecture of Ljubljana University with the Master's thesis 'Ruin as an Architectural Object', which was published as a book in 2013. Miloš completed his PhD in 2019 at Birkbeck College, University of London, with a thesis 'Passivism: Activism and Passivity in Contemporary Architecture'. He is researches, exhibits, writes and publishes articles in professional and academic publications, focusing primarily on architecture, architectural history, political and social aspects of architectural design. Together with the *Outsider Magazine* editorial board, he was one of the recipients of the Plečnik medal for contributions to architectural culture in 2017. Miloš is also a practising architect and landscape designer with a number of landscape realizations. He is a member of the Kabinet architecture group, winning two second prizes in international competitions. In 2018, he was one of the authors of the Slovene pavilion at the Venice Architecture Biennale. He is a member of the editorial board of *Outsider Magazine* and is also a member and a researcher of the international art and research project Nonument, and is a frequent participant in international architecture conferences and events.

Note on the Essays

Chapter 1. Architectural Deleuzism: Neoliberal Space, Control and the 'Univer-City' was first published, in 2011, in the journal *Radical Philosophy*.

Chapter 4. Less Than Enough: A Critique of the Project of Autonomy, was originally published under the title 'Less than Enough: A Critique of Aureli's Project', in *This Thing Called Theory,* edited by Teresa Stoppani, Giorgio Ponzo and George Themistokleous (London and New York: Routledge, 2016).

Chapter 5. The Limits of Limits: Schmitt, Aureli and the Geopolitical Ontology of the Island, first appeared in *New Geographies 08, Island*, 2016, edited by Daniel Daou and Pablo Pérez-Ramos.

Chapter 6. 'Out of the Loop: Architecture, Automation and Cognitive Disinvestment, was originally published in the journal *Volume* 49: Automation, September 2016.

Chapter 7. 'Architecture after California', was originally published in *e-flux architecture* in 2017.

Chapter 8. 'Going to Ground: Agency, Design and the Problem of Bruno Latour', was first published in the collection *Landscape as Territory*, edited by Clara Olóriz Sanjuán (Barcelona: Actar, 2019).

Chapter 9. 'Returns on the City: Detroit and the Design of Late Fordism', was originally published in *Harvard Design Magazine*, Fall/Winter 2018.

Illustrations

Front cover: Fulton Center Metro, Manhattan, New York. Grimshaw Architects, 2014. Photo: Douglas Spencer, 2016.

Section 1. title page: NOX – Lars Spuybroek, Maison Folie, Lille, France 2001–4, photo: Douglas Spencer, 2004.

Fig 1.1: Korean Presbyterian Church of New York, Greg Lynn Form, 1999. Queens, New York City, USA. Photo: Douglas Spencer, 2006.

Fig 1.2: BMW Central Building, Leipzig, Zaha Hadid Architects, 2001-2005. Leipzig, Germany. Photo: Douglas Spencer, 2008.

Fig 1.3: South-East Coastal Park, Barcelona. Foreign Office Architects, 2004. Photo: Douglas Spencer, 2005.

Fig 1.4: Ravensbourne College, Greenwich, Foreign Office Architects, 2010. London, UK. Photo: Douglas Spencer, 2010.

Fig 1.5: Ravensbourne College, Greenwich, Foreign Office Architects, 2010. London, UK. Photo: Douglas Spencer, 2010.

Fig 3.1: Centre Pompidou, Paris, France. Photo: Joan, 2018, licensed under CC BY 2.0, desaturated from original.

Fig 3.2: 'Centre Georges Pompidou at night_1'. Photo: Sean X Liu, 2014, licensed under CC BY-SA 2.0, desaturated from original.

Fig 3.3: Oslo Opera House, Snøhetta, 2000-2008. Photo: Henning Klokkeråsen, 2008, licensed under CC BY 2.0, desaturated from original.

Fig 3.4: 'Inside the Vessel NYC'. Photo: lorna, 2019, licensed under CC BY-SA 2.0.

Fig 3.5: The Museum of Art, Architecture and Technology, Amanda Levete Architects, 2016, Lisbon, Portugal. Photo: Ahmed Elsherif, 2020.

Section 2. title page: EUR District, Rome. Photo: Douglas Spencer 2010.

Section 3. title page: Fulton Center Metro, Manhattan, New York. Grimshaw Architects, 2014. Photo: Douglas Spencer, 2016.

Fig 9.1: Michigan Central Station, Detroit. Warren and Wetmore, and Reed and Stern, 1914. Photo Douglas Spencer, 2018.

Fig. 9.2 Renaissance Centre, Detroit. Portman Architects, 1977. Photo: Douglas Spencer, 2018.

Fig 10.1: Mosaic mural by Eduardo Paolozzi, Tottenham Court Road Underground Station, London. Photo: Roger Marks licensed under CC BY-NC-ND 2.0, desaturated from original.

Fig 10.2: Tottenham Court Road Underground Station, London. Photo: Douglas Spencer, 2017.

Fig 10.3: Daniel Buren, Tottenham Court Road Underground Station, London. Photo: Douglas Spencer, 2017.

Fig 10.4: Iidabashi Station, Tokyo. Makato Sei Watanabe, 2000. Photo: Douglas Spencer, 2017.

Fig 10.5: Fulton Center Metro, Manhattan, New York. Grimshaw Architects, 2014. Photo: Douglas Spencer, 2016.

Fig 10.6: Westminster Underground Station, London. Hopkins Architects, 1999. Photo: Douglas Spencer, 2016.

Interview title page: Library of Birmingham, Mecanoo Architects, 2013. Photo: Douglas Spencer, 2014.

Back cover: Hyatt Regency Atlanta, Portman Architects, 1967. Photo: Douglas Spencer, 2017.